Death Comes in Yellow

Death Comes in Yellow
Skarżysko-Kamienna Slave Labor Camp

by
Felicja Karay

Translated from the Hebrew by Sara Kitai

 harwood academic publishers
Australia • China • France • Germany • India • Japan
Luxembourg • Malaysia • The Netherlands • Russia • Singapore
Switzerland • Thailand • United Kingdom • United States

Copyright © 1996 by OPA (Overseas Publishers Association) Amsterdam B. V.
Published in the Netherlands by Harwood Academic Publishers GmbH.

Emmaplein 5
1075 Aw Amsterdam
The Netherlands

British Library Cataloguing in Publication Data

Karay, Felicja
   Death Comes in Yellow: Skarżysko-Kamienna
   Slave Labor Camp
   I. Title   II. Kitai, Sara
   940.547243

   ISBN 3-7186-5741-4

To all of the Jewish men and women,
Slave laborers at Hasag-Skarżysko –
To those who survived
And to those who died
of starvation,
hard labor,
squalor,
disease,
beatings,
and bullets,
those the tyrant called "Maccabees",
And "such extraordinary workers" –
I dedicate this book,
to serve as the memorial
Never raised to them.

Contents

Abbreviations   x
Comparative Army Ranks   xiv
Introduction   xv

1. **The Hasag Enigma**   1
   The Early Days – From Lamps to Mortar Shells   1
   The Debate over the Fate of the Polish Armaments
   Industry and its Consequences   6
   How Hasag Gained Control of the Polish Industries in
   the Radom District   11

2. **Establishment of the Jewish Forced Labor Camp at**
   Skarżysko-Kamienna: Background and Contributing
   Factors   17
   Recruitment of Polish and Jewish Workers for the Hasag
   Plants up to Early 1942   17
   Budin's Personnel Policy at the Skarżysko Plants as a
   Factor in the Establishment of the Slave Labor Camp   23
   Changes in the Labor Market in the Generalgouvernement
   and the Early Days of the Skarżysko Camp   29

3. **The Hasag–Skarżysko Camp During the "Radom**
   Period" (August 1942 to July 1943)   34
   The "Final Solution" in the Radom District and the "Jew
   Exchange" System in the Camp   34
   Skarżysko's Role in the Nazi Camp System and Principles
   of its Organization   40

Security in the Radom District and its Effects on the
Recruitment of Jewish Workers for the Skarżysko Plants   47

4.   **Reinforcement of the Camp: Transports from
     Majdanek and Płaszów**   52
     The Enigma of the Transports from Majdanek
     (Summer, 1943)   52
     In the Shadow of the "Erntefest": Circumstances
     Surrounding the Recruitment of Jews from Płaszów   59
     Hasag-Skarżysko Becomes "Katyń in
     Generalgouvernement"   63
     Why Was the Camp at Skarżysko not Made into a
     Concentration Camp?   65

5.   **The History of the Camp at Werk A and the
     "Radom Tier"**   74
     "Ekonomia" – Living Conditions and Early Adjustment   75
     Camp Authorities and Internal Organization   79
     The Hasag Plants – A Source of Life or Death   88

6.   **The Struggle to Survive**   98
     To Submit or Resist   98
     Was there Help to be Found in the Shadow of the
     Gallows?   106
     New People – New Problems   112
     Shattered Hopes   116

7.   **The Kuehnemann–Pollmer Partnership**   122
     The Arrivals from Płaszów and the Start of a New Era   122
     Aid from Outside and its Effect on Camp Life   128
     Singing and Card Games – The "Cultural Life" of Werk A   132

8.   **The History of Werk B**   141
     In the "Dance Halls" of Werk B   142
     In the Camp of the Unknown Commander   147
     Between the Lifegiving Flakes and the "Furrows of Passion" 150
     The Pseudo Revolution of the Płaszówites   154
     Sober Reality   160

9. **Under a Cloud of Picric Acid and TNT**   162
    The Green Corridor to Hell   163
    The Six Circles of Hell of the Shell Department   166
    "Schmitz" – The Refuge   172
    Kingdom of the Damned   175

10. **The Yellow Kingdom of Lady Markowiczowa**   181
    Rise to Power and Establishment of the Dynasty   181
    The Devious Paths of the "Kingdom of Death"   184
    The "White House" and its Subjects   188
    The New Pariahs – "Kaelniks" in Werk C   192

11. **"Life Can Be Good – Even in Werk C"**   199
    Meetings at the Cannons   199
    The Deadly Typhoid Epidemic   208
    The Three-Part Revolution and its Consequences   211
    Singing in the Shadow of the "Frying Pan"   217
    The Final Whistle   224

12. **The Last Act**   229
    The Fate of the Survivors   229

Conclusions   234

Bibliography   249

Index   258

Abbreviations

AGKBZHwP Archiwum Głównej Komisji Badania Zbrodni Hitlerowskich w Polsce – Archives of Main Commission for Investigation of Nazi Crimes in Poland

AOKBZN Archiwum Okręgowej Komisji Badania Zbrodni Niemieckich – Archives of Regional Commission for Investigation of German Crimes

AHJF Archives of Ghetto Fighter's House, Kibbutz Lohamey Haghettaot

AK Armia Krajowa – Home Army. The underground military right-wing organization in occupied Poland.

AL Armia Ludowa – see Gwardia Ludowa

Anklageschrift (Kamienna Prozess) – indictment (Kamienna Trial)

BA Bundesarchiv Koblenz

BeWi Hasag's Supply and Economic Division

BGKBZHwP Biuletyn GKBZHwP – Bulletin of Main Commission for Investigation of Nazi Crimes in Poland

BZIH Biuletyn Żydowskiego Instytutu Historycznego – Bulletin of Jewish Historical Institute, Warsaw

COP Centralny Okręg Przemysłowy – Central Industrial Zone in Poland

DAW Deutsche Ausruestungswerke – German Equipment Works, a WVHA enterprise

Doc. occup. Documenta occupationis teutonicae

GG Generalgouvernement

GL Gwardia Ludowa – People's Guard underground military left-wing organization in occupied Poland, later: Armia Ludowa – AL (People's Army)

GRW Grossraumwirtschaftsplan – Spacial Economic Plan in occupied Europe

HSSuPF Hoeherer SS und Polizeifuehrer – Higher SS and Police Leader

HWaA Heereswaffenamt – Ground Forces Armaments Office

ITS International Tracing Service, Arolsen

JUS Juedische Unterstuetzungstelle – Jewish Social Relief, Kraków

KK Komisja Koordynacyjna – Coordinating Committee of ŻKN, Warsaw
Ktb Kriegstagebuch – War diary
MA Militaerarchiv Freiburg – Military Archive Freiburg
Munitionsstop a halt in ammunitions production
NSZ Narodowe Siły Zbrojne – National Armed Forces, the extreme right wing organization of the military underground forces in occupied Poland
Nur. doc. Nuremberg documents
OKH Oberkommando des Heeres – High Command of the Army
OKL Oberkommando der Luftwaffe – High Command of the Air Force
OKW Oberkommando der Wehrmacht – High Command of the Armed Forces
OSTI Ostindustrie GmbH – Eastern Industry. SS company exploiting Jewish manpower in the GG, especially in the Lublin District
Oświadczenie deposition
RMfBuM Reichsminister fuer Bewaffnung und Munition – Ministry of Munitions and Armaments
RMfRuK Reichsminister fuer Ruestung und Kriegsproduktion – Ministry of Armaments and War Production
RPŻ Rada Pomocy Żydom (Żegota) – Council for Aid to Jews "Żegota". Underground organization in occupied Poland
RSHA Reichssicherheitshauptamt – Reich Main Security Office
Rue-Betrieb Ruestungsbetrieb – Munitions Plant
Rue In Ruestungsinspektion – Armament Inspectorate
Rue Kdo Ruestungskommando – Armament Command
Ruestungskomission Armament Commission
Rue Wi Lgb Ruestungswirtschaftlicher Lagebericht – Report on the situation in the Armament Economy, by Armament Inspectorate GG
SA Sturmabteilungen – Storm Troopers
Sitz. Sitzungen (Kamienna Prozess) – Sessions (Kamienna Trial)
SS Schutzstaffel der NSDAP – Elite Guard of NSDAP
SSuPF SS und Polizeifuehrer – SS and Police Leader
SS-WVHA SS-Wirtschaftsverwaltungshauptamt – SS Economic and Administrative Main Office
SS-Wirtschafter SS Economist
Staerkemeldung daily report of the number of prisoners in the camp
SWK Sąd Wojewódzki Kielce – District Court of Justice at Kielce
STAL Staatsarchiv Leipzig
Sygn. sygnatura – signature
Tagebuch Hans Frank's Diary
UK Unabkoemmlich – exempt from military service because of work in industry essential to the war effort
VJP Vierjahresplan – Four Year Plan

Volksdeutsche   Ethnic Germans, a term applied to German minority groups in Europe who had been living in their countries of residence for centuries

Urteil   (Kamienna Prozess) – Verdict (Kamienna Trial)

W-Betrieb   Wehrmachtsbetrieb – Military Plant

Wi Rue Amt   Wehrwirtschafts und Ruestungsamt des OKW – Economy Armament Office of the High Command of the Armed Forces

WiG   Wehrkreisbefehlshaber im GG – Defense District Commander in the Generalgouvernement

WWiStab   Wehrwirtschaftsstab – Military Economy Command

ZBOWiD   Związek Bojowników o Wolność i Demokrację – Fighters' Society for Freedom and Democracy

ŻKN   Żydowski Komitet Narodowy – National Jewish Committee in Warsaw, Underground umbrella organization of ŻOB, Poalei Zion and Bund.

ŻOB   Żydowska Organizacja Bojowa – Jewish Fighting Organisation

Comparative Army Ranks

German	SS	British	American
*Generalfeldmars-chal Generaloberst	Reichsfuehrer-SS SS-Oberstgruppenfuehrer	Field Marshal General	General of the Army General
General	SS-Obergruppenfuehrer	Lieutenant-General	Lieutenant-General
Generalleutnant	SS-Gruppenfuehrer	Major General	Major General
Generalmajor	SS-Brigadefuehrer	Brigadier	Brigadier General
*Oberst	SS-Oberfuehrer	Colonel	Colonel
Oberst	SS-Standartenfuehrer	Lieutenant-Colonel	Lieutenant-Colonel
Oberstleutnant	SS-Obersturmbannfuehrer	Major	Major
Major	SS-Sturmbannfuehrer	Captain	Captain
Hauptmann	SS-Hauptsturmfuehrer	Captain	Captain
Oberleutnant	SS-Obersturmfuehrer	Lieutenant	First Lieutenant
Leutnant	SS-Untersturmfuehrer	Second Lieutenant	Second Lieutenant

*There were no field-marshals in the SS, but Himmler held the special supreme rank of Reichsfuehrer, equivalent to Goering's rank of Reichsmarschall as senior officer of the Armed Forces. Many of the higher SS officers had double ranks as members both of the SS and the Police, e.g., 'Obergruppenfuehrer and General of the Police'.

Introduction

The time was May, 1989. Accompanying a youth delegation visiting Poland, I toured the length and breadth of the country, my primary aim being to honor the memory of the victims of the Holocaust in the ghettos and concentration camps. As the bus left Kielce on its way north to Radom, my eyes caught a sign by the side of the road reading "Skarżysko-Kamienna". I asked our Polish guide to tell the youngsters of the Jewish camp once located in the woods outside the town. "What?", he asked in surprise, "I never knew there was a Jewish work camp in Skarżysko."

This was two years after I had completed my dissertation on the history of that camp. In its original form, the study filled two thick volumes, in itself a source of surprise to many scholars. How could there be so much to research and write about a small, out-of-the-way camp forgotten even in its own country? And what was so special about Skarżysko-Kamienna?

Without a doubt, the personal side to the story played a role here, for I myself went through the "hell of Kamienna." I had a particular interest in the question of why I, along with thousands of other camp prisoners, had survived, while at the same time millions were being exterminated in the crematoria of Auschwitz and Treblinka. I could not find the answer in other books, and indeed few such exist. Hundreds of anonymous slave labor camps across the face of Europe have remained a blank page in the history of the Third Reich. The lack of scholarly interest in the subject stemmed from a dearth of German documentary sources, which had either been lost or deliberately destroyed, the unappealing nature of the subject, and language difficulties (the testimonies of former prisoners have been recorded in every European language imaginable and never translated into English).

This volume presents the history of one labor camp in an attempt to shed light on various aspects of all the Jewish slave labor camps established in the Generalgouvernement (G.G.) under German occupation. The camp was set up by the German armaments company Hugo Schneider Aktiengesellschaft "Hasag" of Leipzig which was granted "commissary management" of the national munitions plants of Poland (Państwowa Wytwórnia Amunicji) located in the town of Skarżysko-Kamienna, district of Radom. The factories, spreading over an area of some 3,500,000 square meters (the area of the Hasag plant in Leipzig was only 383,000 square meters), were divided into three sections called by their German appellations of Werk A, B and C. In 1942, a small Jewish labor camp was set up beside each of these sections. Together they were known as Judenzwangsarbeitslager Hasag Skarżysko-Kamienna.

Hasag-Skarżysko was one of hundreds of slave labor camps scattered throughout occupied Poland. They were distinguished only by size, the nationality of the prisoners, their location, the date of their establishment, and the authority in charge. The large number of camps reflected the German policy to exploit the work forces of the occupied and annexed countries to advance the war effort. These camps were part of a continental system of forced labor covering the face of Europe and made up of four levels:

1.   the population of the occupied country, on which compulsory labor for the Reich was imposed;
2.   slave laborers, including prisoners of war, brought to work camps within Germany itself either as voluntary recruits or as the victims of terror tactics;
3.   the prisoners of the large concentration camps controlled by the SS who were hired out to private employers;
4.   the prisoners of labor camps, most of which were small in size and existed for a limited period as required by the economic task for which they were established.

The entire system was noted for differences in the treatment of the workers by the German authorities in accordance with ideological-racist and political criteria, that is, in line with the German attitude to each of the enslaved nations. This was equally true for the labor camps. In most cases, when the task for which the camp was established was completed, the camp was dismantled and the workers released. This, however, was not the fate of the Jewish labor camps. They were designed from the start to be obliterated by means of the extermination of the entire prisoner population.

This approach derived directly from the National-Socialist philosophy, which regarded the various nations' attitude to work as one of their national characteristics. According to this view, "constructive work" (*Schaffende Arbeit*), with all of its virtues, was typical only of the German race. The antithesis was to be found in the forced labor of all the other European nations, save for the Jews, since the very idea of "Jewish labor" was considered a contradiction in terms.

As a result, the Jews were not assigned any function in the Spacial Economic Plan (*Grossraumwirtschaftsplan*) designed to be implemented throughout occupied Europe. Even before the inception of the Final Solution, the Nazi economic theoreticians, among them Werner Daitz, Fritz Nonnenbruch, and Axel von Gadolin, advocated the expulsion of the Jews from Europe since they did not constitute a vital work force.

This philosophy constituted the basis of labor relations in the Generalgouvernement. In the case of Germans, the labor laws of the Third Reich, founded on the principle of "work service" (*Arbeitsdienst*), were in force. In regard to Poles between the ages of 18 and 60, "compulsory labor" (*Arbeitspflicht*) was imposed by means of a directive issued by Hans Frank on October 26, 1939, with the authority for carrying out the order placed in the hands of the Civil Administration. On the same day, another directive was issued imposing "forced labor" (*Arbeitszwang*) on the Jewish population between the ages of 14 and 60. Unlike the edict relating to the Poles, that concerning the Jews contained no details as to the type of work, wages, or social benefits. Responsibility for implementing this directive was given to Higher SS and Police Leader, HSSuPF Friedrich Wilhelm Krueger.

On December 12, 1939, Krueger issued his Second Executive Order which makes it clear that the purpose of Jewish labor was entirely different from that allocated to Poles. The Jews were to be rounded up and enclosed in camps under the direct supervision of the SS for a period of at least two years in order to achieve the educational goals of forced labor. The phrasing of the order indicates that the Nazi authorities did not regard the actual work performed by the Jews as particularly important, but were rather concerned with destroying the Jewish economic base as the first step toward their final extermination.

Did the German authorities always achieve their aims in actual practice? In the manner of its establishment, organization and development, did this Jewish camp represent the archetype of the slave labor camp envisioned in Krueger's order, or was its nature and history unique in any way? These are not the only questions that demand answers. What, for example, was the connection between the Third Reich's armament policy and the camp's history? How much truth is there in the theory that the use of Jewish labor was dictated by a lack of manpower? And why did Wilhelm Krueger harbor a special protective policy toward the Hasag camps?

The first section of this book deals with these questions while reviewing the external history of the camp. The second section, concerning the camp's "internal" history, is quite different in nature and includes an analysis of the features of prisoner society in each of the three Werks and a description of the individual prisoner's struggle to survive. This struggle was waged within the framework of the work crew in the Skarżysko plants which was composed of five national units: Germans, Poles, Volksdeutsche, Ukrainians, and Jews. It is hoped that we will be able to shed light on the unspoken mechanism directing the complex relations among the workers.

Sources for the history of the Hasag Concern and the Skarżysko factories were found in the reports and war diaries (*Kriegstagebuch*) of the Wehrmacht Generalgouvernement authorities located in archives in Freiburg and Koblenz. The protocols of the Leipzig trial, conducted against 25 German workers at Skarżysko in 1948, as well as records from the trial of Herbert Boettcher, the SS and Police Leader (SSuPF) of the Radom district, were found in the Yad Vashem archives in Jerusalem. The GKBZHwP archive in Poland produced files of the trials of Jerzy Adryanowicz, the commander of the Ukrainian guard in the camp, and of the Polish overseers in the plant. In addition, use was made of the diaries of Hans Frank and Georg Thomas, underground press, both Jewish and Polish, commemorative volumes issued by Jewish communities, memoirs and document collections. The testimony of the Skarżysko camp prisoners also provides a vast amount of information despite the many inaccuracies. An attempt was made to validate this evidence by comparison with other sources.

At least 25,000 Jews passed through the Skarżysko camp, and the large majority of them never lived to see its liberation. Research into the history of the camp and the factors associated with its existence is sure to make a contribution, be it only a minor one, to our understanding of the labor camps under National–Socialist rule. It was in those camps that the prisoners frequently discovered hidden strengths enabling them to fight for their survival and to preserve their human dignity. Such displays cannot but add to our appreciation of the Jewish fight against the Nazi extermination machine.

Acknowledgements

The original Hebrew edition of this book was made possible with the assistance of numerous people and institutions and I am, again, grateful to them all.

As for this English edition, I would like to express my deepest appreciation and sincere gratitude to Prof. Yehuda Bauer, Chairman of the Vidal Sassoon International Center for the Study of Antisemitism — SICSA — of the Hebrew University, Jerusalem, who first gave me the idea of publishing this book in English and who did much to make this possible. The Copyright of the Hebrew edition is held jointly by Tel Aviv University and Yad Vashem.

Thanks are also due to Prof. Mina Rosen, Director of the Diaspora Research Institute of the Tel-Aviv University and Prof. Yisrael Gutman, Head of the International Center for Holocaust Studies, Yad Vashem, Jerusalem, for their unfailing support in this project.

I would also like to thank Dr. Dalia Ofer of the Hebrew University and Ms Sue Fox, Assistant Director of SIVSA for their help. I owe a special word of thanks to Ms Sara Kitai who managed to convey the true spirit of my text in her English translation.

Last but not least, I am, as always, grateful to my husband Hayim Karay, who took it upon himself to deal with all the technical problems involved in bringing the book to final form.

Chapter 1

The Hasag Enigma

The Early Days – From Lamps to Mortar Shells

Testifying before the Nuremberg court on July 31, 1946, Oswald Pohl, the head of the SS-Wirtschaftsverwaltungshauptamt, SS-WVHA (SS Economic and Administrative Main Office), admitted that the Hasag Concern was the *third largest* private industry to employ prisoners of concentration camps, surpassed only by Herman Goering Werke and I.G. Farbenindustrie. This is a very surprising statistic, since unlike the industrial giants dominating the German economy, Hasag was a relatively modest enterprise. It is equally odd that as late as the summer of 1944, Hasag was the only firm which still operated six Jewish slave labor camps, among them Skarżysko-Kamienna, in what was by then a *Judenrein Generalgouvernement.*

What was the nature of this concern and what was the secret of its success in the most problematic of realms – Jewish labor? Why did Himmler refrain from demolishing the Hasag camps as he did all the others? The extensive literature on the munitions industry in the Third Reich could provide no answers to these questions: the name Hasag is either totally absent, or merits only a few short lines. Scholars of the Holocaust to whom I turned for advice had never heard of it. Why is there so little information on this mysterious company?

In the course of my search, I came across a book entitled "*Die Hoelle von Kamienna*" in which the journalist Hans Frey reports on the trial in

Leipzig in 1948 against Hasag employees. According to Frey, in April 1945, when the Allied forces stood at the gates of Leipzig, the outskirts of the city were shaken by a tremendous blast: the main Hasag building was reduced to a pile of rubble. From word of mouth it was soon learned that the general manager of Hasag, Paul Budin, had set the explosion and was himself buried under the ruins. In the process, the entire archives and all of the company documents were destroyed. What secrets was Budin trying to hide from future researchers? Must this question remain eternally unanswered what with the mystery of Hasag literally nothing but dust and ashes? No, a tenacious search through archives in Germany, Poland and Israel can provide a solution, if only a partial one, to the riddle.

The Hasag Concern had a modest beginning. In 1863 a lamp factory by the name of Haeckel und Schneider was founded in Leipzig. In the 1880s, the plant was converted into a metalworks, and in 1899 the Hugo Schneider Stock Company *(Aktiengesellschaft)* was established. The First World War hastened the growth of the firm so that in 1930 its annual turnover was in excess of five million marks.[1] With Hitler's rise to power and the inception of the "Four Year Plan" in 1933, new regulations were issued in July of that year regarding compulsory cartelization. It was made clear to thousands of small and middle-sized companies that their continued independent existence would be assured only if they found themselves a patron. One such was the army of the Third Reich. Paul Budin, a spirited SS functionary, had been appointed general manager of Hasag in 1932.[2] He was a shrewd businessman who quickly understood the implications of the new regulations. In 1934 he converted part of the plant to munitions production and simultaneously established a close relationship with the director of the ordnance division of the Ground Forces Armaments Office *(Heereswaffenamt–HWaA)*, General Emil Leeb.[3] That very year, Hasag was granted the status of a military plant *(Wermachtbetrieb)*, beginning a new chapter in its history.

---

[1] Hans Frey, Die Hoelle von Kamienna, unter Benutzung des amtlichen Prozessmaterials, (Berlin-Potsdam: VVN-Verlag, 1949,) pp. 4–5.

[2] Oeffentlichen Sitzungen der Leipziger Straffkammer des Landgerichts, Kamienna-Prozess, (hereafter Sitzungen), Yad Vashem Archives (YV), TR-10/7, p. 8.

[3] Emil Leeb, Chef des Heereswaffenamtes, Wolf Keilig, Das Deutsche Heer 1939–1945, (Bad Nauheim: H.H. Podzun, 1956) B.3, p. 193.

In August, 1936, the second "Four Year Plan" *(Vierjahresplan – VJP)* was issued. One of its stated aims was to "speed up the arming" of the military.[4] Since this objective directly relates to the development of the Hasag Company, let us consider briefly the various approaches to the Third Reich's armament policy.

1. The ideological–political approach of Goering was based on Hitler's *Blitzkrieg* strategy and advocated the need for the recruitment and arming of the greatest possible number of new army units ("broad arming" – *Breiteruestung*) with a stress on the technological development of munitions.

2. The professional military approach represented by General Georg Thomas, the head of the Economy Armament Office of the Wehrmacht's High Command (*Wehrwirtschafts und Ruestungsamt im OKW-Wi Rue Amt*), warned against the illusion of a *Blitzkrieg* and called for the increased mass production of personal weapons ("deep arming" – *Tiefe-ruestung*) in order to insure the supply of munitions and replacement of worn parts.[5]

The clash between these two camps had direct bearing on the resulting rivalry between the two forces controlling the implementation of armament policy: the army and industry. In principle, following a tradition dating back to the Prussian war, the military was responsible for arming its divisions. In 1933, the Military Economy Command (*Wehrwirt-schaftsstab – WWiStab*) was established, and was charged, among other functions, with supervision of the armaments industry. To this end, a network of Armament Inspectorate Units (*Ruestungsinspektion*) and Armament Commands (*Ruestungskommando*) were set up.[6]

Industrial circles took a stand against the Wehrmacht's desire to assume control of armament production planning. These groups, however,

---

[4] Dietmar Petzina: Vierjahresplan und Ruestungspolitik, Wirtschaft u. Ruestung am Vorabend des. 2. Weltkrieges, hrsg. von Friedrich Forstmeier und H.E. Volkmann (Duesseldorf: Droste Verlag, 1975), p. 75.

[5] Anja Bagel-Bohlan: Hilter's industrielle Kriegsvorbereitung 1936 bis 1939, Beitraege zur Wehrforschung, Band 24, (Koblenz: Wehr und Wissen Vlg, 1975), p. 87.

[6] Georg Thomas: Geschichte der deutschen Wehr- und Ruestungswirtschaft (1918–1943/45), hrsg. von Wolfgang Birkenfeld (Boppard am Rhein: H. Boldt, 1966), p. 234.

suffered from a time-honored contest for control of the German economy waged between the iron, steel and coal monopolies on the one hand, and the chemical industry giants led by IG–Farbenindustrie on the other. Both industries were involved in the production of weapons, particularly ammunition, and each sought to dominate the planning and implementation stages of the process. With a lack of coordination between the two branches of industry, many firms refused to accept orders from the army for fear of production problems. Thus Hasag's consistent reliability in munitions production strengthened the ties between the company and General Leeb. At his recommendation, Hasag was chosen to supply arms to the air force as well.[7] Paul Budin's organizational and financial skills soon earned him the nickname "Economic Strategist of the SS."[8]

What were Hasag sources of capital and who were its stockholders? According to the list of Hasag stockholders from 11th October 1943, 80% of the stock kapital was in the hands of three financial institutions: Deutsche Bank, Allgemeine Deutsche Credit Anstalt (ADCA) and Dresdner Bank.[9] Hasag had a specially close link with the latter two, as is obvious from the composition of the six-members Board of Directors (Aufsichtsrat): the Chairman Dr. Ernst von Schoen von Wildenegg and Felix Basserman who were also members of the Board of Directors of ADCA, Hugo Zinsser and Adolf Hartman, both managers in Dresdner Bank, Carl Hoehn and dr Richard Koch.[10] The direction (Vorstand) of Hasagwerke-Leipzig included Paul Budin as general manager and his three assistants: Gustav Hessen, Dr. Georg Mumme and Hans Fuehrer (see Figure 1.1).[11]

Budin was supposed to consult with the board members on all major matters, including the appointment of managers to the firm's subsidiaries, and his signature alone was not sufficient on contracts and appointments.

---

[7] "Luftwaffenwehramt Firmen Kartei", RRK, Bundesarchiv Koblenz (BA), R 3/3127, p. 150.

[8] Kamienna-Prozess, Anklageschrift (hereafter Anklageschrift), YV, TR-10/7, p. 20.

[9] "Verzeichnis der in der ordentlichen Hauptversammlung der Hugo Schneider Aktiengesellschaft vom 11. Oktober 1943 erschienenen Aktionaere", Staatsarchiv Leipzig, (STAL) AG Leipzig, HRB 169.

[10] HASAG, Handbuch der deutschen Aktiengesellschaften, Das Spezial-Archiv der deutschen Wirtschaft (Berlin: Verlag Hoppenstedt & Co, 1943), Band 5, p. 5259, STAL.

[11] Hugo Schneider A.G. Leipzig, Reichsbetriebskarte, BA, R 3/2014.

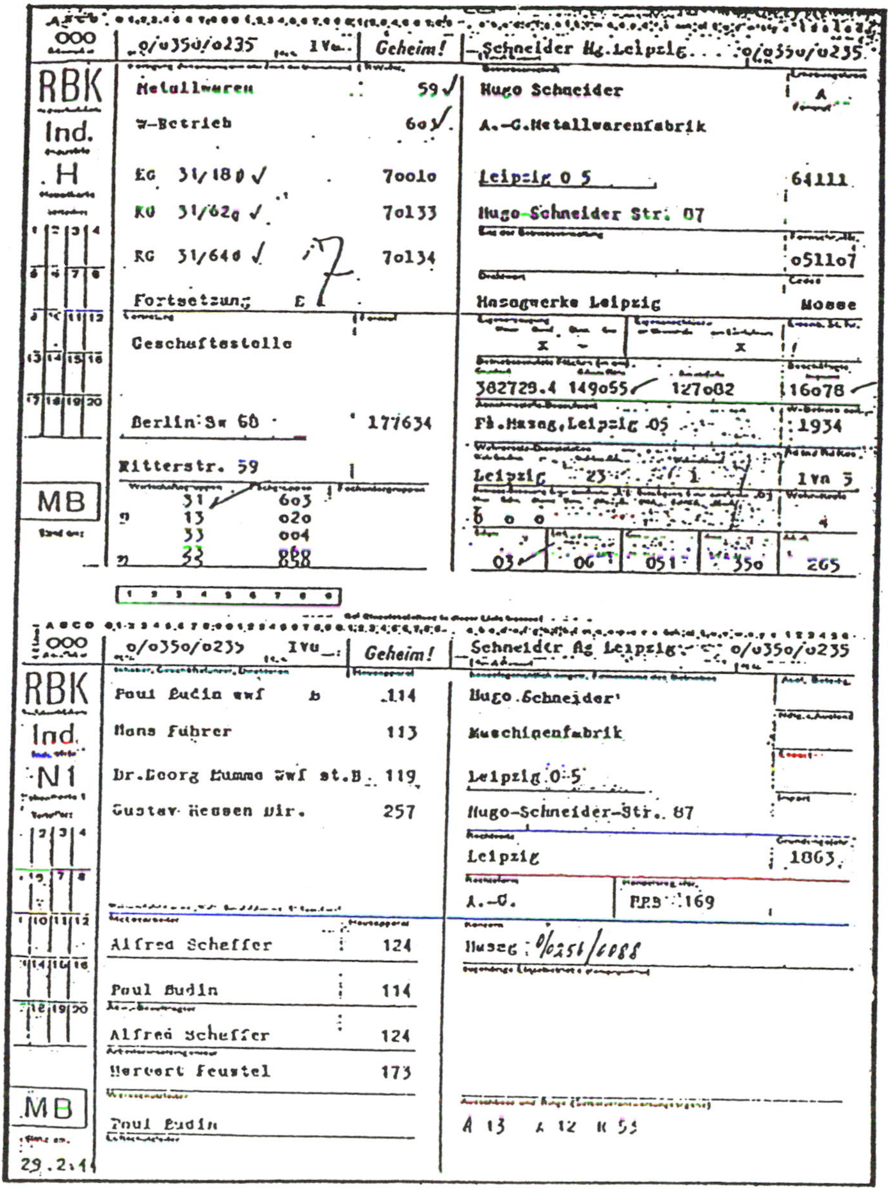

Figure 1.1 The "Reich's Factory Card" of Hasagwerke – Leipzig February 1944 (Reichsbetriebskarte Hasagwerke – Leipzig, BA, R3/2014)

In practice, however, the decisions were his, and were approved on the plants outside of Leipzig, and did not invite his partners to join him retroactively by the board and directors. He was not in the habit of reporting on his visits there. To give him credit, Budin always seemed to find the right person for the right job, and he brought together a very loyal staff. As an SS-Sturmbannfuehrer, he often appointed members of the SS to executive posts in the Hasag plants,[12] but when it came to blue-collar workers, he looked only for professional skills, even hiring former communists. He thus created a team of shop stewards ready to lay their lives on the line for Hasag.

As a devout Nazi, Budin could claim that "Hasag is me." Under his management, the company prospered. By 1939, its annual turnover had reached 22 million marks and its work force had grown to 3,700. With the granting of the status of official munitions plant *(Ruestungsbetrieb)*, Hasag was ready to begin economic operations in the occupied lands as well, and this led to a dizzying boom. In February, 1944, the company's plants in Leipzig alone employed 16,078 workers. For his achievements, Budin was dubbed "Leader of the War Economy" *(Wehrwirtschaftsfuehrer)*, and in 1944 Hasag-Leipzig was awarded the status of Model National-Socialist Factory *(Nationalsozialistischer Musterbetrieb)*.[13]

This, then, was the company and the man who were "waiting in the wings" when the Wehrmacht invaded Poland in 1939, ready to follow up the military rout with an economic rout.

The Debate Over the Fate of the Polish Armaments Industry and its Consequences

With the outbreak of the war, arming the military became the primary objective of the "Four Year Plan," and it was against this background that the future role of the Polish armaments industry became the subject of debate immediately following the occupation of that country. Goering, as agent of the VJP, represented Hitler's doctrine designating Poland

---

[12] SS-Standartenfueher Hugo Dalski, the manager of Hasag-Skarżysko plants, SS-Gruppenfuehrer Karl Zech, the manager of Hasag-Altenburg in Germany, (YV, TR-10/8, p. 9).

[13] Hugo Schneider A.G. Leipzig, 18 August 1944, BA, R 3/3232.

for military and political annihilation,[14] and thereby demanded the dismantling and transfer of all plants vital to the German economy, including, of course, munitions factories, to the Reich. This demand was founded on economic grounds: Poland's swift defeat was seen as proof that the end of the war was near and so there would no longer be a need to expand armament production. With the war over, there might be widespread unemployment and the Polish munitions industry could develop into a competitor to German concerns.

The Wi Rue Amt, headed by General Thomas, was opposed to this liquidation program. The Wehrmacht viewed the Polish armaments industry, as they did that within the Reich itself, as one of the cornerstones of its power, and thus advocated its continued existence under Wehrmacht supervision and control. Fearing that the war would spread to two fronts, Thomas demanded that the industrialists step up military production,[15] and considered the Polish munitions plants an important back-up in light of the danger of aerial bombing of Germany. When England declared its embargo, however, Goering altered his position. At a meeting held on December 4, 1939, it was decided to promote the armaments industry in the Generalgouvernement, particularly in the southern region which included the district of Radom (see Figure 1.2).[16]

At this same time, the WWiStab began to take several practical measures. In December, 1939 the Armaments Inspectorate – Eastern Command – was established in the Generalgouvernement and its major tasks defined as: accepting orders from the Wehrmacht divisions and distributing them among the various munitions plants, responsibility for the external and internal security of these plants, and supply of manpower to the factories where necessary. The post of inspector of armaments was given to General Barckhausen, with his headquarters in Kraków, and three Armament Commands under his authority in Warsaw, Kraków and

---

[14] Arbeitssitzung, 19 January 1940, Documenta occupationis teutonicae, vol. 6, K.M. Pośpieszalski, Hitlerowskie prawo okupacyjne w Polsce, vol. 2, Generalna Gubernia (Poznań: Instytut Zachodni, 1958) p. 14.

[15] Sitzung der Reichsgruppe Industrie am 29.11.1939, Anatomie des Krieges, Dokumente, hrsg. von Dietrich Eichholtz u. Wolfgang Schumann, (Berlin: VEB Deutscher Verlag der Wissenschaften, 1969), p. 231.

[16] Besprechung, 4.12.1939, Berlin, Hans Frank Tagebuch, (hereafter Tagebuch) YV, JM/21/NR. 1, p. 84c.

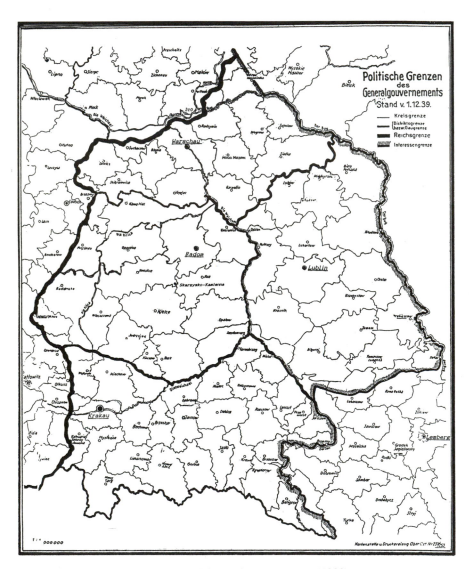

Figure 1.2   The political borders of Generalgouvernement (1939)

Radom. A "technical squad" was set up in each of the army divisions charged with seizing and controlling factories and other facilities vital to the military.[17] The squad patrols relied on precise intelligence, which included extensive information on the munitions factories in Poland.

The "Assessment of Polish Economic Strength" of September 25, 1936 reveals that one of the major ammunition factories was located in Skarżysko-Kamienna.[18] It was founded in 1926 on hilly, wooded land at a critical junction of railway lines and roads, and was part of the Polish national concern "*Państwowe Wytwórnie Uzbrojenia*". The plant began to prosper in 1936 with the implementation of the Central Industrial Zone *(Centralny Okręg Przemysłowy – C.O.P.)*, one of whose objectives was to expand the network of munitions factories in southern-central Poland. In 1939 the number of workers at the Skarżysko plant was 4,612, all of them Poles.[19]

Skarżysko fell on September 6, 1939, and that same month the 23rd Technical Squad issued a report on the condition of the factory. The number of bullets seized at the site was in the millions; the storerooms contained some 10,000 tons of raw materials, and the shop floors around 2,000 machines.[20] The Ground Forces Armaments Office applied incessant pressure to be allowed to begin ammunition production in Skarżysko immediately, but the Wehrmacht lacked the necessary means to accomplish this task. The only available alternative was to make use of the resources of private industry. A formal solution was contained in an order issued by General von Brauchitsch, the supreme commander of the ground forces, regarding appointment of a "commissary management" *(Komissarische Verwaltung)* over confiscated Polish or Jewish property. The authority to make such appointments was granted to the supreme commander-East or to the economic offices of the Wehrmacht empowered by him to do so.[21]

---

[17] Georg Thomas: Geschichte, op. cit., pp. 163–164.

[18] "Beurteilung der Wirtschaftlichen Kraft Polens", 25.9.1936, Militaer Archiv, Freiburg, (hereafter MA), W Wi IV B, p. 6.

[19] Piotr Matusak, Ruch oporu w przemyśle wojennym okupanta hitlerowskiego na ziemiach polskich w latach 1939–1945, (Warszawa: Ministerstwo Obrony Narodowej, 1983), p. 236.

[20] Werkbericht, Skar.-Kam., 19.9.1939, MA, Wi ID 1/165a, pp. 215–217.

[21] C. Madajczyk, Polityka III Rzeszy w okupowanej Polsce, (Warszawa: Państwowe Wydawnictwo Naukowe, 1970), vol. 1, p. 61.

As a result, and in the wake of the recommendation of the Ground Forces Armaments Office, Roechling in Berlin and Hasag in Leipzig were approached on October 31, 1939 with the offer of commissary management of the munitions plants in Skarżysko.[22] Both companies accepted.

With preparations being made for Germany's invasion of Western Europe, urgent steps were taken to step up military production. By the end of 1939, all of the heavy industries and armaments factories in the Radom district (as in the districts of Kraków, Warsaw and Lublin) were turned over to German companies. The Skarżysko plants, along with the steel factories at Starachowice run by the Braunschweig Company, the gun factory at Radom run by Steyr-Daimler-Puch AG, and others, were declared directly subject to the G.G. Armaments Inspectorate and responsibility for their daily affairs was placed in the hands of the Armaments Command – Radom under General von Winterfeld.

The economic policy of the occupation authorities took into account the natural resources and population of each region. The Radom district, covering an area of 25,260 square kilometers, was a depressed region populated largely by small farmers eking out a meager existence. The trades and small commercial enterprises were in Jewish hands. According to statistics published in March, 1940, the population of the district numbered 2,726,516, of these:

Poles	2,409,660
Jews	282,380
Volksdeutsche	33,347
Others	1,129[23]

As a first stage, a meeting of mayors of the Radom district towns resolved on November 25, 1939 to reconstruct the transportation system vital to the military, to set up labor exchanges for Polish workers, and to impound Jews for temporary forced labor.[24] In the second phase, the

---

[22] OKW (W Stab), an Ministerpraesident Goering, Berlin, den 20 Maerz 1940, "Wehrmachtauftraege 27.2 – 26.3.1940", MA, Wi ID 1/95.

[23] "Das deutsche Generalgouvernement Polen", hrsg. von dr. Max Freiherr du Prel, (Wuerzburg: K. Trueltsch, 1942), p. 29.

[24] Sitzung in Radom am 25 November 1939, YV, 0-53/99, pp. 443–447.

authorities planned the rational reorganization of agriculture, industry, the trades and commerce in order to increase productivity and free manpower reserves for the Reich, as well as to reduce the size of the labor component in production, particularly in regard to Jewish labor. Underlying this program was the fundamental desire to reduce to a bare minimum the number of productive residents of the Generalgouvernement which the authorities would have to feed.

In order to implement German policy, an administration system headed by a governor was set up in the Radom district. Ernst Kundt filled this post between 1941 and 1945. Key positions in the local government were manned by Germans, while the junior posts were filled by Poles. From 1942, SSaPolice Leader Herbert Boettcher served as head of the security services in the district, and Jewish affairs under his command were handled by Paul Feucht.[25]

How Hasag Gained Control of the Polish Industries in the Radom District

Having accepted the Armament Office's offer of commissary management of the Skarżysko plants, Hasag chose to produce munitions for the infantry and artillery divisions, leaving Roechling responsible for production of hand grenades and mortar shells. Budin appointed Egon (Hugo) Dalski as general manager of the Hasag industries. Providing a description of Dalski today is a matter of some difficulty, since he disappeared entirely after he was removed from his post in August, 1943. He appears on the roster of SS members dated December 1, 1938 with the rank of Obersturmbannfuehrer,[26] but by 1939 had already achieved the rank of SS-Standartenfuehrer. It is surprising how little information on Dalski appears in Polish documents where he is mentioned as "an SS officer and organizer of Polish executions." [27] The scarcity of information on such a central figure is particularly odd in view of the fact that Dalski

---

[25] "Geschaeftsverteilungsplan der Sipo-Radom, den 27 Oktober 1942, YV, JM/4771, p. 9345228.

[26] Egon Dalski, geb. 2.1.1898, Partei-Nr. 605214, SS-Nr. 18286, "Dienstalterliste der Schutzstaffel der NSDAP" Berlin, 1938.

[27] Państwowa Fabryka Amunicji w Skarżysku-Kamiennej, 18.2.1947, YV, JM/3700, p. 12.

was rumored to be of Polish extraction.[28] According to Jewish sources, he was one of the plant managers even before the war and revealed himself as a German immediately following the occupation.[29] Gustav Kuhne, a long-standing Hasag employee, was appointed to the post of Dalski's assistant. A German staff, both professional and administrative, was also assigned to each of the production divisions. The Poles remained as laborers and low-level shop stewards.

Although the Polish scholar Piotr Matusak claims that the Poles did not cooperate with the German management in running the plant, reports of the Armaments Inspectorate indicate that the factory was fully operative by late December, 1939.[30] The management's secret of success was its "stick and carrot" policy whereby it sought reasonable food allotments for the workers while at the same time employing harsh terror tactics. To implement the first half of this policy, the two companies were compelled to improve the diet at their own expense since all of their requests in this regard to the Generalgouvernement authorities were refused.[31] The food shortages and difficult winter flamed anti-German sentiment in the region, already known as a bastion of Polish nationalism. When Polish underground activity was uncovered in the Radom district in the winter of 1940, mass arrests followed and some 500 Poles from Skarżysko and the vicinity were summarily executed.[32] Consequently, and as a result of the growing unemployment accompanying the influx of thousands of refugees from Wartegau, there was an abundance of available manpower and the number of laborers at the plant increased steadily. The Plant Guard *(Werkschutz)*, recruited from amongst the Volksdeutsche and Ukrainians, was in charge of plant security and guarding the Polish laborers.

---

[28] "Akta Prokuratora Wojewódzkiego w Kielcach w sprawie Jerzego Adryanowicza", Archiwum Głównej Komisji Badania Zbrodni Hitlerowskich w Polsce, (hereafter AGKBZH), Sąd Wojewódzki Kielce (hereafter SWK), sygn. 217, p. 115.

[29] Chaim Milchmann, Testimony, YV, M-1/E/1972/1793.

[30] "Ruestungswirtschaftlicher Lagebericht (hereafter Rue Wi Lgb) fuer die Zeit vom 20.12.39 bis 24.1.1940," MA, RW 23/7, p. 74.

[31] "Bericht ueber die Ernaehrungsfrage in Skarżysko-Kamienna", Skar.-Kam., 10.5.1940, MA, Wi IF 5/103a.

[32] "Polnische Geheimorganisation", Rue Wi Lgb, Krakau, 26.2.1940, MA, RW-23/7, p. 92.

The Skarżysko operations of Hasag and Roechling constituted only one small part of the struggle for control and profits waged by German concerns in the Reich and the occupied countries. With the outbreak of the war, the Reich government became even more dependent on the firms supplying it with military equipment, and the latter in turn endeavored to exploit the circumstances to advance their own interests: immediately following the Polish campaign, the leaders of the armaments industry proposed the principle of linking the rate of production to developments at the front. In other words, *war production was to be stepped up only directly before the attack on each individual country*. Underlying this demand was the industry's desire to maintain sufficient reserves for a rapid transition to an economy of peace following victory by the Reich. Since the military was strongly opposed to such a notion, the German firms brought about the establishment in March, 1940 of the Reich government's Ministry of Munitions and Armaments headed by Dr Fritz Todt. In March, 1940, implementation of the revised plan for munitions production was placed in the hands of newly formed institutions consisting entirely of industrialists. Among these were five national committees responsible for the production of special types of munitions. Special Committee 2 was headed by Paul Budin.[33]

Budin's status in Germany was enhanced by the victory of the Third Reich over France, which led to a sharp revision of internal politics in the Generalgouvernement. Wishing to reinforce his power, Hans Frank planned to transfer ownership of the property of the former Polish state, including its military industries, to the Generalgouvernement. The latter had been promised to the Wehrmacht by order of Hitler in a directive dated October 19, 1939.[34] Although all confiscated basic industry remained officially the property of the Third Reich, in practice in the rights of the former owners were transferred to interim managers known as "trustees" *(Treuhaender)* who were responsible only to whichever German entity had appointed them. There was, in fact, a "gentlemen's agreement" between the authorities and the trustees, particularly of the German concerns who had been granted commissary management, that

---

[33] Schreiben von Philipp Kessler, 25.5.1940, Anatomie des Krieges, op. cit., p. 255.
[34] Besprechung, 1.8.1940, Krakau, Tagebuch, YV, JM/21, nr. 2, p. 751.

they would be given priority if and when the plants under their control were to be sold.[35]

When the "ownership fight" between the Armaments Inspectorate and the G.G. authorities broke out in the summer of 1940, there were two bones of contention: who was entitled to appoint "trustees" and who owned the munitions factories and was thus authorized to supervise their operations and lease them to a third party. In July, 1940, Frank declared that the munitions factories would not constitute an independent force in the Generalgouvernement,[36] thus confronting the Wehrmacht's economic authorities with the real danger of losing their primary source of support – the military industries – in the Generalgouvernement, as had already happened in the Reich. In that same month, the Division of War Economy and Ordnance framed its counter-demands accordingly:

a) to be granted unrestricted operational authority over the munitions plants;

b) to be granted authority to appoint and supervise trustees to the military industry and to approve leasing contracts to third parties.[37]

A new armaments inspector was also appointed in the G.G. This was Gen. Maximilian Schindler, known as a stern and determined man. As preparations for the invasion of Russia in August, 1940 began, the Wehrmacht again gained the upper hand and Schindler launched an attack on Frank: the Armaments Inspectorate was given sole responsibility for the executive management of the munitions plants and all visits from anyone outside this authority were forbidden. At the same time, he presented the G.G. authorities with a list of 11 plants in which the Wehrmacht was especially interested. Although they included enterprises such as the Braunschweig Stahlwerke steel factories linked to Herman Goering's concern, the Skarżysko munitions plants were surprisingly missing from the list.[38]

---

[35] Dietrich Eichholtz: Geschichte der deutschen Kriegswirtschaft 1939–1945, (Berlin: Akademie Vlg, 1971,) B.1, p. 192.

[36] Besprechung, 12.7.1940, Krakau, Tagebuch, YV, JM/21, nr. 2, p. 654.

[37] Aktenvermerk ueber die Besprechung beim OKW Wi Rue Amt am 22.7.1940 Krakau, 29.7.1940, MA, RW 23/6a, p. 79.

[38] Besprechung, 29.11.1940, Krakau, Tagebuch, YV, JM/21, Nr. 2, p. 1088.

Why did Schindler avoid infringing on Hasag's interests? The answer can be found in the fact that in June, 1940, Roechling had relinquished commissary management of the Skarżysko plants and the Armaments Inspectorate now wished to establish Hasag in its place. This became a matter of some urgency when, following the armistice with France in June, 1940, the German industrialists decided to suspend munitions production. The Skarżysko plants, situated in the Generalgouvernement, thus became that much more vital. It appears to have been Budin, a cunning tactician, who made his consent to run all of the Skarżysko plants conditional on Schindler's acquiescence to several of his demands: Hasag would operate the factory as a sub-contractor with the assurance of a purchase option in the future, the transfer of the Raków foundry at Częstochowa to Hasag management, and Schindler's support in all matters of production, including recruitment of workers.

Schindler agreed to all Budin's conditions: up until 1943, Hasag ran the Skarżysko plants as a sub-contractor (Regiebetrieb) of the Wehrmacht's Supreme Command, meaning that its production was contracted for in return for costs plus commission. In September, 1940, the Rakow foundry was placed under the commissary management of Hasag.[39] The third plant to fall into Budin's hands was the "GRANAT" grenade factory in Kielce, where Hasag's Supply and Economic Division *(Beschaffung und Wirtschaftsabteilung der Hasag – BeWi)*, in charge of the company's financial affairs, was established.[40] Thus for Hasag, 1941 began with a tremendous spurt of development since, counter to all military logic, munitions production within Germany fell off to a dangerous low,[41] compelling the Ordnance Division to increase its orders in the Generalgouvernement. However, in the wake of the victories in the east in the Autumn of 1941, orders for munitions were reduced here as well and for the first time in the history of war, the daily consumption of munitions exceeded daily production.

---

[39] Rue Wi Lgb, Krakau, 12.9.40, MA, RH 53–23/27, pp. 100, 118–119;

[40] Beschaffungs – und Wirtschaftsabteilung der Hugo Schneider Aktiengesellschaft, Kielce, 12 November 1942, YV, 0-6/37-3.

[41] Deutschland-Produktion des wichtigen Kriegsgeraetes (1940–1944), Hans Jacobsen, Der zweite Weltkrieg in Chronik und Dokumenten, (Darmstadt: Wehr u. Wissen Vlg, 1961), p. 562.

When it became clear that there would be no Blitzkrieg on the eastern front, the Reich authorities were forced to change their armaments policy, and in February, 1942, Albert Speer was appointed Minister of Armaments. Speer sought the fullest possible cooperation of the industrialists in order to reorganize the munitions industry to ensure massive production of arms and ammunition. Ironically, Gen. Thomas took the same position, thus putting the lie to any theoretical basis for the separate existence of the Wehrmacht's economic offices. In May, 1942, Speer removed the Economy Armament Office from Thomas's control and transferred it to the authority of his Ministry, including the Armaments Inspectorate in Germany and the Generalgouvernement.

Hasag also enjoyed the preferential treatment afforded the industrialists in Speer's new organizational configuration: in Germany, Budin was reappointed head of Special Committee 2.[42] In the Generalgouvernement its status became immeasurably more secure: of the 64 factories defined as "armaments plants" in early 1942, **only two** specialized in munitions, the Skarżysko plants and "Granat" in Kielce whose iron came from the Raków foundry – all three under Hasag management. As orders began to flow in during March, 1942, the Hasag-Skarżysko storehouses gradually filled up with 14 different types of munitions.

These production achievements also had a bearing on the organizational structure: Speer appointed Egon Dalski accredited agent for matters of munitions production in the Generalgouvernement. In September, 1942, an Armaments Commission was established in the G.G., its members consisting of representatives of Speer's office and of the Generalgouvernment, with Gen. Schindler as chairman. Listed among the commission's functions was the recruitment of workers for the military industry in the Generalgouvernement[43] – a fact which represented a major turning point in the annals of the Hasag plants.

---

[42] "Hauptausschuss-Munition" Organisationsplan, Stand vom 28.2.1943, BA, R 3/1030, pp. 18–19, 20–23.

[43] G. Thomas, Geschichte, op. cit., p. 312; Besprechung, 3.11.42, Krakau, Tagebuch, YV, JM/21, Nr. 7, p. 1197.

Chapter 2

Establishment of the Jewish Forced Labor Camp at Skarżysko-Kamienna: Background and Contributing Factors

Recruitment of Polish and Jewish Workers for the Hasag Plants up to Early 1942

Up to the end of 1941, three major factors were affecting the labor market in the G.G.: the increasing involvement of the German private sector in the various branches of commerce and industry; intensified preparations for the Barbarossa Campaign; and the Reich's need for seasonal workers. With this increased demand for laborers, recruitment was centralized in the hands of the Central Labor Department of the G.G. government, headed by Max Frauendorfer. Throughout the Generalgouvernement, 356 labor exchanges were opened – their tasks: to register the entire working population, to issue work permits, and to act as agents for the supply of manpower. All plants (including those under commissary management) were required to apply to the local labor exchange for any workers they might need.[1] The employment of Jewish workers was still in the hands of HSSuPF Krueger and his subordinates.

---

[1] Verordnung ueber die Beschraenkung des Arbeitsplatzwechsels, Doc. Occup., vol. 10, Praca przymusowa Polaków pod panowaniem hitlerowskim 1939–1945, ed. A. Konieczny, H. Szurgacz, (Poznań: Instytut Zachodni, 1976), p. 446.

The first signs of a labor shortage in Germany became apparent in Spring, 1941 when recruitment to the Wehrmacht was stepped up. When, in February 1941, the High Command withdrew its opposition to the employment of foreign workers in the war industries,[2] the Armaments Inspectorate gave permission to recruit Polish workers at German subsidiaries in the G.G. for transfer to the main plant, on a voluntary basis. The Hasag concern alone took advantage of this opportunity and, in April, 1941, sent 1,961 Poles from its factories in Skarżysko and Kielce to its plants in Germany.[3]

It is worthy of note that of the 13 million residents of the General-gouvernement in 1941, only 700,000 (none of them Jews) were registered with the labor exchanges.[4] Nevertheless, the Skarżysko plants had no trouble finding workers to replace those who had been sent to the Reich. In a memo of November, 1941 describing the "diet of the industrial workers in the Radom district," Dr Haeussler, head of the district Industrial Department, explained that as a result of wage benefits and food supplements supplied to their staffs by the military industries, workers were leaving the small factories to work in the munitions plants. The example given was the Hasag plants in Skarżysko, "formerly a region whose influence was limited to the immediate area, while workers now come from as far as 35 kilometers away."[5]

No wonder the Skarżysko plants became a source of pride for Paul Budin who, in May 1941, decided to invite Himmler to visit: "This is the largest of the three factories I run for the Wehrmacht in the General-gouvernement on behalf of Hasag. In this plant alone we employ 9,000 Poles in the production of ammunition and explosives. This is clear proof of the pioneering function and duty being fulfilled by the German munitions industry both in terms of labor management and in terms of production..."[6] (see Figure 2.1). The report of the Armaments Inspectorate from February 1, 1942 reveals that the work force of the

---

[2] Hans Pfahlman, Fremdarbeiter und Kriegsgefangene in der deutschen Kriegswirtschaft 1939–1945, (Darmstadt: Wehr u. Wissen Vlg, 1968), p. 231.

[3] Rue Wi Lgb, 14.5.1941, MA, RW 23/8, p. 117.

[4] Arbeitsmarktlage, Rue Wi Lgb, 14.2.1941, MA, RW 23/8, p. 30.

[5] Ernaehrungslage der Industriellen Arbeiterschaft, 14.11.1941, Doc. Occup., vol. 6, pp. 361–367.

[6] Paul Budin, "An die SS-Reichsfuerung", Leipzig, 29 Mai 1941, YV, JM/4440, p. 2655323.

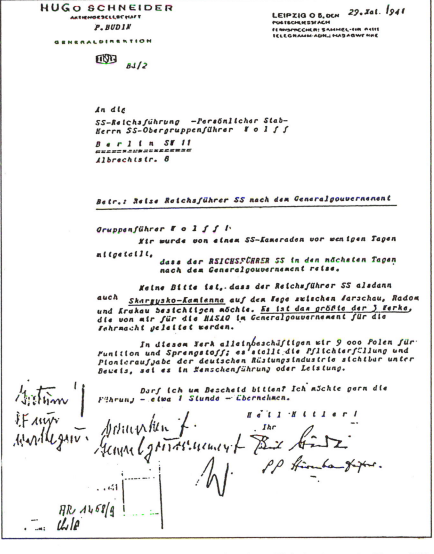

Figure 2.1 Invitation from Paul Budin to Himmler to Visit the Skarżysko Plants (YV, JM/44440, p. 2655323)

Hasag-Skarżysko plants already numbered 10,267. With the addition of the "Granat" factory and the Raków foundry, Hasag employed 13,850 workers.[7] This success in recruiting Polish laborers raises the question of why Hasag needed any Jews at all.

According to the directive of December, 1939, which marked the first stage in the program of Jewish slave labor in the Generalgouvernement, the Jews were to be enclosed in camps under the supervision of the SS. Forced labor was to be implemented by means of camps, and any other type of arrangement was merely a short-term divergence from this principle. Until the end of 1941, three frameworks were in operation: ghetto workshops, work brigades sent outside the ghetto, and temporary camps.[8] Moreover, Jews continued to be abducted (*Abschleppung*) from the streets for any number of "public works."

The plan to enclose the bulk of the Jewish population in work camps supervised by the SS failed dismally because of the problems involved in financing, maintaining and policing the camps. In the wake of this failure on the part of Krueger and his subordinates, there was total chaos in all matters concerning the employment of Jews throughout the first half of 1940. Several groups took advantage of this situation to benefit from free Jewish labor. Thus, throughout the G.G., open work camps sprang up, created by Wehrmacht, police or SS units, construction and road building companies, private Polish and German sewerage firms, private farms, etc. Each camp remained in existence for however long it was needed. Living and sanitation conditions were terrible, and maintenance of the camps was made the responsibility of the Judenrat of whichever ghetto the Jews were drawn from. They were guarded by the Polish police, SS units, Werk-schutz, or hired guards. Only in the Lublin district were closed work camps set up at the initiative of SSuPF Odil Globocnik.

In view of the chaotic situation, an agreement was concluded between Frank and Krueger. A memo sent to the directors of all the labor exchanges in the Generalgouvernement on July 4, 1940 marked the start of

---

[7] Statistischer Ueberblick ueber die W-Betriebe der Rue In im GG, Stand 1.2.1942, Anlage nr. 59, MA, RW 23/6a, p. 143.

[8] Israel Gutman: Avodat kviyah shel Yehudim b'sherut hagermanim b'misrach Europa b'tkufat milchemet olam hashnia, (Hebrew), *Zion*, A–B, (Jerusalem: Hachevra haartziisraelit l'historia w'etnografia, 1978).

the second stage in the program of Jewish slave labor camps in the G.G.[9] The memo directed that any request for and employment of Jewish workers, whether freely or in the form of forced labor, was the exclusive province of the labor exchanges. Moreover, since the Judenrats which until now had paid Jewish workers' wages were bankrupt, all employers of Jews in the free market were to pay them 80% of the wages paid a Polish worker in a comparable job (this order was never put into effect). As for the Jews conscripted for forced labor on large-scale projects and already in camps under SS control, they would receive only token wages. This was undoubtedly a gesture made for the benefit of Krueger and Globocnik.

In July, 1940, Hasag was naturally interested in keeping its production costs to a minimum. As long as the Judenrats were footing the bill for Jewish workers, the use of Jewish work brigades was the cheapest solution. The new directive altered Hasag's situation since, as a commissary manager, it was now required to recruit Jewish workers as well through the labor exchanges and to pay their wages out of its own pocket.[10] The simplest solution was to set up a closed Jewish work camp, but to do this they would have to prove that the Skarżysko plants were about to expand operations, a notion which, in July, 1940, was unrealistic in view of the drop in orders.

Nevertheless, it appears that by August talks were already underway between the Skarżysko management and the directors in Leipzig regarding the "rehabilitation of the Kamienna plants."[11] This project may have been the basis for the permission granted Budin to maintain Jewish slave labor camps. Evidence can be found in the underground press from September, 1940 which reported that the Skarżysko plants employed free workers (i.e., Poles) as well as forced laborers who slept within the factory grounds,[12] apparently a reference to Jews. I would suggest that Budin and Dalski maintained a sort of "dummy camp" in order to employ Jews

---

[9] Arbeitseinsatz der juedischen Bevoelkerung, Krakau, 5. Juli 1940, Doc. occup., vol. 6, pp. 568–572.

[10] Gazeta Żydowska, 26.2.1940.

[11] Gustav Kuhne, Sitzungen, p. 11.

[12] "Informacje z Polski t.j. ze Skarżyska-Kamiennej z września 1940", YV, M-2/240.

without having to pay them, and this is the source of the false contention
that a labor camp already existed in Skarżysko in mid-1940.[13]

In 1940–41, the recruitment of Jewish laborers for the Skarżysko
plants was of a seasonal nature and was affected by the attitude of the
Polish workers at any given time, as well as by their numbers: in the
winter of 1940, when mass arrests of Polish workers led to a shortage of
manpower in Werk C, a group of Jews from Skarżysko was immediately
recruited for construction jobs. When in late 1941 there was again
increased unrest among the Poles, the Hasag management responded with
a series of arrests, and Dalski hung notices stating: "Workers! You
continue to listen to trouble-makers whose slogans are 'Go slow,' 'Don't
report for work,' etc. We've known about this for a long time and we do
not intend to sit back and turn a blind eye to your behavior toward us....
The names of shirkers have been reported to the Gestapo in Radom. We
are trying to get food for you ... and are doing as much as we can for you
despite the difficulties.... If the only gratitude you know is to foment
unrest and sabotage a vital military plant, there's a very good chance that
in winter you will find the gates of the factory locked in your faces. Let
those who incite you today supply you with bread then."[14]

The Hasag management was not unaware of the large concentrations
of Jews near Skarżysko resulting from the hardships imposed on the
Jewish population in the Radom district, then numbering nearly 400,000.[15]
In Spring, 1941, the ghettos were established, most of them in the central
region, among them the ghettos of Bodzentyń, Końskie, Opatów,
Suchedniów, Szydłowiec, and Skarżysko. A directive issued on December
11, 1941 ordered the closing off of all the ghettos in the Radom district,[16]
and a simultaneous directive of the G.G. Labor Department formally
cancelled all benefits and social rights for Jews.[17]

---

[13] International Trace Service, (ITS) Katalog I, (Arolsen, 1949), p. 324.; ITS, Katalog III,
1969, p. 424.

[14] "Odezwa", Muzeum Miejskie w Skarżysku-Kamiennej, Dział dokumentów.

[15] Alfred Rosenberg, Testimony, YV, JM/3573, rol. 275, p. 190.

[16] Rundschreiben, betr. Bildung juedischer Wohnbezirke, Radom, 11 Dezember 1941, BA,
R 52 II/254, pp. 116–117.

[17] Regelung von Arbeitsbedingungen der Juden im Generalgouvernement vom 15 Dezember
1941, Doc. occup., vol. 6, p. 572.

Thus a potential reserve of workers, imprisoned and starving, became readily available to Hasag. All that was needed was the initiative of the plant management to turn this into an actual work force.

Budin's Personnel Policy at the Skarżysko Plants as a Factor in the Establishment of the Slave Labor Camp

From 1939 Hasag employed Germans, Volksdeutsch, Ukrainians and Poles in the Skarżysko plants as permanent workers, and Jews on a temporary basis (see Introduction). From observing relations among their staff over a period of three years, the management learned that successful control of thousands of workers of different nationalities depended on a calculated personnel policy: familiarity with the specific complexities of each national unit, exploitation of the ancient conflicts between them, and handsomely rewarding outstanding workers. It was no less important for them to find some common ground for the Poles, Ukrainians and Volksdeutsch without encouraging their anti-German solidarity. It is my considered opinion that Budin realized just how the Jewish camp could become a political tool par excellence, the perfect answer to all of his problems.

The first obstacle to orderly production was the shortage of German shop stewards resulting from the Wehrmacht's recruitmentrive. Hasag was virtually the only company to find enough Germans, since Budin was able to promise those in his employ in the G.G. the status of "essential production worker." [18] Since this was very hard to achieve in Germany, Budin sought to transfer vital Hasag employees in the Reich to Skarżysko. A "Letter of Referral" sent by Karl Herold from Leipzig in June 1942 reveals the benefits granted the Skarżysko workers: promotion, free housing and food, 54 marks per week before taxes (to be sent to the families in Germany), and an allowance of 200 zlotys per month. The Letter of Referral stresses that *"all of these benefits apply only to the period of your employment within the borders of the Generalgouvernement and regular terms will be resumed upon your return to the plant in Germany"* [19] [original emphasis].

---

[18] "Arbeiterstand in den W-Betrieben", Rue WI Lgb, 15.4.1941, MA, RW 23/8, p. 87.

[19] "An das Gefolgschaftsmitglied Karl Herold", Leipzig, den 19 Juni 1942, Die Hoelle, op. cit., Dokumente.

Although the Germans were united by the solidarity of the controlling minority, they still had to find a common ground with the thousands of Polish workers vital to production. In this context, the existence of the Jewish camp offered limitless possibilities if only because of the anti-Semitism shared by the two nations. The presence of Jews enabled each and every German to prove his exceptional efficiency, not to mention the opportunity for quick profits.

In May 1942, there were 118 German men at the Skarżysko plants employed in administrative, supervisory and instructorship posts, and 23 German women, most of them in secretarial jobs.[20] Budin was forced to include Volksdeutsch on his staff as well. Throughout the years of their operations, the Hasag plants employed a total of 690 Volksdeutsche.[21] In May 1942, there were 71 Volksdeutsch in the factory, 31 employed as *Werkschutz* and the rest as overseers. They held a lowly status since the Germans feared they had "returned to the fold" only for the financial benefits and the Poles viewed them quite simply as turncoats. It was to Budin's advantage to find this denigrated minority an arena in which they could enhance their status without detracting from the privileged rank of the Germans. Supervision of the Jews seemed the easiest solution.

The problem which aroused the greatest concern for the Hasag management was the composition of the *Werkschutz* since they were well aware of the fierce hatred between the Ukrainians and the Poles. Skarżysko was no exception, but here the management had no choice but to accept the situation. In 1942, the Hasag *Werkschutz* consisted of 180 men, 28 German commanders, 31 Volksdeutsche, and the remainder Ukrainians.[22] In September, 1941 the Armaments Inspectorate transferred all authority for the *Werkschutz* to the plant managements in order to tighten supervision of the Ukrainians.[23]

This order increased the *Werkschutz's* dependence on the Hasag management which in turn sought out ways to reduce the expense of maintaining this crew. They received an average of 38 zlotys a week, their own kitchen, and certain benefits. Although these seemed fairly poor

---

[20] "Stand der reichsdeutschen Gefolgschaft am 31.5.1942", YV, JM/3700, pp. 14–15.

[21] "Pismo Rady Zakładowej P.F.A. w Skar.-Kam.", 2.4.1946, YV, JM/3700, p. 20.

[22] Werkschutz, Lohnzahlung, YV, JM/3700, pp. 17–18.

[23] Rue In im GG, Krakau, 29.9.1941, betr: Ukrainischer Werkschutz, MA, RW 23/6a, p. 122.

conditions, the *Werkschutz* had learned from experience that any seizure of Jews for work at the plant was accompanied by the plundering of their property. The Hasag management was well aware of this fact, and regarded the Jewish camp as an opportunity to grant the *Werkschutz* extra benefits at no cost to the company. Moreover, they hoped that having the Jews as free game would blunt the Ukrainians' hatred for the Poles.

No manipulations of personnel policy could change the fact that all other nationalities were very much in the minority as compared to the thousands of Poles. Poles were required to sign a pledge undertaking to perform their jobs responsibly and to report any instance of sabotage.[24] A number of their social benefits were cancelled, and the work day was extended to 10–14 hours in two shifts. The average wage of a Polish worker was 15–35% lower than that of his German counterpart. In October 1941, a skilled worker at the Hasag plants was receiving 1.30 zloty an hour, and an unskilled worker 1 zloty.[25]

These conditions could not keep pace with rising inflation, although not all Poles suffered equally. Pre-war social distinctions between the intelligentsia and the laborers were still maintained in the plant. The former, engineers, technicians, low-level administrators, etc., largely remained in their previous posts, the majority in Werk A. It was here that the "nobility" worked as well, people from the rich families of Skarżysko and the vicinity who bribed the officials of the labor exchanges and the German managers and thus found a haven at Hasag from the danger of conscription for work in the Reich. The most severely hit were the thousands of factory workers and unskilled laborers. Absenteeism was high among this group, and Hasag employed harsh terror tactics against them. In Autumn 1942 a "Education for Work Camp" *(Arbeitserziehungslager)* was set up to deal with those Poles who were negligent or shirkers.[26]

A similar state of affairs prevailed at the other munitions factories as well. Why did so many Poles shirk their work? Polish historiography regards "mass absenteeism" above all as the expression of a national

---

[24] Longin Kaczanowski, Hitlerowskie fabryki śmierci na Kielecczyźnie, (Warszawa: Książka i Wiedza, 1984), p. 104.

[25] Arbeitsamt Lublin, 21 Oktober 1941, Doc. occup. vol. 10, p. 465.

[26] L. Kaczanowski, Hitlerowskie fabryki, op. cit., p. 44.

struggle aimed at sabotaging the Third Reich's war production. German sources present an entirely different point of view: a report of the Armaments Command of the Radom district from July 1942 lays responsibility at the feet of the Poles and the Jews alike. The Jews, given no legal food allowance, were forced to turn to the black market, using Poles as their middlemen. The latter, in turn, garnered rich profits from these transactions. "Opportunities for Jews to do business have been gradually eliminated and they are increasingly being replaced by Aryans who have proved themselves to be quick Students producing excellent results. *The number of people making their living in this way has increased in direct proportion to the drop in the number of available jobs*"[27] [my emphasis – F.K.].

The close link between absenteeism and the black market becomes clearer in view of the fact that *the black market in the Generalgouvernement grew to the proportions of an independent economy existing almost legally alongside the official economy*. It was unmatched in any other occupied country in Europe in terms of the extent of the population involved, the methods of operations, and the sophistication of its organization. This was made possible by the tolerant attitude of the German authorities and administrators who worked in partnership with the Poles, making easy profits for themselves. Thus, despite the war officially waged on the black market by the police, it continued to flourish.

In 1942 two processes associated with the Jews played a part in the growth of the black market. The first was the completion of the Aryanization of small businesses whereby Poles replaced Jews in nearly every branch of small and mid-size commerce and industry. Since profits from these businesses were considerably higher than the minimal wages paid by the munitions plants, skilled laborers preferred to absent themselves from their jobs in the plants – despite the risks – and to turn their homes into workshops for goods they could sell for a high price on the black market.

The second process furthering the growth of the black market was the start of implementation of the "Final Solution". In June 1942, HSSuPF Krueger declared that the deportation of Jews was causing a drop in

---

[27] "Ueberblick des Dienststellenleiters", Juli 1942, MA, RW-23/16, p. 8.

prices.[28] In point of fact, the lower prices resulted from the cessation of police activities against those supplying the black market, which occurred around the same time as the first large deportations. Each ghetto aktion was accompanied by the plundering of the remainder Jewish property, some of which reached the black market and brought prices down. This was also true for the gold, foreign currency, and jewelry.[29]

The huge proportions of the black market offered opportunities even for the poorer sectors of the population to find a niche in it, thus again leading to greater absenteeism. The suggestion of the American scholar, Homze, that by April 1942 no reserves of workers remained in the G.G.[30] can not, therefore, be accepted. The shortage of manpower did not derive from the increased war effort or from shipments to the Reich, but from the Poles' extensive involvement in the black market. Hasag realized that intimidation alone could not solve the problem of absenteeism. In December, 1942 Budin informed the Skarżysko employees that anyone absenting himself from work would not receive his food allowance which would instead be divided up among the conscientious workers[31] (see Figure 2.2). Hasag also tried to compensate "outstanding" Poles with promotions, but so long as there were no other workers in the plant, this was difficult to carry out.

It was this series of difficulties, which might be termed "the Polish problem", on which Budin's personnel policies hinged, and it is here that the primary motives for the establishment of the Jewish camp at Skarżysko should be sought. In political terms, it was reasonable to suppose that placing responsibility for supervision of the Jews in Polish hands would make it easier for the Germans to control the Poles themselves. In economic terms, the Jews represented a reserve of manpower which could be employed when needed should the Poles be transferred to Germany or absenteeism increase. The camp was to serve another economic function as a link in the chain of the black market

---

[28] Arbeitstagung 18.6.1942, Stanisław Piotrowski, Dziennik Hansa Franka, (Warszawa: Wydawnictwo Prawnicze, 1956), p. 318.

[29] C. Madajczyk, Polityka, op. cit., 1, p. 624.

[30] E.L. Homze: Foreign labor in Nazi Germany (Princeton: Princeton University Press, 1967), p. 165.

[31] Bekanntmachung an die Belegschaft in Skarżysko-Kamienna, Kielce, 7.12.42, Muzeum Miejskie, see note 14.

Kielce, den 7. 12. 42

Bekanntmachung

an die Belegschaft in Skarżysko-Kamienna

Eine wirksame Verbesserung der Ernährung greift mit sofortiger Wirkung Platz. Darunter befindet sich zufolge der Vorlteile, die wir durch die eigene Kartoffel-verarbeitung haben

1. die Erhöhung der Brotration, wie folgt:

    a) Ausgesprochene Schwerstarbeiter (z.B. Transportarbeiter in der Granatenfertigung und Presserei usw.) 2.500 gr
    b) Schwerarbeiter wie bislang 2.000 gr
    c) Normalarbeiter von 1.400 gr ebenfals durchweg auf 2.000 gr

2. Die Unterstützung der in Kamienna wohnenden Familienmitglieder in der Form, dass auch sie, die bislang leer in der Kartoffelversogung ausgegangen waren,

    1 Dz pro Kopf Kartoffeln

    zugewiesen erhalten, und zwar

    a) 1/2 Dz Kartoffeln vor Weinachten,
    b) den weiteren 1/2 Dz Kartoffeln am 1 April 1943, zuferlässige Arbeit vorausgesetzt.

3. Verstärkung des warmen Werksküchenessens durch Erhöhung der Ration von 1/2 Ltr. auf durchweg 3/4 Ltr., und zwar nicht durch Wasser, sondern durch Ernährungszusatz, wie Kartoffeln und Gemüse.

BESONDERE BEMERKUNG:
Strengste Anweisung habe ich gegeben dadurch, dass von jetzt ab grundsätzlich alle Männer und Frauen der Belegschaft, die unpünktlich sind oder unentschuldigt fehlen, ihre Sonderzuteilungen sowie die Vorteile des Konsums strikte eingeschränkt bezw. zeitlich gesperrt erhalten, denn sie verdienen es nicht besser.

Diese eingesparten Sonderzuteilungen werden im vollem Umfang den fleisigen und zuverlässigen Arbeitskräften durch die Betriebsführung überschrieben, wobei ich mir selbst die Kontrolle vorbehalte.

Paul BUDIN
Generaldirektor der HASAG

Figure 2.2   Notice of the Workers of Skarżysko-Kamienna

system, bait attracting Poles to the plant because of the opportunity they offered for doing business on the premises.

Changes in the Labor Market in the Generalgouvernement and the Early Days of the Skarżysko Camp

Although the idea of setting up a Jewish slave labor camp at the Hasag plant was born of a long series of events, the fact of its establishment stemmed from changes in the labor market in the G.G. that began in the Spring of 1942. Hitler assigned Fritz Sauckel the task of organizing the recruitment of slave laborers in all of the occupied countries of Europe, particularly Russia. Factory owners in the Reich, however, refused to employ Russians. As a result, urgent orders went out to the General-gouvernement to conscript Poles if enough volunteers could not be enticed.[32]

The term "conscription" offered new opportunities for Budin. In March, 1942, armed with letters of recommendation from the Reich's Labor Ministry, he requested the necessary approval of the Labor Department of the G.G., but was met with strong opposition. Never-theless, Budin organized the transport of Polish workers to the Reich, resorting even to "police measures" to do so. Frank, despite his harsh complaints against the "shocking exploitive methods employed by German concerns in the Generalgouvernement,"[33] submitted to the coalition formed by Budin, the army, and the Reich, all of which were interested in limiting his authority.

The transport of Polish workers to the Reich occurred around the same time as the issuance of new restrictions on the Jews in the Radom district: in February, 1942 they were forbidden to leave the ghetto, offenders to be put to death.[34] About one month later, around late March to early April 1942, the nucleus of the Skarżysko camp was established when 2000 Jews were suddenly brought into the area of the plant to serve as permanent workers.[35]

---

[32] Dienstverpflichtungsverordnung, 13.5.1942, Doc. occup. vol. 6, p. 322.

[33] Arbeitstagung, 18.3.1942, Tagebuch, YV, JM/21, nr. 6, p. 194.

[34] Gazeta Żydowska, 21.3.1942.

[35] G. Kuhne, Sitzungen, p. 8; cf. Henryk Zając, Testimony, YV, 0–16/1157.

Were the camp's establishment and organization part of the program of slave labor camps in the district, or was this a unique phenomenon?

There were, within the district, three models of Jewish slave labor camps, each of them typical of a different stage in the program:

1. open work camps *(Arbeitslager)*, some 25 in number,[36] existed for various lengths of times from early 1940 to mid-1942 for "work brigades";

2. "residual ghettos" *(Restghetto)*, which appeared in 13 towns in Autumn, 1942 after the large-scale deportations occupying the areas of the former ghettos, were forced labor camps in all respects, subject to the authority of the District SS Leader; [37]

3. "factory camps" *(Betriebslager)* established on factory grounds in eight towns during the Summer, 1943 for Jewish laborers, which operated until they were dismantled in 1944.

Based on my research, I calculate that a total of around 50 slave labor camps of different sorts existed at one time or another in the Radom district.

At this time there were still open work camps scattered around the district, so that the action of the Hasag management appears somewhat premature. What were their motives? There can be no doubt that Budin and Dalski, both senior SS officers, had prior knowledge of the approaching date for implementation of the "Final Solution" in the Radom district. In March 1942, Martin Bormann sent a memo to the directors of the munitions factories stating that the industry could not yet let its Jewish workers go, "and no complaints could be leveled at a plant manager still employing Jews." [38] It would thus appear that Budin was attempting to

---

[36] Zofia Czyńska, Bogumił Kupść: "Obozy zagłady, obozy koncentracyjne i obozy pracy na ziemiach polskich w latach 1939–1945", Biuletyn GKBZHwP, (hereafter BGKBZH), (Warszawa: Wydawnictwo Prawnicze, styczeń 1946), p. 13.

[37] Adam Rutkowski: Hitlerowskie obozy pracy w dystrykcie radomskim, Biuletyn Żydowskiego Instytutu Historycznego, 17–18, (hereafter BZIH), (Warszawa: ZIH, 1956), pp. 114–120.

[38] Rundschreiben nr. 35/42, betr. Einsatz von Juden in Ruebetrieben, Partei Kanzlei, 14 Maerz 1942, YV, JM/4139, p. 12152.

establish facts on the ground *before* the "Final Solution" reached the Radom district.

The primary reason for the urgent establishment of the camp, however, seems to have been the opening of the SS-WVHA in February, 1942, an organization which sought to gain control of all the Jewish labor camps in the G.G. This led to the anti-Himmler coalition joined by all the other authorities exploiting Jewish labor. The Generalgouvernement's Labor Department preferred to see small camps established near the factories,[39] and the Armaments Inspectorate wished to maintain the status quo in regard to the Jews. The coalition also attracted SS and local commanders in the G.G. districts, since their control over the Jewish camps was jeopardized by Himmler's centralization plan.[40] The private companies also joined in opposition to the plan since it was not in their interest to have to hire Jewish concentration camp prisoners from the WVHA.

Budin was able to take advantage of this favorable political constellation in order to set up the Skarżysko camp *before* the WVHA had time to gain exclusive control of Jewish labor. Starting in April, the district labor exchange began to assign groups of Jews to the Skarżysko plants. The Judenrats lent their cooperation since they no longer had responsibility for the wages and food allotments once the Jews were transferred to closed camps.[41] In June, 1942, as news of the death transports in other districts began to reach Radom, panic broke out in the ghettos. Some Jews tried to get the Judenrats to bribe labor exchange officials to recommend their recruitment for work in the munitions plants. Hasag seized the opportunity to spread rumors of its willingness to accept volunteers. Arrangements were made by the head of the local labor exchange together with the Judenrat. In order to encourage Jews to volunteer, Hasag paid them a token wage and allowed them to exchange letters with their families remaining in the ghettos.[42]

Thus, in the Summer of 1942, Skarżysko was the one and only factory camp to be established. Sources indicate that at least 17 transports of Jews,

---

[39] Arbeitssitzungen am 13.4.42, 11.5.1942, Krakau, Okupacja i ruch oporu w Dzienniku Hansa Franka, ed. Zofia Połubiec, (Warszawa: Książka i Wiedza, 1970), pp. 455, 459.

[40] Joseph Billig, Les camps de concentration dans l'économie du Reich hitlerien, (Paris: Presses Universitaires, 1973) pp. 199–220.

[41] Gazeta Żydowska, 31.5.1942, p. 2.

[42] Pamiętnik Dawida Rubinowicza, (Warszawa: Książka i Wiedza, 1987), pp. 92–96.

whether conscripts or volunteers, were brought to Skarżysko between March and July from Radoszyce, Biała-Rawska, Staszów, Chęciny, Kielce, Stopnica, Raków, Opatów, Włoszczowa, Ożarów, Lelów, Końskie, Bodzentyń, Opoczno, and Zwoleń. Even if we treat the reliability of these sources with some caution, we can state that even before the official establishment of the camp in August, Hasag had managed to gather around 5,500 Jews.[43]

In preparation for the implementation of the "Final Solution", instructions were sent to all the G.G. labor exchanges on June 25, 1942 directing that from this time on Jews could be employed only with the approval of the local SS and police commander. The military industries were not exempt from this requirement.[44] This was the start of the third stage in the program of Jewish slave labor in the Generalgouvernement. Schindler reached an agreement with Karl Schoengarth, commander of the security police in the G.G., and Herbert Boettcher, SS and Police Leader of the Radom district, whereby the Jews employed in the munitions plants would be issued special documents by the plant managements, and the Armaments Inspectorate would be responsible for any negotiations with HSSuPF Krueger regarding the recruitment of Jewish workers.[45]

Himmler, however, refused to approve the various agreements pertaining to the Jews. Krueger was forced to notify Schindler on August 17, 1942 that according to the latest orders, all Jewish manpower was to be transferred to the exclusive authority of the SS and only then would be made available to the munitions plants.[46] But the order arrived too late: by the end of August, construction of all three *werks* of the Skarżysko camp was complete, and the Jews within were under the control of Hasag and not the SS.

At the time of its establishment, the Skarżysko camp was therefore clearly unique as the first *Betriebslager* not only in the Radom district, but throughout the Generalgouvernement. It came into being as a function of

---

[43] See the list of transports between Mars and July 1942, Felicja Karay, Hamavet b'tzahov, mahane avoda Skarżysko-Kamienna (Hebrew), (Jerusalem: Yad Vashem & Tel-Aviv University, 1994) p. 57.

[44] Arbeitseinsatz der Juden., Krakau, 25.6.1942, BA, R 52 II/255, p. 35.

[45] Fernschreiben an O. F. K. Kielce, 8.8.1942, MA, RH 53-23/87.

[46] Kriegstagebuch des Ruestungskommando (hereafter Rue Kdo) Warschau, 17.8.1942, BA, RW 23/19.

the specific interests of the private companies, Frank's government, and the Wehrmacht authorities. Even the timing was particularly convenient, since the power of the G.G.'s local administration was on the wane, while that of the WVHA had yet to reach its height. Budin enjoyed the full support of Herbert Boettcher, appointed to his post in the Radom District in May, 1942. Hasag-Skarżysko was followed in the autumn by the establishment of two more "factory camps": one at the explosives plant in Pionki and the other at the "Granat" factory in Kielce, it, too, managed by Hasag.

Chapter 3

The Hasag-Skarżysko Camp During The "Radom Period" (August 1942 to July 1943)

The "Final Solution" in The Radom District and The "Jew Exchange" System in The Camp

The establishment of the Skarżysko camp in August 1942 marks the start of its "external history" – the policies of the Hasag management and other pertinent authorities regarding the camp and the manner in which Jewish workers were recruited. The two years of the camp's existence may be divided into three periods differentiated by the place from which prisoner transports originated and the time of their arrival:

1. **The Radom Period** – From August 1942 to late Summer 1943, when transports arrived from towns in the Radom district;
2. **The Majdanek Period** – From June to late November 1943, when prisoners from the Majdanek concentration camp were brought to Skarżysko;
3. **The Płaszów Period** – from November 1943 to August 1944, when transports of thousands of Jews from the Płaszów camp arrived.

In August 1942, overall command of deportations in the Radom district was placed in the hands of Herbert Boettcher and his subordinates, the most notorious of whom was Franz Schippers, the communications officer.[1] During the final *aktion* in most of the ghettos, representatives of the German plants in the vicinity, led by Hasag, were invited to a last "selection" and allowed to choose from among the masses of deportees those most fit for work. The only transports to Skarżysko at this time of which we have certain knowledge are those mentioned in recorded testimony, although there can be no doubt that there were additional transports of which no record remains.

Even where mention is made of a specific transport, we can only estimate its date and extent since no relevant German documentation exists. If we check the list of transports (see Table 3.1; notes 2–11) against the map of the ghettos in the Radom district (see Figure 3.1), we will see that Hasag did not get Jews from every town. Nonetheless, the estimated 8,000 workers they did acquire is very high in comparison to other plants. This would seem to be attributable to the cooperation between Hasag and SS commanders of all ranks, from Herbert Boettcher down to the local commander of each town or village *(SS-Gebietsfuehrung)*. For example, testimony regarding the last aktion in Szydłowiec under the command of Franz Schippers states that the SS announced that anyone paying 1,000

---

[1] Akta w sprawie Franz Schippers, YV, JM/3786, nr. 602.

[2] **Brzeźnica-Koczelnice:** Mitteilung von Werk Skarżysko-Kamienna, Abt. Lohnbuero, Skar.-Kam., 10.11.42, YV, 0–6/37–3.

[3] Widerstand und Untergang des Ghettos in **Tschenstochau**, YV, M/32-A-4, Nr. 159/76; Pinkas **Chmielnik**, p. 844; **Dąbrowa Górnicza**, Obozy hitlerowskie na ziemiach polskich 1939–1945, Informator encyklopedyczny, (Warszawa: Państwowe Wydawnictwo Naukowe, 1979), p. 150.

[4] Testimonies YV, **Kielce:** Fiszgarten Daniel, 0-16/254; **Opatów:** Szlomo Grinszpan, M-9/16 (2); Bela Grossman, M-1/E/1612/1492; C. Erlichman, Sefer Apt, p. 226; **Końskie:** Icchak Figlarczyk, 0-3/3154.

[5] Testimonies YV: **Ożarów:** Jakow Lustig, M-1/E/377/33; **Ostrowiec:** Mosze Korngold, M-21/1-16, p. 9.

[6] **Pacanów:** Icchak Friedman: Bletlech fun a leben, (Yiddish), (Tel Aviv, "Naj Leben", 1981), p. 113.

[7] **Policzner Hojf:** Israel Chustecki: Testimony, YV, M-1/E/348/264; **Radomsko:** Genia Fogelman: Notes and letters, YV, B/44-3, nr. 5677.

[8] Eliezer Lewin: Skarżysko Book, p. 90; Elchanan Erlich: Sefer **Staszów**, p. 370.

[9] **Stopnica:** Martin Gilbert: Atlas of the Holocaust, (London: Michael Joseph, 1982) p. 132.

Table 3.1 Transports to Skarżysko-Kamienna Camp between August and November 1942 (in alphabetical order)*

Date	From	Number of transports	Quote	Note
10. Nov.	Brzeźnica & Koczelnice	2	400	2
Okt.	Chmielnik	1	500	3
Sep.	Częstochowa	1	50	3
Okt.	Dąbrowa Gornicza	1	650	3
Nov.	Kielce "Granat"	1	200	4
Nov.	Końskie	1	70	4
Aug.–Okt.	Opatów	2	1,200	4
Sep.–Okt.	Ostrowiec	2	200	5
Okt.	Ożarów	1	600	5
Okt.	Pacanów	1	200	6
Nov.	Policzner Hof	1	100	7
Okt.	Radomsko	1	200	7
Sep.–Okt.	Skarżysko-Kamienna	2	550	8
Okt.	Staszów	1	300	8
Okt.	Stopnica	1	1,500	9
Aug.–Sep.	Suchedniów	2	570	10
Okt.	Szczawnica	1	100	10
Sep.–Nov.	Szydłowiec	3	180	10
Sep.	Wodzisław & Jędrzejów	1	200	11
Aug.–Nov.	Zwoleń	3	580	11
	Total	29	8,350	

* Not all of the sources employed for Table 3.1 are edited here. For the others, see F. Karay, Hamavet b'tzahov, op. cit., Chapter 5, notes 6–53. All Yizkor-Books cited here in the notes for the table of transports see: Bibliography.

---

[10] **Suchedniów**: Szmuel Herling: Sitzungen, p. 92; **Szydłowiec**: B. Kagan, Szydlowcer Book, p. 19; **Szczawnica**: Zahawa Sztok: Testimony, YV, 0–33/1843.

[11] **Wodzisław-Jędrzejów**: "Fahrplan fuer Judentransporte aus dem Distrikt Radom ins Vernichtungslager Treblinka, September 1942", Faschismus-Getto-Massenmord, edited by T. Berenstein, A. Rutkowski, A. Eisenbach, (Berlin: Ruetten u. Loening, 1960), Dok. 248, p. 322; **Zwoleń**: Chaim Szlufman, Zwoliner Book, p. 331.

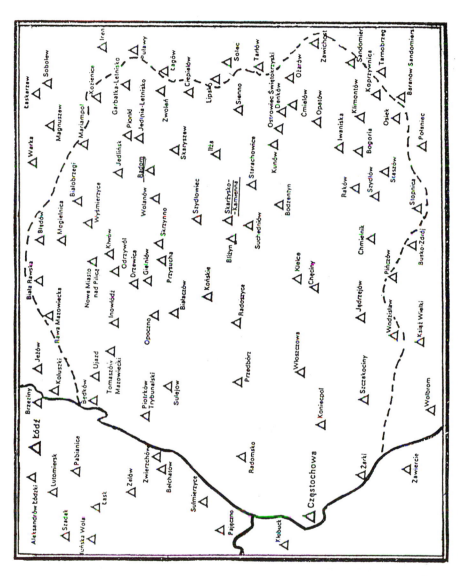

Figure 3.1 Map of the Ghetto's in Radom District

zloty would remain in the region [i.e. would be sent to the Skarżysko camp
– F.K.], but the Jews, not believing them, did not pay this sum.[12]

Another example regards the deportation from the Skarżysko ghetto. At
Schippers's orders, a list of debilitated workers at the Hasag camp was
made up in late September on the pretext that they would be allowed to
return home to the ghetto. On October 3, 1942, there was a "selection" in
which 1,000 prisoners, including those on the list, were sent to one side.
Some 500 of them were taken to a nearby wood and shot to death. The rest
were taken to the Skarżysko ghetto where Franz Schippers and a group of
SS officers brought especially for the purpose from Radom, were already
carrying out the aktion. Around 3,000 Jew were gathered in the town
square, where the German and Polish managers of the Hasag plants
conducted a "selection." Some 500 people, most of them young, were
chosen and sent to the camp, while the other members of their families
were herded into the death cars together with the prisoners newly
"returned" to the ghetto from the Skarżysko camp.[13]

The significance of these events can be learned from the rumors which
spread throughout the camp maintaining that the "Jew exchange" was the
result of bribes paid to the SS commanders by Skarżysko Jews who
regarded employment by Hasag as their only means of survival. In view
of the prevalence of similar rumors concerning other transports, it seems
reasonable to assume that there was some sort of "gentlemen's agreement" between the Hasag management and the Radom SS which all sides,
including the Jews, preferred to keep under wraps. According to this
arrangement, whenever Jews managed to find the means and the money
to bribe the SS officers commanding the *aktion*, the latter would notify
Hasag who would then send its *Werkschutz* to collect the spoils. The SS
made a handsome profit from these transactions, and the prime mover
behind them seems to have been Franz Schippers who was well-known
for looting Jewish property to line his own pocket.

The term "Jew exchange" (Austausch der Juden), used before the court
by Artur Rost,[14] was explained as the need to "re-examine veteran
prisoners of the camp in terms of their fitness for work since new people

---

[12] Szlomo Rosenzweig: Testimony, YV, 0–2/999.

[13] Anklageschrift, pp. 21–32; cf. E. Lewin, see note 8.

[14] Artur Rost: Sitzungen, p. 12.

were continually arriving." [15] The figures for munitions production in Autumn, 1942, however, reveal that the initial successes of the Wehrmacht led to a renewal of the *Munitionsstop*. From July to November 1942, the production index of the German munitions industry remained at the same level. [16] In the Generalgouvernement as well, Wehrmacht orders for munitions were not increased, which means that production at the Skarżysko plants, employing over 7,000 Poles, was not stepped up. Why, then, were thousands of Jews brought into the camp?

There can be only one unequivocal answer – in order to plunder their property. The Hasag managers launched their own initiative and scurried about throughout the Radom district in search of Jews (see example in Figure 3.2). Even elderly people were brought to the camp, on the logical assumption that they would possess the greater wealth. As long as the ghettos remained in existence, parcels were sent to relatives in the camp in return for a fee paid to the go-between. Moreover, rumors claiming that recruitment for work at Hasag was the only means of survival were planted in order to attract volunteers who arrived together with all their belongings. Jewish money and property thus flowed into the camp under the watchful eye of the Hasag management. The plant's "liberal policies" fanned the prisoners' hope that here, indeed, their survival was ensured.

These hopes were dashed by the "grand search" *(grosse Filzaktion)*. On October 25, some 800 Jews were ordered to present themselves with their belongings in hand. Rumor had it that they were to be transferred to a different camp. The shop stewards, including Willi Seidel, Taubert, Bosch, and others, were there as well. At the command of Egon Dalski, the prisoners were ordered to hand over their parcels, and all valuables and clothes were confiscated. Both men and women were ordered to remove their clothing and were body searched. [17] The suitcases packed with clothes and watches were taken to the apartments of Seidel and Dalski, and trunks filled with money and jewels to Dalski's office. No lists were made of this property which simply disappeared. [18] These, then, were Hasag's "production needs". It is thus not surprising that one of the Germans later

---

[15] Willi Seidel: Sitzungen, p. 46a.

[16] Karl Ludwig: Technik und Ingenieure im Dritten Reich, (Duesseldorf: Droste Vlg, 1979), p. 422.

[17] Dawid Dziadek: Sitzungen, p. 82; Karl Herold, ib. p. 60.

[18] Willi Seidel: Sitzungen, p. 61; Elise Kiessling, ib., p. 135a.

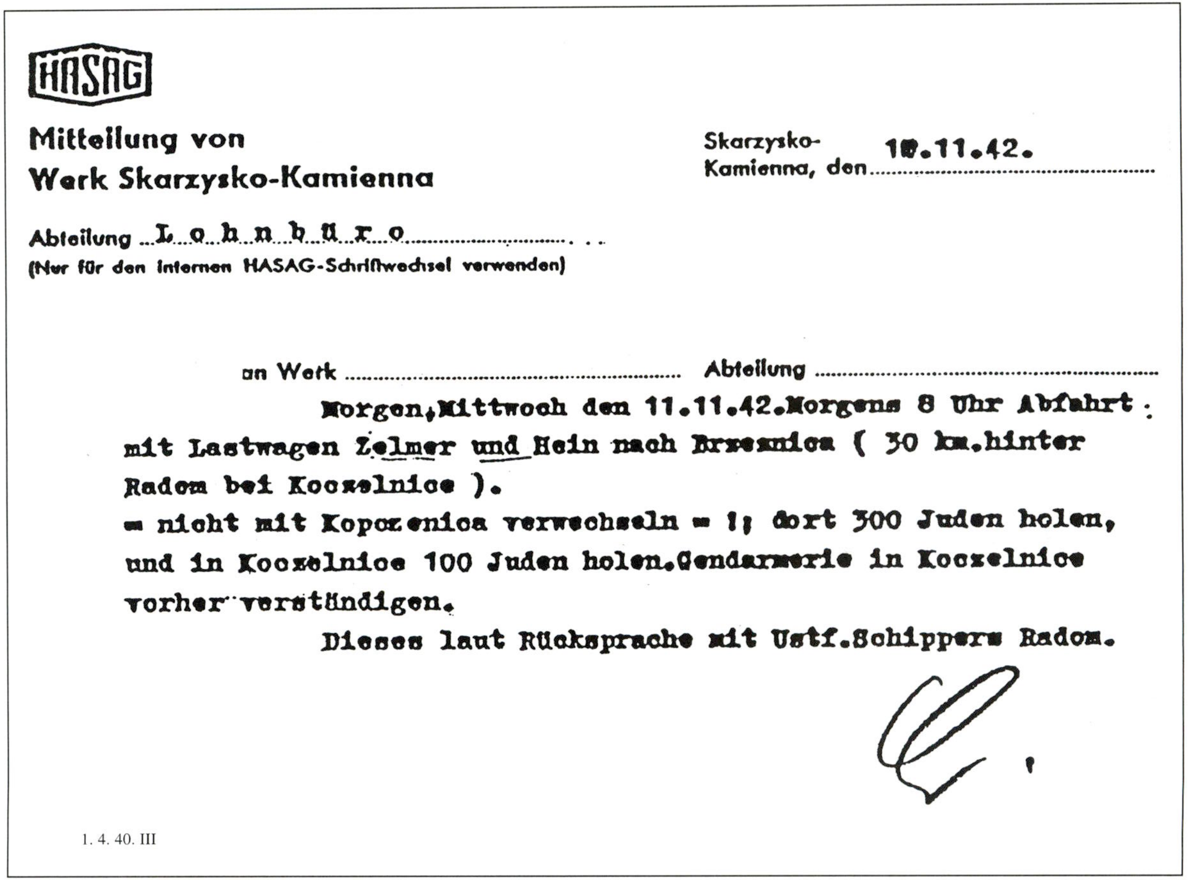

Death Comes in Yellow

HASAG

Mitteilung von
Werk Skarzysko-Kamienna

Abteilung ..L.o.h.n.b.ü.r.o..............
(Nur für den Internen HASAG-Schriftwechsel verwenden)

Skarzysko-
Kamienna, den ....1 0.11.42.

an Werk .... Abteilung ....

Morgen,Mittwoch den 11.11.42.Morgens 8 Uhr Abfahrt ;
mit Lastwagen Zelmer und Holm nach Brzeznica (30 km.hinter
Radom bei Koczelnice).
= nicht mit Kopczenica verwechseln = !; dort 300 Juden holen,
und in Koczelnice 100 Juden holen.Gendarmerle in Koczelnice
vorher verständigen.

Dieses laut Rücksprache mit Ustf.Schippers Radom.

1. 4. 40. III

Figure 3.2 Document of the Hasag-Werke Paymaster's office from November 10, 1942, directing 300 Jews to be brought from Brzeźnica and 100 from Koczelnice (and bearing the approval of Ustf. Schippers). (YV, 0-6/37-3)

confessed that "the people [i.e. the Germans] were totally unconcerned with what was happening in the plant."[19] The tragic epilogue to this "grand search" followed the next day, when as a result of a "selection" in the three *werks*, 195 Jews were "dismissed" and shot to death.[20]

Skarżysko's Role in the Nazi Camp System and Principles of its Organization

At the time of the large transports, the ultimate fate of the Jewish workers in the military industries had not yet been determined. At the insistence of Sauckel and Speer, it was decided that, in opposition to Himmler's demands, munitions plants would not be established in the concentration camps but would be left in private hands. Furthermore, in view of the need to send 140,000 Poles to work in the Reich, skilled Jewish laborers would not yet be removed from the military factories.[21] Himmler had no choice but to waive his demands, and issued directives whereby two agreements were signed on October 14–15, 1942 between the SS and the Military Command in the G.G. formalizing the legal status of the Jews employed on behalf of the Wehrmacht. The provisions of these agreements included the following:[22]

1. All of the Jewish camps established at Wehrmacht work sites would be transferred to the authority of the G.G. SS and Police Leader;

2. All matters concerning the armaments plants under the supervision of the Armaments Inspectorate *(Rue-Betriebe der Ruestungsinspektion)* would be decided between HS-SuPF Krueger and General Schindler.

3. Factories working for the Wehrmacht but not under supervision of the Armaments Inspectorate would be defined as "Munitions Plants of the Army District Commander in the Generalgouvernement" *(Rue-Betriebe des Wehrkreisbefehls-haber in GG – WiG)*;

---

[19] Felix Krebs: Sitzungen, p. 21b.

[20] Entlassene Juden, Skar.-Kamienna, 27.10.42., YV, 0–6/37–3.

[21] Besprechung Speers mit Hitler vom 20.9.1942, BA, R 3/105.

[22] WiG im GG, den 14–15 Oktober 1942, betr. Ersatz der juedischen durch arische Arbeitskraefte, MA, RH 53–23/70.

4. Jews would receive no wages and no taxes or social in-
    surance would be paid for them. However, every employer
    would transfer a fee for each Jewish worker into the SS
    account.

Hasag, which enjoyed the supervision of the Armaments Inspectorate,
had established a camp which was a unique precedent in terms of the
classification of work camps in the G.G. According to the Polish
"Encyclopedic Informer," there were three major categories of work
camps in Poland:

1. 1,750 "ordinary" work camps *(Arbeitslager)*, including **437
    Jewish work camps;**
2. 21 penal camps *(Straflager)*;
3. 21 "Education for Work" camps *(Arbeitserziehungslager)*.

Camp supervision was of two primary types: the first, consisted of
camps subject to administrative, economic, military or SS authorities,
with 27 subcategories including "company camp" *(Fabrikslager, Betriebslager)*; and the second, consisted of camps subject to the Gestapo, such
as the "Education for Work" camps.[23] The term *Betriebslager* used in the
present volume to refer to the Skarżysko camp, does not appear in German
sources which employ the appellation *Judenlager*.

In what way was the organization of Skarżysko unique? The answer
must be sought in Germany, where, in 1941, at Himmler's initiative,
"Education for Work" camps were established for criminal classes of
foreign workers. Since these camps were controlled by the Gestapo,
workers who had completed their sentence were often sent to concentration camps rather than returned to the plants from which they had come.
Not wishing to lose their workers in this manner, concerns such as Krupp,
Hasag, Flick, and others began in 1942 to set up their own "private" penal
camps at their factories.[24] The *Werkschutz*, wage laborers subject only
to the plant management, were in charge of administering and guarding
these camps.

---

[23] Informator, see note 3, p. 44, 617; cf. Raul Hilberg: The Destruction of the European
Jews, (Chicago: Quadrangle Books, 1961), p. 336.

[24] Eva Seeber: Robotnicy przymusowi w faszystowskiej gospodarce wojennej, (Warszawa:
Książka i Wiedza, 1972), pp. 220–224.

Hasag established the camp at Skarżysko along the same lines. In organizational terms, it was in no way like a concentration camp. Although according to the October agreements, the camp came under the authority of the Radom District SS and Police Leader, its organization, supervision and daily administration were in the hands of the *Werkschutz* subject only to the Hasag management. The *Werkschutz* consisted of approximately 180 guards, around 80 in Werk A, 30 in Werk B, and 40 in Werk C. The rest were functionaries and *Stosstrupp* men.[25] The *Werkschutz* was commanded by SS-Haupsturmfuehrer Kurt Krauze, with Fritz Bartenschlager as his second-in-command. Each *Werk* had its own commander of the guard *(Wachfuehrer)*. All positions of authority and administration were held by Germans.

The *Werkschutz's* functions included:

1. Protecting the plant and its German staff from acts of sabotage or attack;
2. Supervision of the Polish workers, including responsibility for arrests and punishment;
3. Responsibility for all matters concerning the Jewish camp in the three werks.

The commando unit for special tasks *(Stosstrupp)* numbered up to 10 men and was under the command of Kurt Krauze. Its members were armed with pistols and semi-automatic weapons (regular *Werkschutz* members were issued only rifles) and only they were allowed to conduct policing operations outside the area of the plant. It was almost exclusively this unit which carried out the mass executions of Jewish prisoners as well. The unit's commander is listed as Leo Strenk,[26] and those of its members whose names are known were Roman Hławacz, Georg Sander, Jarosław Hławacz, Mirosław Biłas, Petro Kozłowski, Iwan Romanko, Stefan Woźny, and Teodor and Stefan Czopyk.[27]

In Autumn, 1942, Anton Ipfling was appointed general commander of the Jewish camp. It was he who organized the recording of the names of the prisoners in the three *Werks* and oversaw the "Jew File" *(Judenkartei)*

---

[25] Sentencja wyroku w sprawie Jerzego Adryanowicza, Kielce, 20.10.1967 "Uzasadnienie", AGKBZH, SWK, sygn. 236, p. 120.

[26] Jaroslaw Zadorecki: Testimony, AGKBZH, SWK, sygn. 236, pp. 15–17.

[27] "Komunikat Prokuratury w Kielcach", Kurier Szczeciński, 20.1.1966.

in his office in Werk A. He also fulfilled policing functions, which were shared by the commanders of the camps in Werk A and Werk C: guard duty in the "watch house" *(Wache)*, patrolling the camp perimeter and gate, escorting prisoners on their way to and from work, arrests, carrying out sentences of whipping or execution passed on individual prisoners, recapturing escapees, conducting spot checks and searches at the plant gate and within the camp, overseeing "selections" and mass executions. The camp commanders were invariably Germans of the rank of Wach-fuehrer. They served in principle as officials of Hasag rather than on behalf of the SS, so that Artur Rost was correct in testifying that the SS among the German staff of the *Werkschutz* "could not be considered genuine SS men."[28] For want of German sources, it is difficult to determine the names of the actual commanders of each of the three camps and the dates of their posting.

Systematic recording of the names of prisoners seems to have begun only on October 15, 1942 when it became necessary to calculate the fees to be transferred to the Radom SS authorities. The "daily reports" of the number of prisoners in the three *werks (Staerkemeldung)* initially bear the signature of Jerzy Adryanowicz, and later of Ipfling. The reports gave the number of men and women by the place of their incarceration at the start and end of the day, additions, losses, the ill, and the total number of prisoners fit for work (see for example Figure 3.3). On October 15, 1942 there were a total of 4,361 prisoners in all three camps: 2,590 men and 1,771 women. Attached to the report were lists of the names of the sick, escapees, prisoners killed, etc.[29] Hasag paid the Radom SS a fee of 5 zlotys a day for a man and 4 zlotys for a woman. From this, 1.60 zlotys were deducted for the cost of the prisoner's daily maintenance.[30] Since we do not have the exact dates of transports into the camp, it is difficult to verify the accuracy of these lists. It is my belief that in order to save on the fees to the SS, some of the transports went unrecorded.

In formal terms, the fact that each Betriebslager was under the authority of the SS and Police Commander of the Radom district had the following ramifications:

---

[28] A. Rost: Sitzungen, p. 98.

[29] Staerkemeldung, Juden, Skar.-Kam., 15.10.42, YV, 0–6/37–3.

[30] R. Hilberg: The Destruction, op. cit., p. 336.

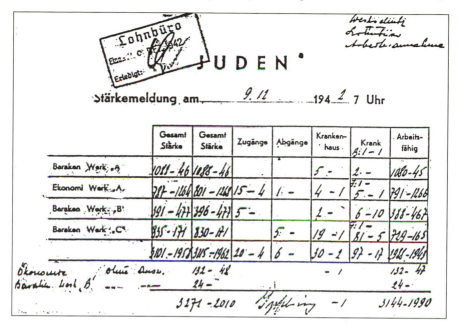

Figure 3.3 The "Daily Report" of the Number of Prisoners in the Three Werks (A, B, C) (YV, 0-6/37-3)

1. The Radom SS and Police Leader conveyed his instructions to the Werkschutz commander and the plant manager;
    2. The SS command was responsible for the internal security of the munitions plants, supervised guarding procedures, and received regular reports of Jewish escapees;[31]
    3. Money and valuables confiscated from Jews by the Werkschutz in the course of "official" searches were deposited in the SS and Police account;[32]
    4. The Hasag management and Werkschutz commander were required to report to the SS command any instances of Jewish offenses of the order of sabotage attempts, relations between the Jews and the Poles in the plant, etc.;

---

[31] Besprechung bei den Hasag-Werken, Skar.-Kam. 20.9.43, YV, JM/4530, p. 2–765122.

[32] Hasag-Werk Skar. Kam., 3.11.1943, betr. Judengelder, Zentrale Stelle Ludwigsburg, "Verschiedenes", Heft 6, Band 109, p. 260.

5. Germans charged with sabotage, aiding Jews, having sex-
    ual relations with Jewish women, etc. were handed over to
    the Gestapo.

From what we have said, it seems obvious that the Jews were the *de
facto* property of Hasag. The prisoners themselves were well aware of
this: "The Jews belong to the plant and are subject to the authority of
the Werkschutz and the Hasag shop stewards, so what is the SS doing
here?"[33] Any doubt regarding who was actually in control of the camp was
erased when Hasag purchased the Skarżysko factories along with those at
Kielce and Częstochowa.

Negotiations for Hasag's purchase of the plants had begun in July 1942
when Budin submitted the following offer to Emmerich, the head of the
Economic Department of the G.G. government:[34]

1. Częstochowa factories – up to 4,500,000 zloty
2. "Granat" at Kielce   – up to   500,000 zloty
3. Skarżysko factories   – up to 4,500,000 zloty

The G.G. authorities rejected the ludicrous offer (the value of the
Skarżysko plants alone was assessed as at least 30 million zloty). However, in late November 1942, with the attack on Stalingrad halted, the
Armaments Inspectorate increased its orders for munitions. Budin
announced that expanding production would be contingent on the signing
of a purchase agreement, and as a result pressure was applied on Frank
by both Speer and the Wehrmacht authorities. In January 1943, the
G.G. government sold Hasag the Skarżysko plants as a "thoroughly
exceptional transaction" for 10 million zloty: "practically for free."[35]
(The "Granat" factory was sold for one million zloty and the Raków
foundry at Częstochowa for 5.5 million.) Skarżysko now became a
corporation, Hasag Eisen u. Metallwerke – Werk Skarżysko Kamienna,
with a founding capital of 20 million zloty.[36] The company's shares were

---

[33] Mordchai Strigler: Goirolois, (Yiddish), (Buenos-Aires: Zentral Farband fun pojlisze
Jiden in Argentine, 1952), vol. 2, p. 150.

[34] Sitzung bei der Hauptabteilung Wirtschaft, Krakau, 23.10.42, MA, RW 23/2, Bl. 23.

[35] Arbeitssitzung im Belvedere am 26. Januar 1943, "Verkauf von Ruestungswerken",
YV, Tagebuch, JM/21, nr. 10, p. 29.

[36] Ludwik Landau: Kronika lat wojny i okupacji, (Warszawa: Państwowe Wydawnictwo
Naukowe, 1962), vol. 2, p. 140.

divided up between Hasag and Budin, its business manager, with Paul Geldmacher as his assistant. Budin objected to the sale of company shares to the members of the board of directors of Hasag-Leipzig and so gained what was in fact sole control of the Skarżysko plants.[37]

Underlying this close cooperation between the private concerns and the Wehrmacht authorities was the redoubling of their rivalry with the WVHA. In January 1943, at the prodding of the WVHA, the Eastern Industries Co. *(Ost Industrie GmbH – OSTI)* was established and planned to set up factories within the territory of the G.G. using Jewish workers held in camps under the direct supervision of the SS. The first such camps were erected by Odilo Globocnik in the Lublin district, and Osti's plans called for additional slave labor camps as well. Objections were raised by both the Armaments Inspectorate and the private concerns. Hasag's purchase of the Skarżysko plants reduced the danger that "its" Jews would be carted away to SS work camps. Jews were now transferred *en masse* to all of the production departments. In meetings with Wehrmacht representatives in Spring, 1943, it was decided that production of munitions for the infantry would be increased from 6 million to 20 million units per month![38] From this time on, the Hasag concern held a monopoly over the armaments industry in the Generalgouvernement.

Security in the Radom District and Its Effects on the Recruitment of Jewish Workers for the Skarżysko Plants

Until mid-1942, security in the Generalgouvernement posed no particular problems to the occupying forces. Their status reports maintained that the territory was quiet and the population loyal and "cooperating in a thoroughly satisfactory manner in the realms of administration and economics." [39] The impotence of the Polish underground stemmed both from internal rifts and from the fact that they were passively awaiting the "call to rebellion" in accord with the policies of the Polish government-in-exile in London. The most telling factor, however, seems to have been the Polish hatred for the Bolsheviks, demonstrated, for example, by the appeal to the Poles issued by the right-wing journal "Warta" in 1941 not to resist

---

[37] Gustav Hessen: Sitzungen, pp. 119–120.

[38] Kriegstagebuch (hereafter Ktb) des Rue Kdo Radom. 11.5.43, MA, RW 23/17, p. 20.

[39] Wehrkreiskommando GG, 2.6.1943, "Beurteilung der Lage", MA, RH 53-23/66, p. 84.

the Germans since they were fighting the Soviet Union and helping the Poles to solve the Jewish problem.[40]

These views were equally current within the Skarżysko plants, and so long as the Poles entertained the hope that Germany would wear down the power of the Soviet Union and vice versa, they had no real reason to sabotage the Reich's war effort. Underground activities were thus primarily passive in nature, and took the form of the theft of ammunition, minor acts of sabotage, and absenteeism. This state of affairs did not change even after the right-wing faction, the *Armia Krajowa – A.K.*, (Home Army) gained hegemony of the local underground.

The turning point came only in the Autumn, 1942: the pacification of the Polish villages in the Zamojszczyzna district, part of the plan to prepare the area for the arrival of German settlers, aroused panic in the Radom district. The Poles were also thrown into turmoil by the mass deportation of Jews to extermination camps, since many believed the Poles would be next in line. The German source states: "The ridding of the country of Jews, which caused little distress to the Poles as such, became a horrifying image of their own fate due to the way in which it was carried out." [41] The underground stepped up its attacks on financial institutions and local transportation arteries, but these activities were in no way damaging to production at the Hasag plants.

Signs of a change in the overall mood were only felt in Spring, 1943, when, following the defeat at Stalingrad and the uprising in the Warsaw ghetto, the Polish government-in-exile gave its permission to launch a "limited campaign." In May 1943, the number of attacks on German targets, including labor exchanges, rose to 1,300. Fearing the vengeance of the underground, Polish functionaries became reluctant to collaborate with the occupation. Things were still going well in the munitions industry, however, where 42,000 Poles were employed, because "the large munitions plants had great drawing power for the local working population." [42] They held out the bait of exemption from work in Germany

---

[40] Mieczysław Adamczyk: Prasa konspiracyjna na Kielecczyźnie w latach 1939–1945, (Krakow: Wydawnictwo Literackie, 1982), pp. 141, 112, 137.

[41] "Die Entjudung des Landes, die die Polen an sich wenig beruehrte wurde in der Art ihrer Ausfuehrung zum Schreckbild eigenen Schicksals", Wehrkreiskommando GG, 2.6.43, MA, RH 53-23,/66, p. 84.

[42] Arbeitssitzung, Radom, 26.5.43, Tagebuch, YV, JM/21, Nr. 8, p. 334.

as well as wage and food benefits. In the case of Skarżysko, close to half of the 19,400 Poles (aged 14–60) living in the city in mid-1943[43] were associated with Hasag, as were residents of other towns in the vicinity. Nevertheless, the number of Poles employed in the plant was continually dropping: from 7,000 in January 1943 to 6,576 in July of that year, when the Jewish workers in the plant numbered 6.408[44] (See Figure 3.4). Why was this so?

The answer can be found in a secret report sent by General Schindler to Albert Speer on May 25, 1943 in which he used somber terms to describe the state of security in the G.G. in general and in the Radom district in particular. The most outstanding example was the munitions factories at Skarżysko. In the wake of communist propaganda threatening capital punishment for anyone aiding in reinforcing the Wehrmacht, the Poles were afraid to appear for work and "overall absenteeism today is 1,700 workers out of a total of 13,000." [45] The Poles, previously sympathetic to the German cause, were now reluctant workers, and the shop stewards were apprehensive about prodding them. The undisciplined *Werkschutz* overseers were ineffectual, and there were even cases of desertion to the partisans. The only solution Schindler saw was to send in Wehrmacht units to combat the Polish "gangs."

Schindler knew that Hitler had given Himmler authority over the war against the "gangs" and that he had made pacification of the G.G. contingent on the "evacuation" of all Jews, including workers in the munitions industry.[46] Schindler sought to forestall this at any price, even refraining from any mention whatsoever of the existence of Jews in what was a secret report. When Frank called a meeting on May 31, 1943 to discuss security problems in the G.G., attended by Gen. Schoengarth, Krueger, Haennicke, and Himmler's deputies, Schindler took advantage of the opportunity. When Himmler's men raised their chief's demand to evacuate the Jews, all of the others present voiced their objections.

---

[43] "Od krzemienia do maszyny"," Nasze Słowo", Skar.-Kamienna, 1962.

[44] Betriebskarte Werke Skar.-Kamienna, Stand am 30.6.43, BA, R 3/2040.

[45] Der Vorsitzer der Ruestungskommission im GG, Krakau, 24.5.1943, MA, RH 53-23/ 66, pp. 67–73.

[46] "Lage im Generalgouvernement", Berlin, 10.5.1943, Eksterminacja Żydów na ziemiach polskich, edited by T. Berenstein, A. Eisenbach, A. Rutkowski, (Warszawa: ZIH, 1957), p. 327.

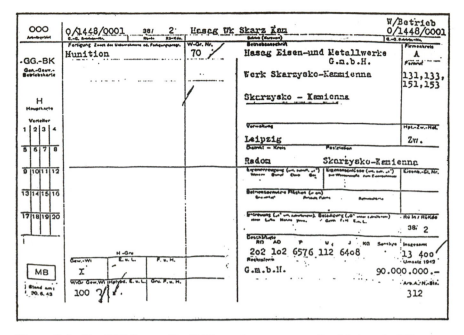

Figure 3.4 The "GG-factory Card" (Generalgouvernement Betriebskarte) of Hasag-Werke Skarżysko-Kamienna (BA, R 3/2040)

Krueger declared that the information he had received from Schindler indicated that this was an impossible task. There were among the Jews skilled workers and experts in special fields for whom Polish replacements could not be found. "The Jews remaining in production are in the best possible physical condition; they are known as 'Maccabees' and are excellent workers, and the women as well have already been seen to be physically stronger than men."[47] Gen. Haenicke, supreme commander of the Wehrmacht in the G.G., again gave the example of the Skarżysko plants which were encountering severe production problems due to the fact that 2,000 workers were "striking"!

We may assume that Himmler was persuaded by the report submitted by his deputies since the evacuation of Jews from the munitions plants was postponed indefinitely. The Skarżysko factories continued to suffer a

---

[47] Arbeitssitzung, Krakau, 31.5.1943, Das Diensttagebuch des deutschen Generalgouverneurs in Polen 1939–1945, hrsg. von W.Praeg und W. Jacobmeyer, (Stuttgart: DVA, 1975), p. 682.

shortage of 1,700 workers, at least half of them Jews who had died of hunger and disease, despite additional transports: 120 Jews from the town of Białobrzegi, a group from the work camp at Kruszyna, and 250 from Radomsko.[48] Some 500 Jews volunteered for work in the plant when the Sandomierz ghetto was obliterated in January 1943,[49] and around 1000 young people were brought to Skarżysko from the Szydłowiec ghetto.[50] In Spring 1943, two transports bearing 550 workers arrived from Piotrków Trybunalski and another 200 or so from Jędrzejów.[51] Hasag even transferred groups of workers from its plants in Częstochowa and Kielce to the Skarżysko factories.[52] The last to arrive during the "Radom Period" were 150 prisoners from the camp at Poniatowa and 200 from the "Amler" camp near Staszów.[53] Between November 1942 and mid-June 1943, a total of 12 transports bearing 3,360 Jews arrived in the Skarżysko camp.

Even relying on estimated figures alone, it is clear that during the "Radom Period" a total of 58 transports with 17,210 Jews were brought to the camp. With 6,408 remaining at the end of June, this means that during the first 15 months of its existence, 10,802 prisoners had died in the Skarżysko camp.

---

[48] Zev Sabatowski: Sefer Radomsk,, p. 372; Chaim Kohn: Testimony, YV, 0-53/74, p. 718.

[49] Benjamin Zweig: Testimony, YV, 0-33/2826; Jakow Zając, 0016/291.

[50] Staerkemeldungen, Januar 1943, see note 29.

[51] Menachem Horowicz: Testimony, YV, 03/1316.

[52] Wolf Szymkowicz: Sitzungen, p. 93a.

[53] Awraham Weingarten: Skarżysko-Book, p. 127; Sefer Staszów, pp. 379, 502.

Chapter 4

Reinforcement of the Camp: Transports from Majdanek and Piaszów

The Enigma of the Transports from Majdanek (Summer, 1943)

In April 1943, a total of 112,499 workers were employed in the Generalgouvernement's munitions plants (under supervision of the Armaments Inspectorate). Of these, 15,538 were Jews in plant camps[1] (see Table 4.1).

Table 4.1   Labor Forces in the Armament Industry

	Jews only	Total workers
January, 1943	15,091	105,632
April, 1943	15,538	112,499
July, 1943	21,643	123,588
October, 1943	22,444	130,808
January, 1944	26,296	140,057
April, 1944	28,537	179,244
May, 1944	27,439	172,781

[1] "In der Ruestungsindustrie eingesetzte Arbeitskraefte im GG, Juni 1944, MA, RW 46/ 494, p. 171 (11); see "Labor forces in the armament industry", R. Hilberg, op. cit., p. 341.

Table 4.2 Workforces in the Radom district Munitions Plants June 30, 1943 (BA R 3/2040)

	Factory	City	Total	Number of the workers				
				Polish	Jews	Ukrainian	German	Other
1.	Stahlwerke Braunschweig	Starachowice	12,449	10,765	1,239	193	252	—
2.	Lackfabrik "Dorsa"	Radom	148	143	—	—	5	—
3.	J. Meissner Werk Niewiadow	Niewiadów	844	595	—	—	40	209
4.	Ludwigshütte Zieleniewski	Kielce	2,050	1,465	546	4	25	10
5.	Beru Werke	Kielce	228	204	—	—	24	—
6.	Hochöfen u. Wk. Ostrowiec	Ostrowiec	7,409	6,385	738	117	38	131
7.	KB Metallurgia	Radomsko	1,191	1,161	—	2	28	—
8.	Ericsson Elt. AG.	Radom	315	305	—	3	5	2
9.	Steyr Daimler Puch	Radom	4,485	3,223	1,008	125	129	—
10.	Hasag Wk. Skarz.-Kam.	Skarżysko	13,400	6,576	6,408	112	304	—
11.	Hasag Wk. Kielce (Granat)	Kielce	2,012	1,520	404	11	77	—
12.	Hasag Eisenhütte	Częstochowa	3,160	2,551	521	13	75	—
13.	Hasag Apparatebau	Częstochowa	4,462	985	3,350	35	89	3
	Total		52,153	35,878	14,214	615		

As Table 4.1 demonstrates, the number of workers rose steadily throughout 1943. In the Radom district alone, the"factory cards" (Be-triebskarten) from June 30, 1943 (see Table 4.2) reveal 14,214 Jews to be working in thirteen plants.[2] Another 1,500 or so were put to work in the explosives factory in Pionki,[3] and some 2,700 in the two other Hasag plants, Częstochowianka and Warta.[4] Thus, the 18,414 laborers in the Radom district constituted 72–75% of all the Jews employed in the munitions industry in the Generalgouvernement. Table 4.2 and 4.3 show their distribution by places of work.

Table 4.3   Workers in the June 30, 1943

	Poles	Jews	Total
9 firms (excluding Hasag)	24,246	3,531	27,777
Pionki explosives factory	3,500	1,500	5,000
Hasag (6 plants)	13,632	13,383	27,015
	41,378	18,414	54,792

These figures reveal that Hasag had become the largest employer in the Radom district, with a work-force nearly equal to that of all the other plants combined. Fully 75% of all the Jews in local industries were employed by Hasag. Yet despite this seeming prosperity, in May 1943 a crisis in production loomed at the Skarżysko plants due to the high mortality rate of the camp prisoners and the continued absenteeism of Polish workers. In order to combat widespread absenteeism, the Hasag management, like that of the other German companies in the G.G., was forced to purchase food on the black market for their Polish staff and to increase their wages. Although these measures succeeded in containing the problem, they also raised production costs. Therefore, as Schindler

---

[2] Gen. Gouv., Betriebskarten, Stand am 30. Juni 1943, BA, R 3/2040.

[3] Stanisław Meducki, Przemysł i klasa robotnicza w dystrykcie radomskim w okresie okupacji hitlerowskiej, (Warszawa: Państwowe Wydawnictwo Naukowe, 1981), p. 114.

[4] Hasag-Warta, Statistischer Ueberblick ueber die W-Betriebe der Rue In im GG, Stand vom 1.3.1944, YV, JM/4530, p. 2760497; Hasag-Częstochowianka, Informator enc., p. 147, nr. 705.

claimed, "the munitions plants in the G.G. were no longer competitive since they were compelled to invest too heavily in their work-force."[5]

This may explain why Budin was so eager to obtain Jewish workers, notwithstanding the number of Poles available for work at Hasag. His chances, however, were slim: all of the labor camps in the Lublin district were under the exclusive control of Odilo Globocnik, and even the few Jews remaining in the Warsaw ghetto after suppression of the uprising were sent here as well; the Płaszów labor camp was subject to the authority of the Kraków district SSuPF; liquidation of the camps and ghettos of the Galicja district was completed in June 1943; no Jews could be obtained from the ghettos of Łódź or Białystok.

In the Summer of 1943, Globocnik was hoping to put the OSTI concern on its feet with the help of Jewish labor. However, he encountered several difficulties. In his report to Himmler of June 21, 1943, he complained that the 45,000 Jews in his camps were not being used productively because of the refusal of Schindler and Speer to place military orders with the WVHA plants.[6] Krueger (a member of the OSTI board of directors) was aware of this situation, and it may have been he who suggested to his friend Schindler that he look into the possibility of obtaining Jews for Hasag from Majdanek. Krueger, however, did not have the official authority to help Schindler since Erich Schellin, as agent of the WVHA, was responsible for all of the SS's economic affairs in the G.G., as well as for the transfer of prisoners.[7]

Procuring Jews from Majdanek would seem to have been an impossible task since the transfer of any prisoners from a concentration camp required the approval of Gerhard Maurer, the head of the WVHA Department for Concentration Camps, and it was highly unlikely that Globocnik would allow the transfer of thousands of Jews to a private concern, particularly one which enjoyed the support of Speer, his opponent and rival. Hence we may assume that the transports from Majdanek to Skarżysko were arranged "under the table" at a lower level of command. Budin may have bribed the commander of Majdanek, Herman Florstedt, known in SS circles for his greed and corruption. The

---

[5] Besprechung, 27.1.1944, Krakau, Tagebuch, YV, JM/21, nr. 10.

[6] Pohl case, Nur. doc. NO-485.

[7] SS-Standartenfuehrer Erlich Schellin, see Pohl case, NO-485.

covert nature of these activities seems to be borne out by the total lack of reference to them in any German sources. Thus, the War Diary of the Radom Armaments Command makes no mention whatsoever of transports from Majdanek to Skarżysko, although it does record the transport of Jews from the Płaszów camp six months later.

Given the lack of German documents, the only source of information regarding the Majdanek transports is the testimony of former prisoners who differ widely as to the number, dates and sizes of the transports:

1. According to one version, two transports were sent from Majdanek in late June 1943 containing 3,000 Jewish men and women. The first shipment also included 46 workers in the printing trades being sent to work in German presses in Radom.[8]

2. According to other testimony, 1,700 men and women were sent in June and another 500 men in early July.[9] Mordchai Strigler, who himself was brought to Skarżysko from Majdanek, mentions a transport of 1,500 men and women in June and another 500 women in July.[10]

3. According to yet another version, one transport containing 500 men was sent on July 6, 1943.[11]

In addition to the inconsistency of the sources, it is unclear why transports of prisoners from Majdanek were sent to Auschwitz at the same time as those to Skarżysko and how the recruitment of workers in the printing trades for Radom presses was connected to these transports.

An attempt to reconstruct the events reveals that the affair began in June 1943 when a group of Jewish workers in the printing trades at Majdanek were selected for Radom. On June 15, 1943, notice that their transfer was to be delayed was received.[12] Hasag may have heard of this transport and

---

[8] T. Berenstein, A. Rutkowski, "Żydzi w obozie koncentracyjnym Majdanek, 1941–1944", BZIH, 58, (IV–VI, 1966), p. 20.

[9] Aleksander Donat: The Holocaust Kingdom, (London: Becker and Warburg, 1965), p. 215.

[10] Mordchai Strigler: Majdanek, (Yiddish), (Buenos-Aires: Union Central Israelita Polaca en la Argentina, 1947), p. 174.

[11] Testimonies, YV: Arie Jagoda, 0-3/1649; Simcha Engerest, 0-3/3158.

[12] A. Donat: The Holocaust, op. cit., pp. 213–214.

decided to investigate the possibility of using this opportunity to obtain Jewish workers for itself. At around the same time, orders arrived in Majdanek from Gerhard Maurer, instructing them to prepare 5,500 Jews to be sent to the Buna plants at Auschwitz. On June 20, 1943, a "selection" was begun in which 500 suitable prisoners were chosen.[13] The procedure lasted for several days and was accompanied by rumors that the transport was being sent "somewhere good."

None of those who signed up knew where they would be sent or to which transport they were to be assigned. If we compare the description of the "selection," registration procedures and other details in Strigler's memoirs with those appearing in the book by Tadeusz Stabholz, himself transported to Auschwitz,[14] it would appear that on June 20, 1943, the camp commanders initiated a "selection" designed to fill two simultaneous transports: one to Auschwitz and the other to Skarżysko. In the women's camp as well, a group of workers in the printing trades destined for Radom was put together, and on June 22, 1943, while this group was still awaiting transport, there was a call for factory workers (with no mention of which factory was involved), and some 700 women signed up.[15] On June 24, 1943, when two officers from Auschwitz arrived in Majdanek to pick up "their" Jews, they were astounded to discover that "from amongst the 5,500 prisoners who were to be made available to them, 1,700 had already been selected for a labor camp at ... Radom."[16]

When and how was this done? The solution to this puzzle can be found in the testimony of Strigler, who stated that the Majdanek officials recorded the names of the print-shop workers and the candidates for "the good camp" together on a single list for one transport to Radom.[17] This was done in order to conceal the transport to Skarżysko which had not been approved by higher authorities. Thus, 1,700 Jews (1,000 men and

---

[13] Zofia Leszczyńska: Kronika obozu na Majdanku (Lublin: Wydawnictwo Lubelskie 1980), p. 181.

[14] Tadeusz Stabholz: Siedem piekieł (Stuttgart: "Ojf der Fraj", 1947), pp. 71–72. cf. M. Strigler: Majdanek, op. cit., pp. 192, 201.

[15] Regina Finger, Obozy, Dokumenty i materiały, edited by N. Blumental, (Łódź: Centralna Żydowska Komisja Historyczna w Polsce, 1946), p. 39.

[16] "Bericht ueber die Auswahl der zu ueberstellenden Haeftlinge im KL Lublin, Auschwitz, 6.7.1943," Dokumenty i materiały, ib., p. 138.

[17] M. Strigler: Majdanek, op. cit., p. 224.

700 women) designated for Hasag were added to the 46 printing trades workers destined for Radom. Globocnik was surely unaware of this ruse, so that Gerald Reitlinger's assertion that in June 1943 Globocnik sent 1,700 Jews to the OSTI camps in the Radom district is mistaken.[18]

Meanwhile, the Majdanek officials were forced to organize three urgent additional transports to Auschwitz. On July 7, 1943, the third transport was sent on its way.[19] Alexander Donat says, that one day before, on July 6, 1943, 46 printing trades workers together with 1,700 prisoners for Hasag- Skarżysko had set out for Radom. Lejb Bornes, one of these prisoners, was given "temporary documents" *(Vorlaufiger Ausweis)* upon arrival at Skarżysko. They bore the date July 12, 1943.[20] In August 1943, another transport of 500 men[21] arrived in Skarżysko, bringing the total number of prisoners brought from Majdanek to 2,200.

With the help of the new transport, Hasag hoped to expand its munitions production. However, in late summer 1943, counter to expectations, Schindler again received troubling reports from the Radom Armaments Command regarding production problems resulting from the continuing high mortality in the camp. Budin, who arrived in Skarżysko in August to rectify the situation by himself, dismissed the general manager, Egon Dalski and his assistant Kuhne.[22] In their stead he appointed Paul Geldmacher as manager and Artur Moehring as his assistant.[23] In response to rumors of demoralization and drunkenness among the *Werkschutz*, their commander Kurt Krause was replaced by Walter Pollmer. In October 1943, Anton Ipfling was fired from his post as commander of the camp in Werk A, and Paul Kuehnemann appointed in his place.

Changes in personnel alone could not alter the state of affairs in production which was contingent on the physical condition of the camp

---

[18] Gerald Reitlinger: Die Endloesung, (Berlin: Colloqium Verlag, 1956), p. 332.

[19] Danuta Czech: Kalendarium der Ereignisse im Konzentrationslager Auschwitz-Birkenau, Hefte von Auschwitz, Nr. 4, (Państwowe Muzeum w Oswięcimiu, 1961), pp. 109–110. ibid. Nr. 6, 1962, p. 43.

[20] "Vorlaufiger Ausweis", Kamienna, den 12.7.43, Juda Lejb Bornes, Testimony, YV, 0-3/3763.

[21] Szymon Rozenblat: AGKBZH, SWK, sygn. 217, p. 134.

[22] Gustaw Hessen: Sitzungen, p. 119; cf. Anklageschrift, p. 21.

[23] Ktb des Kdo Radom, 2.8.43., MA, RW 23/17, pp. 84, 114, 128.

prisoners. Officially, by mid-1943, no food was rationed for Jews in the Generalgouvernement. Thus the only food supplied to the prisoners were the starvation rations provided by Hasag. For purely economic reasons, as long as a live Jew could be found to replace each dead Jew, Hasag was in no hurry to spend money on food for the prisoners.

In the Shadow of the "*Erntefest*": Circumstances Surrounding the Recruitment of Jews from Płaszów

In June 1943, Himmler declared all of the Generalgouvernement an "area of anti-gang warfare." As a result, Skarżysko and the vicinity became closely guarded. The concentration of German forces in the region was directly responsible for the paucity of military actions launched by the local Polish partisans. The turning point in local security came in late August 1943 when, in the wake of the Jewish uprisings in Treblinka and Białystok, the number of attacks on German targets rose throughout the Generalgouvernement.

The threat posed by the "gangs" compelled Gen. Schindler and Hans Frank to call an emergency meeting of all the managers of the G.G. munitions plants for Sept. 16, 1943. The dilemma facing all of those present was how to maintain the independence of the G.G. industry while security was in the hands of the SS, rather like setting the wolf to guard the sheep. The continued existence of the company camps was also of concern in view of Himmler's demand that the remaining Jews be held in concentration camps. Schindler and his colleagues therefore preferred to have the Wehrmacht rather than the SS responsible for plant security. Frank added his demand that the problems of the munitions industry in the G.G. be solved "autarkically."[24]

The independence of the munitions industry and future of the factory camps thereby became a factor in Frank's struggle to free the General-gouvernement from the authority of Himmler and his subordinates. This conflict was apparent throughout the discussions at the symposium organized by the Commission for Security Affairs in the G.G. on September 22, 1943 at which SS representatives were also present. When the

---

[24] Betriebsfuehrertagung der Ruestungsindustrie des GG, Krakau, 17.9.1943, Tagebuch, YV, JM/21, nr. 9. p. 945.

industrialists implied that only the Wehrmacht could deal with the "gangs", Erich von dem Bach Zelewski, speaking for the SS, replied that the Fuehrer alone could decide such issues. In his opinion, security in the Generalgouvernement was quite satisfactory, and he had not promised police assistance in guarding the plants.[25] From von dem Bach's remarks it would seem that the SS had no interest in protecting the capitalists calmly raking in the profits from their factories. Ultimately, the external security of the munitions plants was reinforced by units of the Ostlegionen. In regard to internal security, the demands of the RSHA *(Reichssicherheitshauptamt)* were met and supervision of the *Werkschutz* was transferred from plant management to the district SiPo commanders.[26]

The Jewish uprisings in August were taken as a warning by the authorities, so that in his speech at Posen on October 4, 1943, Himmler already hinted at a new stage in the "Final Solution." The uprising in Sobibor on October 14, 1943 supplied the excuse to put his plan into action: without warning, between November 3 and 8, 42,000 Jews were murdered by special SS units in the "Erntefest" campaign at the Majdanek, Poniatowa and Trawniki camps in the Lublin district.

Why did Himmler decide to annihilate camps which were the basis of the OSTI's economic programs he himself had supported in February of the same year? Unquestionably, the German leaders were alarmed by the Jewish insurrections which undermined the Nazi axiom concerning "Jewish germs" lacking in any spirit to fight for their honor or their lives. In the eyes of Hitler and Himmler, this threat to Nazi ideology was even more dangerous than potential economic damage.

We may assume that ideological considerations were accompanied by pragmatic ones: in September 1943, Speer was accorded exclusive authority over all matters pertaining to the war economy, including manpower.[27] He was to assume this post on November 1, 1943, and represented a serious threat to the OSTI development plans. Accordingly, at a meeting of the WVHA management on September 7, 1943, it was decided that in the future all Jewish labor camps in the G.G. would be

---

[25] Sitzung des W Wi Stabes, Krakau, 22.9.1943, Okupacja i ruch, op. cit., p. 202 ff.

[26] Ktb des Kdo Radom, 19.10.43, MA, RW 23/17, p. 116.

[27] "Erlass des Fuehrers ueber die Konzentration der Kriegswirtschaft", RGBl, 1943, vol. 1, pp. 529–531.

turned over to the WVHA, on condition that the camp guards would be subject to the WVHA and would be reinforced by the SS.[28] On October 22, Pohl ordered the expedited transfer of eight camps to the WVHA: Trawniki, Poniatowa, Radom, Budzyń, Płaszów, Lwów-Janowska, Alter Flughafen, and D.A.W. near Lublin.[29] However, on October 29, 1943, Speer relegated responsibility for manpower, including Jews, to the G.G. Armaments Inspectorate.[30] Might the slaughter of the "*Erntefest*" have been perpetrated in order to prevent Speer and the private concerns from gaining control of 42,000 Jews?

Gen. Schindler had good reason to celebrate, since the slaughterers did not come anywhere near the "company camps" under control of the Armaments Inspectorate. At a meeting of the Armaments Commission on November 10, 1943, he used carefully chosen words to refer to the "unanticipated dissolution" of the Jewish work-force in the Lublin camps.[31] He was concerned that other labor camps would also be destroyed, bringing to naught the assurances of Krueger, who, on November 2, 1943, had promised to transfer 10,000 Jews from SS camps to the plants in the Radom district.[32] Krueger was about to leave his post as HSSuPF of the Generalgouvernement, and his replacement, Wilhelm Koppe, was still an unknown quantity for Schindler.

For these reasons, Schindler was determined to set his plan in motion before Koppe assumed his new post. In the wake of the November massacres, the only remaining available prisoners were 20,000 in the Płaszów-Jerozolimska camp, most of whom, although officially said to be working in the D.A.W. factories, were chronically unemployed. Two other small camps still in existence, Julag I and Julag III, were dismantled on November 14–15, and 1,700 Jews were transferred to Płaszów.[33] Meanwhile, at Płaszów a list of prisoners to be sent to Skarżysko was being

---

[28] Besprechung im WVHA-Berlin am 7.9.1943, Eksterminacja Żydów, op. cit., p. 254.

[29] Globocnik an Himmler, Triest, 5.1.44, Prozess IV. NO-057.

[30] Erlass ueber die Aufgabenverteilung in der Kriegswirtschaft vom 29.10.1943, YV, JM/4530, p. 2-764778.

[31] Sitzung der Ruestungskommission des GG, 10.11.43, Albert Speer, Der Sklavenstaat, (Stuttgart: DVA, 1981), p. 384; about: "Erntefest", see ibid., p. 283; G. Reitlinger, op. cit., p. 334; J. Billig, op. cit., p. 209.

[32] Ktb der Rue In im GG, 4.11.43., MA, RW 23/3, p. 126.

[33] Testimonies, YV: Mata Hollender, 0-16/1215; Ryszard Aptowicz, 0-3/2712.

compiled with the full cooperation of the camp commander, Amon Goeth. As usual, the prisoners were not told the destination of this transport, and panic reigned.

On November 16, 1943, the train left the station, and that same night 2,500 prisoners from Płaszów arrived in Skarżysko. Two days later, another 1,500 Jews were sent on their way, some to Warta-Hasag in Częstochowa and others to factories in Pionki, Starachowice, Ludwików and Ostrowiec.[34]

This transport from Płaszów concluded the "Majdanek period", during which the local munitions industry had fought to retain its independence, with the following consequences:

1. The attempt to find a solution to the security problems in the G.G. became another aspect of the power struggle between Himmler and the coalition consisting of the industrialists, the Armaments Inspectorate, and Hans Frank's administration.
2. The private concerns in the G.G. won out over OSTI and, led by Hasag, remained the primary munitions suppliers to the Wehrmacht.
3. Even beyond the Radom district, Hasag was able to take advantage of shifting circumstances to recruit Jewish workers. Thus the "Erntefest" facilitated Schindler's acquisition of thousands of Jews from Płaszów who ceased to be of importance to the floundering OSTI and the chronically unemployed D.A.W.
4. As the WVHA gained control of the Jewish slave labor camps in the G.G., a paradoxical situation was created: on the one hand it gained political power by bringing these camps under its sway, but on the other hand it manifestly lost major economic influence by the annihilation of the Lublin camps and the collapse of OSTI. We must therefore conclude that the WVHA did not gain in strength in late 1943 so that in regard to the issue of who would maintain the Jewish work camps in the Generalgouvernement, a balance of power was created between the WVHA and the munitions industry.

---

[34] Ktb der Rue In im GG, 18.11.1943, MA, RW 23/3, p. 127.

Hasag-Skarżysko Becomes "Katyń in Generalgouvernement"

The Russian offensive in early 1944 again threatened the security of the Radom district and brought about a renewed wave of attacks on German targets. There was even a growing number of desertions from the ranks of the Werkschutz at the various plants. On April 15, 1944 the Skarżysko plants were shocked to hear that 25 Tartar guards from Werk C had defected to the partisans, taking their weapons with them.[35] Faced with this growing unrest, the police and local gendarmes launched surprise raids throughout the city and the vicinity. From the beginning of 1944, mass arrests of Polish members of the underground were carried out and there were frequent executions. These terror tactics reached their peak when *Elaboracja* (Werk C) again became the center for mass murder.

In previous years, the woods surrounding Werk C had served as a good place to conceal such activities. From available testimony, it appears that three major mass murder operations had been conducted at various times. The first, which I shall call the "Hasag trenches," was connected with a former school building in Werk A which, in 1940, became a detention hall for Polish political prisoners. From there they were taken to Werk C, shot, and buried in old trenches.[36] These executions seem to have lasted for about 18 months. The identity of only one group of 28 Polish victims is known.[37]

The second operation was the slaughter of thousands of Jewish prisoners executed on the "firing range" *(Schiessplatz)* throughout the period of the camp's existence, and buried in mass graves.

The third operation, "the Bzinek atrocity," apparently began in the Spring of 1944 in response to the evacuation of Majdanek, to which the Radom district's security forces had customarily sent political prisoners. As the front drew closer, an alternative site for their massacre had to be found. Werk C seems to have suited their needs, for in April 1944 a large section of the forest was fenced in. The 2.5 meter high fence bore notices

---

[35] Ktb der Rue In im GG, Zentr. Abt., 15.4.44, MA, RW 23/4, p. 55.

[36] Eliezer Lewin: Testimony, YV, 0-19/9-2.

[37] Andrzej Jankowski: Masowe egzekucje na terenie miasta Skarżysko-Kamienna w latach 1939–1945, Sesja popularno-naukowa, (Skarżysko-Kamienna: Towarzystwo miłośników miasta Skar.-Kam., 1974), p. 45.

threatening anyone approaching with immediate death. It was guarded solely by German gendarmes and was surrounded by an aura of terror and mystery.

During this same period, hundreds of prisoners were locked up in two jails at Rejów and Bzinek. Group by group, they were taken to Werk C in hermetically sealed trucks into which the exhaust fumes were funnelled, killing them on the way.[38] Under heavy guard, the trucks would pull up before the canvas-covered fence behind which was a makeshift crematorium, known by the plant workers as the "*patelnia*" (Polish for "frying pan"). Here the bodies were removed from the trucks and burnt, their ashes scattered in the woods.

Who were the victims of this atrocity, and why did the Germans guard the secret of the "*patelnia*" so jealously? The only remains left intact among the ashes were belt buckles and army insignia from which Polish researchers conclude that soldiers of various nationalities were murdered here, among them English and American prisoners of war who were employed by the SS to build fortifications not far from Skarżysko. Once the work was completed, they were slaughtered.[39] This would indeed explain the secrecy surrounding the operation, which would have been unnecessary were the victims Jews.

As the Russian front drew nearer, the plant management made an effort to destroy all traces of Hasag's crimes. Here the *Sonderkommando* entered the picture as the link between the three mass murder operations. Due to the total absence of any German documentation, the sole source for their part in this affair is the testimony of Mordchai Strigler before the commission of enquiry at Buchenwald.[40] The *Sonderkommando* may have derived from a "special squad" at the Gestapo prison in Radom where condemned political prisoners of different nationalities were held. From among its members, 67 were chosen for the *Sonderkommando*. They were kept in isolation, and their names do not appear on any of the prison registers. This unit, brought under absolute secrecy to Werk C, worked in

---

[38] Władysław Tusiewicz: Testimony, AOKBZH w Radomiu, 26.11.1947, YV, 0-53/103, p. 283.

[39] L. Kaczanowski: Hitlerowskie fabryki, op. cit., pp. 73–74; A. Jankowski: Masowe egzekucje, op. cit., p. 46.

[40] Zeugeenaussage von Motek Strigler, Eugen Kogon, Der SS-Staat, (Muenchen: Kindler Verlag, 1974), p. 220.

the "*patelnia*", burning the corpses of the victims of the "Bzinek atrocity." In addition, they were assigned the job of opening the mass graves from the two previous operations, the "Hasag trenches" and the "firing range," and burning those bodies as well. Their work lasted for some four to six weeks and was completed toward the end of June, 1944.

According to Strigler, members of the special unit managed to convey to him lists of the victims and descriptions of the various operations, employing the services of a Jewish prisoner, Mendel Rubin, who was arrested in Werk C in October 1943 and made to work side by side with the *Sonderkommando*. Amongst these papers was one headed "*Katyń in Generalgouvernement*". Strigler and his fellow prisoners buried the documents inside the camp and today their fate remains unknown. The fate of other reports hidden elsewhere throughout the district by members of the unit is similarly unknown,[41] as is the total number of people murdered in Werk C. Polish researchers estimate the number of victims of all three operations as 35,000.[42]

The *Elaboracja* affair reveals the weakness of the local partisans. There is no evidence whatsoever of any attempt to attack the death convoys or even the prisons in which Poles were tortured. Insofar as the prospect of organizing an uprising in the Jewish camp is concerned, there can be no doubt that the "*patelnia*" was a constant remainder of the fate awaiting anyone daring to try. Paradoxically, the impossibility of plotting an insurrection worked to the prisoners' advantage since it increased the chances for the camp's continued existence. This very sentiment was voiced by a German gendarme who escorted the death convoys. To the terrified prisoners he remarked: "These people are traitors, but you have nothing to fear. You're workers and we have to protect you".[43]

Why was the Camp at Skarżysko not Made into a Concentration Camp?

Although circumstances favored the continued existence of the Skarżysko camp, another danger still lurked: its reconstitution as a

---

[41] M. Strigler, Goirolois, op. cit., vol. 1, pp. 310–329.

[42] L. Kaczanowski: Hitlerowskie fabryki, op. cit., p. 77.

[43] Róża Bauminger: Przy pikrynie i trotylu, (Kraków: Żydowska Komisja Historyczna, 1946), p. 56.

concentration camp by the WVHA which sought in this manner to gain control of all of the Jewish camps in the G.G. Indications of apprehensions regarding this contingency appear in a report sent from SSuPF Herbert Boettcher to Wilhelm Koppe on December 1, 1943. Boettcher stated that "the SS officer in charge of economic affairs" (a reference to Erich Schellin), had informed him that the decision would soon be made as to whether the Jewish camps directly under the Radom district SSuPF would be turned into concentration camps, adding that: "He was unable to answer my question of whether the concentration camps were to include the Jewish camps of the munitions industry."[44]

Boettcher's report goes on to detail the difficulties involved in the external and internal security of the munitions plants, particularly Hasag-Skarżysko. He mentions the drop in the number of escape attempts from the camp and the transfer of supervision of the *Werkschutz* to the Radom SiPo as the particular achievements of himself and his subordinates. The greatest problem, however, appears at the end of the report: "Should the Jewish camps directly under the SS and Police commanders ... become concentration camps, *I would ask that a simultaneous decision be taken as to responsibility for the Jewish camps of the munitions plants*. If, as has recently been suggested, they become *Aussenkommando* of concentration camps, this would be beneficial in the sense that it would reduce the work load of the SS and Police commanders.... *However*, it would also have disadvantages since neither the SiPo nor the *Werkschutz* come under the authority of the concentration camp commander." Therefore, Boettcher states: "He can give no orders to the members of the *Werkschutz* who are charged with guarding the Jewish camp. *In my opinion it would be best to leave these camps, as they have been, under the supervision of the SS and Police commanders who will also continue to handle fiscal accounting regarding the Jewish camps*" [my emphasis – F.K.].

In this manner, Boettcher (holder of a law degree) was able to create a legal basis for his continued control of the company camps by relying on the decisions of the WVHA from September 9, 1943. As a result, in the SS camps such as Płaszów, internal security was effected by SS men and

---

[44] Der SSuPF im Distrikt Radom, an den HSSuPF Ost, Radom, 1.12.1943, betr. Schutz der Ruestungsbetriebe, YV, JM/4530, p. 2-765116, ff.

Askaris reporting to the camp commander,[45] while in the company camps it was in the hands of the *Werkschutz* under the command of the Radom SiPo, i.e., Boettcher.

Boettcher's question went unanswered, and the status quo ante remained unchanged. A number of factors played a role in preserving this situation. First, in early 1944, the WVHA still had its hands full bringing eight SS camps in the Lublin and Krakow districts under its control. At the same time, the importance of the Radom district was becoming increasingly apparent, as demonstrated by the map in Figure 4.1. Moreover, Schindler cultivated the support of the new HSSuPF, Koppe, who considered Hasag-Skarżysko "a factory of extraordinary value."[46] Indeed, in January, 1944, the plant produced 16.6 million rounds of ammunition as compared with 10 million in September, 1943.[47] On March 1, 1944, Hasag-Skarżysko was the second largest of the 104 "military factories" in the Generalgouvernement, with a complement of 15,451 employees,[48] some 7,500 of them Jews.

However, in February 1944 the situation changed. A deadly typhoid epidemic broke out in the camp claiming hundreds of victims. The German foremen's constant complaints of a shortage of workers led to a series of consultations in the Radom Armaments Command concerning the recruitment of new laborers. Although the number of Poles employed by the plant increased relative to June 1943, in March 1944 the plant management concentrated its attention most particularly on the Jewish camp. On March 1, 1944, a military commission paid a visit to the camp. Its conclusion: the extraordinarily high mortality rate among the prisoners was jeopardizing the entire production program.[49]

As a result, Hasag again sought ways to obtain new transports of Jews, but in the Spring of 1944 this was virtually an impossible task. The single large transport was brought from outside the borders of the G.G. In March 1944, with the help of Koppe, Greiser agreed to allocate to Hasag 1,500

---

[45] See note 28; Askaris were police units that consisted of Ukrainians, Lithuaniens and Latviens. They guarded the concentration and extermination camps, Eksterminacja Żydów: op. cit., p. 255, note 3.

[46] HSSuPF im GG an Praesident Bauder, Krakau, 13.1.1944, YV, JM/4530, p. 2-765109.

[47] Allgemeine Ruestungslage, Lgb vom Februar 1944, MA, RW 46/494, p. 82.

[48] Statistischer Ueberblick, see note 4., ib., p. 764905 ff.

[49] Ktb des Rue Kdo Radom, 1.3.1944, MA, RW 23/18, pp. 12, 15.

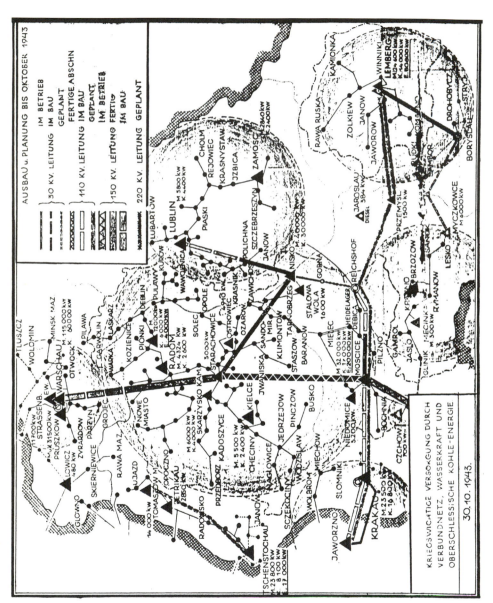

Figure 4.1 Mobilization of Industry in the GG for the War Effort (Kriegseinsatz der Industrie im GG, Oktober 1943) BA. R 52 VI/11)

Jews from the ghetto of Łódź.[50] Some were taken to Skarżysko and the rest divided up among the Hasag company camps in Częstochowa from which around 120 experienced workers were sent to Skarżysko along with three small groups from Radom and probably one from Warsaw. In addition, a transport of 500 women arrived from Płaszów in March 1944.[51] All in all, a total of some 6,270 Jews arrived in Skarżysko between July 1943 and August 1944 (including the transports from Majdanek and Płaszów).

Attempts to obtain further transports were unsuccessful. The danger of the camp being wiped out by disease and starvation thus compelled the authorities to take the only action left them – to attempt to control the mortality rate by improving conditions in the camp. Although Schindler cautioned that a solution would have to be found to the problem of food supplies, the G.G. government refused to provide any assistance and Hasag was unwilling to lay out any additional funds whatsoever. The situation seemed lost.

The turning point came on March 16, 1944. At Schindler's insistence, Boettcher called a meeting in his office to discuss "the uniform handling of food supplies for the Jewish labor force" in the munitions plants in his jurisdiction. Here it was resolved that "from April 1, 1944, food supplies for the Jew would be organized by the unit quartermaster stores of SS units."[52] This decision did not involve taking any measures that would imply increased control on the part of the WVHA. None of the company camps in the Radom district was transferred to the supervision of the WVHA, none was turned into a concentration camp, and there was no change in their formal status until their final evacuation in the Summer of 1944.

In the Summer of 1944, some 50,000 "legal" Jews were still in the G.G., all of them in camps.[53] Of these, around 20,000 were prisoners of the Płaszów concentration camp and several thousand others were held in a number of small secondary camps.(Aussenkommando) Only the Radom

---

[50] H. Biebow an Hauessler, Litzmannstadt, 18.3.1944, Eksterminacja Żydów, op. cit., p. 256.

[51] Helena Schuetz, Testimony, YV, 0-16/329.

[52] "Ab 1.4.44 uebernimmt die SS die Verpflegung der in den W-Betrieben eingesetzten Juden", Ktb des Rue Kdo Radom, 16.3.44., MA, RW 23/18, p. 16.

[53] Fragment sprawozdania dla Delegatury Rządu Londyńskiego, Raport z listopada 1943, Eksterminacja Żydów, op. cit., p. 341.

district alone continued to maintain 14 forced labor camps, 11 of them company camps and one a concentration camp at Bliżyń. Together they contained some 25,000 Jewish prisoners (see Table 4.4). Hasag remained the *single* concern to maintain, to the very end, six company camps for 14,000 Jews, constituting approximately 30% of the entire "official" Jewish population of the Generalgouvernement.

The "external history" of the Skarżyska camp during the two and a half years of its existence reveals that its extraordinary status was made possible by the firm support of all the authorities within the G.G., and first and foremost the Armaments Command. What motives lay behind the tireless efforts of Gen. Schindler, who, for this entire period, assured a steady stream of transports of Jewish workers to the Hasag plants? It was indeed part of his job to ensure increased production to meet the demands of the Wehrmacht, but pressured by the large German concerns who had a vested interest in restricting development of industry in the East, the Reich authorities placed only limited orders with G.G. factories so that the local industrial potential was never fully exploited. According to Speer, the contribution of the G.G. to total munitions production in all countries under German hegemony reached not more than 0.025%.[54] Only in the realm of ammunition did the G.G. play any significant role, with its production in March 1944 supplying fully one-third of the infantry's needs. Of all the other occupied nations and German satellites, only France and Belgium also produced ammunition for the Wehrmacht, and both in much smaller proportions than the G.G.[55] What this means is that Hasag virtually held a monopoly in this field, not only locally, but also throughout Europe (excluding the Reich itself).

It therefore follows that the Hasag plants, with Skarżysko as their flagship, were the cornerstones of Schindler's power base and the very justification for its existence, while for Budin, although Skarżysko was of importance, it was only one of many such factories. Thus it was Budin who, in March 1944, presented Schindler with a list of conditions and made it clear to him that if no authority was found which was willing to take upon itself the task of providing for the Jewish prisoners, production would not be expanded. With the price of ammunition falling, Budin could

---

[54] Sitzung der Ruestungskommission des GG, 12.1.44, A. Speer, Der Sklavenstaat, op. cit., p. 386.

[55] "Wehrmachtsauftraege im 1943", P. Matusak, Ruch oporu, op. cit., p. 50.

Table 4.4 Jewish Labor Comps at Radom district, July 1944

		Number of Jews	Number of all workers	Estimated number of Jews
		30.6.1943	1.3.1944	July 1944
	A. Company camps (W-Betriebe)			
1	Braunschweig – Starachowice	1,239	13,605	1,400
2	Ludwigshuette – Kielce	546	2,737	600
3	Hochoefen Ostrowiec	738	7,989	1,000
4	Dietrich Fischer – Piotrków	—	1,641	800
5	Steyr-Daimler-Puch – Radom	1,008	4,541	1,800
6	Hasag – Skarżysko	6,408	15,451	7,500
7	Hasag – Kielce	404	2,063	400
8	Hasag – Apparatebau	3,350	4,584	3,500
9	Hasag – Raków	521	3,397	500
10	Hasag – Warta	1,200	1,224	1,300
11	Pionki	1,500	5,836	1,500
		16,914	63,068	20,300
	B. Others			
12	Hasag – Częstochowianka	1,500		1,200
13	Henryków – Kielce	400		400
14	Karo-Hortensja – Piotrków	600		600
		2,500		2,200
	C. Concentration camps			
15	Bliżyń	4,000		3,000
	Total	23,414		25,500

only justify such expansion if it was not accompanied by increased expenditure. This was possible only by the massive use of Jews, since unlike the Poles, their maintenance cost Hasag next to nothing, save the fees paid the local SS commander.

Thus, the continued existence of Jewish company camps became a condition of Budin's consent to manufacture ammunition in the Generalgouvernement, and since this branch had always been the Achilles heel of the German war economy – a truism known to all the authorities concerned with munitions – Budin's condition became the primary factor behind both the maintenance of six Jewish company camps and the fact that they did not become WVHA concentration camps. Following the precedent set by Hasag, several additional small company camps were established by other firms. The unusual status afforded Hasag, however, was again obvious when the Jewish camps were evacuated.

In July 1944, Soviet units reached the border of the Radom district and evacuation of the factories was speeded up. On July 20, 1944, Bierkamp, the Generalgouvernement SiPo commander, ordered the evacuation of Jewish prisoners to concentration camps. If conditions at the front obviated this procedure, the prisoners were to be killed on site and their bodies burned. The order stated that "these measures are also to be taken where necessary regarding the Jews still employed in munitions factories." [56] The SS was given the authority to carry out the evacuation and to determine the destination of transports. Jewish workers from munitions plants such as Steyr-Daimler-Puch at Radom, Radom, Braunschweig Stahlwerke-Starachowice, "Krusz"-Pionki, Hochoefen-Ostrowiec, and others, were sent to Auschwitz.

This, however, was not the fate of the Hasag camps. At Skarżysko, following a "selection," some 500 prisoners were slaughtered. On the night of July 30, 1944, around 250 prisoners attempted to escape from Werk C. All were caught and killed in the surrounding woods. On the following day a transport of 1,500 men was sent to Buchenwald,[57] and another of 1,200 women to Leipzig.[58] Several transports containing close to 3,000 Jews arrived in Częstochowa and were divided up among the four local Hasag plants.[59] One thousand men remained in Skarżysko to finish loading the trucks, and were then sent in two transports to dig trenches in the vicinity of Sulejów. On September 9, 1944 they were all transferred to Buchenwald.[60] According to the best estimates, a total of

---

[56] Der Kommandeur der SiPo u. SD fuer den Distrikt Radom, an SS-Haupt-Stuf. Thiel, Radom, 21.7.44, Doc. occup., vol. 6, p. 519.

[57] Neuzugange vom 5.8.1944 vom Zwangslager bei der Firma Hasag in Kamienna, Weimar-Buchenwald, YV, Bu-23, August 44, GCC 2/197/-8-/.

[58] The transport of women from Hasag-Skarżysko to Buchenwald, (Leipzig), YV, JM/3963, 3964.

[59] The story of Mendel Herskovitz, YVA, 0-36/9, p. 1657. cf. Irma Laksberger, Testimony, YV, 0-16/251.

[60] Elhanan Erlich, op. cit., p. 388, cf. Edward Kossoy, Handbuch zum Entschaedigungsverfahren, im Selbstverlag, YV, p. 100.

6,700 Jews were evacuated from Skarżysko, the large majority of them to the various German Hasag plants at Leipzig, Schlieben and Meuselwitz. They constituted part of the 10,000 prisoners supplied to Budin, by special powers afforded him by Hitler, for the production of bazookas.[61]

As to the question of the total number of Jews held in Skarżysko and the number who died in the camp, two answers are possible. According to minimal estimates based, at least in part, on testimony and original sources, 19,360 were brought to the camp and 6,700 evacuated from it, leaving 12,660 who died in the camp. However, since not every transport is documented in existing sources, it may be assumed that at least 25,000 Jews entered the camp and 7,000 were evacuated, giving 18,000 who found their death at Skarżysko.

Some researchers and former prisoners place the number who died in the camp at 20,000 to 23,000.[62] However, even if we rely on minimal figures, we can say that during the 32 months of its existence, approximately 20,000 Jews were brought to Skarżysko and around 14,000, or 70%, died there. These numbers support the conclusion that, at least in its initial stage, the forced labor camp at Skarżysko fulfilled the function of a typical extermination camp.

In January 1945 the last Germans left Skarżysko. No trace of the abandoned camp at the edge of the woods remains today save the ashes from the hundreds of mass graves, all that is left of the Jews whose sole function was to die for Hasag. And those ashes, scattered on the wind, cry out for us to tell their story, the story of their life, their struggle, and their death.

---

[61] Der Chef der SS-WVHA Pohl, an Reichsfuehrer SS, Berlin, 17.10.1944, Ni-315, YV, JM/3720.

[62] L. Kaczanowski, Zbrodnie w przyzakładowym obozie, Sesja, s. n. 37, p. 63; cf. Herszel Kris, Testimony, YV, 0-33/1855.

Chapter 5

The History of the Camp at Werk A and the "Radom Tier"

Throughout the discussion of its "external history", the camp was conceived of as a single entity, one of many such sites on the map of occupied Poland. Repeatedly we followed the route of the dozens of transports until they stopped at the camp gate. The time has now come to go through that gate and observe from close at hand the alien and hostile world known as the Skarżysko-Kamienna camp. What shall we discover – an internal life similar to that which prevailed at other camps, or a different sort of reality?

The "internal history" of the camp reveals that the prisoners brought here, whether by force or as volunteers, were not merely a random collection of individuals each of whom employed his or her own personal strategy in the brutal struggle for survival. Rather, they also became part of a prisoner society characterized by two prominent features. First, in response to the periodic transports, a three-tiered structure evolved, consisting of the "Radom Tier" whose members came from the cities and towns of the Radom district, the "Majdanek Tier" of former prisoners of this concentration camp, and the "Płaszów Tier" of those brought from the Płaszów camp. Yet simultaneously, a class structure also emerged, reflecting the economic distinctions between the prisoners and the different functions they fulfilled in the camp administration.

Thus what evolved was a pluralistic and heterogeneous society divided into a large number of groups which, while allowing for interrelations on many levels, also constituted fertile ground for the sprouting of inner tensions. This situation prevailed in all three, so that the following description of the "internal history" of Werk A may serve to illustrate life in the other two camps as well (see Figure 5.1).

"Ekonomia" – Living Conditions and Early Adjustment

In early 1942, the first huts in Werk A appeared in the vicinity of the German commissary, Konsum, and here groups of Jews abducted for labor gangs were housed. When some 2,000 Jews were brought to the factory all at once in the Spring of 1942, the management had not yet made arrangements for their accommodation. The only available building was a large empty production facility near Ekonomia Street, from which the structure got its name. In the main hall, four tiers of wooden pallets were hastily built, and here the men and women were packed together. Despite the dreadful crowding, those who managed to find a place inside were considered lucky in comparison to others left outside to lie in the mud.

Between April and August 1942, these prisoners were joined by hundreds more Jews put to work in construction. They had the arduous tasks of paving roads and building new fences, huts and production halls. The only latrine facilities were provided by the woods and a few taps scattered around the area of the plant. The backbreaking work, dysentery, and starvation soon thinned the ranks of the "founding fathers." The vast majority of them were from the poorest classes of society, so that the support they received from the Judenrat or from their families was next to nothing. We may assume that the plant recorded the names of only those workers sent by the labor exchanges, and not those abducted from the nearby ghettos, and therefore "official" numbers would be artificially low. As far as we can tell, up to August 1942, some 3,000 to 4,000 Jews passed through "Ekonomia." The sparse testimony from that period provides additional evidence of the virtually total annihilation of these people.

With the large-scale deportations of August 1942, a massive influx of transports began, and the overcrowding grew worse. The greatest concentration remained in "Ekonomia," with separate barracks for men and women alongside it. Rooms were found on the top floor of "Ekonomia" for the families of those employed in the internal Jewish administration and for the wealthy from nearby towns, thus giving rise to

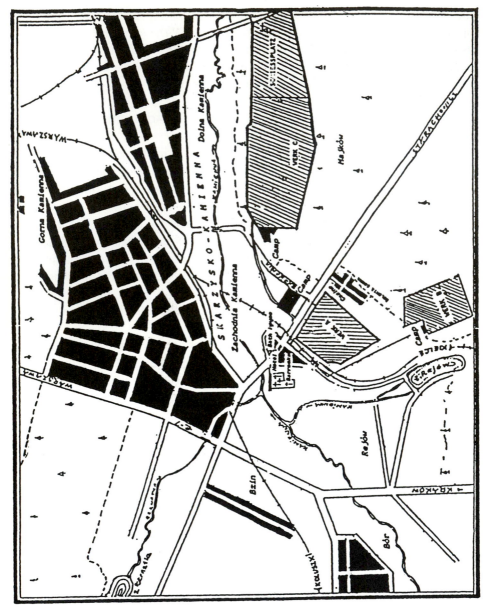

Figure 5.1 "Hasag-Werke" Skarżysko-Kamienna (Werk A, B, C) and the Jewish camps (reconstruction)

the "Skarżysko room," the "Suchedniów room," and other such. In time, some of the men were also housed in the former stables known as the "horse barracks" *(Pferdebaracken)*.

The center of the camp was occupied by the assembly grounds. The Werkschutz guardhouse *(Wache)* stood by the gate. Latrines and bath houses *(Waschraum)* were erected, as was an infirmary *(Revier)* in two remote huts. A special hut was allocated to the Jewish administration and police offices. Minimal lighting was installed in the prisoners' barracks, which contained no tables, benches or heaters. A bit of straw was scattered on the pallets and only those with connections were supplied with mattresses and blankets. The camp grew steadily, so that on September 12, 1942 there was a total of 3,383 prisoners in Werk A.[1]

Food supplies for the camp were obtained in two ways: official and noun-official. Official responsibility was in the hands of the Hasag Supply Division (BeWi) at Kielce. From here provisions were sent to the Konsum storehouse controlled by the German administration known as Schlicht. In theory, the labor camp was allotted enough provisions to meet the minimum calorie requirements of the prisoners, but these were not in fact supplied by the Hasag management. The bakery and kitchen were in the area of the plant and not the camp. Although dark rye flour was provided for baking bread for the Jews, most of it was stolen by the Polish and German bakery managers who used it to bake loaves which the Poles then sold surreptitiously to the Jewish prisoners. The "Jewish bread" was therefore made from the remaining flour to which dried potato flakes, produced at a special mill in Werk B, were added.

The same flakes were used to make "soup" for the prisoners. Twice a week a bit of barley, carrot scrapings or horse meat was added, and twice a week it was made with sugar. This was the famous "sweet soup" of the camp. The soup for the Polish workers was also made from the potato flakes, but other ingredients were often added at the expense of the Jewish ration. When one of the Germans, Hans Schmecher, brought a sample of the "Jewish soup" to Kuhne, stating: "We can't go on this way," he was promised that the cooks would be taught how to use the flakes properly![2] In total, the daily food allotment for a prisoner consisted of 230 grams of bread, 0.75 liters of soup twice daily, and "coffee" in the morning and

---

[1] Staerkemeldung, 9.12.1942, YV, 0-6/37-3.

[2] Hans Schmecher, Sitzungen, p. 9.

evening. Sometimes there was also a spoonful of beet jam. The prisoners were given no cutlery of any kind.

The prisoners wore the clothes they brought with them to the camp, and when these wore out they wrapped themselves in rags and paper bags. For shoes they were given wooden clogs which rubbed and blistered their feet. No other clothing was distributed, nor was soap. Once a month the prisoners from all three werks were brought to the central bathhouse *("łaźnia")* in Werk A where their clothes were also summarily disinfected, but this was no protection against the lice rampant throughout the barracks.

It was a sordid reality which confronted thousands of men and women of the "Radom Tier," a typical cross-section of the population of a Jewish town in Central Poland. Before the war they had been wealthy merchants, farm owners, shopkeepers and wholesalers selling to the local farmers, craftsmen, or poor laborers. A few were religious officials or factory workers. They all shared a conservative provincial character, a pious devotion to religion and tradition, a language (Yiddish), and strong ties to their large families. Politically, however, they were very different, ranging from Hasidim, through the various hues of the Zionist movement, and on to Bund members. They were deeply rooted in their surroundings and had long-standing ties with the local population.

The moment a Jew stepped onto the camp grounds, he began a new life. The entire transport underwent a careful search. The prisoners were ordered to hand over all their money, foreign currency, and valuables. The Germans sometimes knew who to search more thoroughly and who less, as Mejer Rysenberg, one of the prisoners on the transport from Staszów, relates. During the search the local policeman hinted that Meir's group had no reason to fear the threats of the Werkschutz, and thus he and his friends were able to hide money and valuables in their shoes and sneak them into the camp.[3]

The following day the transport underwent its first "selection" in the camp, aimed at weeding out the elderly and debilitated prisoners. The second "selection" was conducted on the plant grounds by the German foremen in the three *werks*. The hardiest individuals with suitable professions were taken to Werks A and B, and the "leftovers" sent to Werk C.

---

[3] Mejer Ryzenberg, Testimony, YV, 0-33/38.

Each prisoner was registered in the camp file and the factory office where he or she received a "work card", containing personal information and an identity number. New prisoners were apparently given the numbers of those who had died in order to obscure the actual number of prisoners who passed through the camp.[4] The prisoner's first concern after registration was to secure a pallet. Here he arranged his meager possessions: a few clothes, perhaps a blanket, a dish or two. Here he would eat, sleep, receive visitors, conduct business, and hide his treasures. From this moment on, his pallet was his castle. The women also brought with them some laundry soap, knitting needles, and sewing materials. However insignificant the item, it now took on the proportions of a prize which might some day save their life.

Most of the prisoners brought to the camp were on their own, but there were cases of married couples, brothers and sisters, or even whole families who arrived as volunteers or whose bribes had kept them together. Each prisoner tried his best to stay close to family members, or at least people from the same town. This desire led to associations of fellow townsmen like the *Landsmannschaft*. Such a group, together with the family, eased the "greenhorn's" pain of adjustment. It was clear that he would have to fight his battle for survival on his own, but if he lacked any kindred spirit, his life would be considerably harder. The veteran prisoners soon warned the newcomers that it wasn't good to look too healthy because they would attract extortionists, and it wasn't good to look too sickly either because no one would give them a second thought. They also learned to assess the German commanders: who was really in command in the camp, who was worth getting close to and who was to be avoided, how to get extra bread, and other vital lessons. This early information would help the prisoner negotiate his way along the paths of his new and dangerous world.

Camp Authorities and Internal Organization

Within the camp the prisoner was subject to three authorities: the German commander and his subordinates; the *Werkschutz*; and the internal Jewish administration.

---

[4] Mordchai Strigler, In di fabrikn fun toit (Yiddish), (Buenos Aires: Union Central Israelita Polaca en la Argentina, 1948), p. 244 ff.

The German officers were perceived by the prisoners much like a band of thieves who treated the camp as if it were their feudal estate. Here, far from the eye of Himmler and under the protection of Egon Dalski, they enjoyed pleasures they would not have dared to imagine were they stationed in a concentration camp. Theodor Eicke's "sacred" principles[5] were reinterpreted in the Skarżysko camp. The officers waged the "political battle against the state's enemies," by pilfering Jewish property for themselves; in the name of "fraternity" they organized a clique of black marketeers; and the "rites of manhood" were expressed in orgies of drunkenness and gang rapes of Jewish girls.

The head of this group was Kurt Krause, 52, known for his weakness for beautiful women. The prisoners estimated the value of his personal wealth at 5 million marks! Like a feudal squire, he kept a firm grip on "his" Jews, such as Ajzenberg, the shoemaker from Skarżysko, who made him "the best pair of boots in the world." [6] Among his deputies were Otto Eisenschmidt, a member of the SA suspected of taking part in the orgies, and Paul Kiessling, whose major concern was his own pocket and thus appropriated anything he could get his hands on. As watch commander, he also oversaw Werk C where he was notorious for his ruthlessness.[7] He avoided the orgies, however, probably because of the watchful eye of his wife, Else, Dalski's secretary.

The most dreaded of all was Fritz Bartenschlager, a member of the SA and a war criminal feared even by the Poles. His rape and murder of Jewish girls earned him the smoldering hatred of the Jews. As one testimony has it, after the deportation from the Skarżysko ghetto in October 1942, Franz Schippers, Willi Seidel, and Iwan Romanko arrived in the camp. At Bartenschlager's invitation, they picked out six girls at roll call and brought them to his rooms. The names of Cesia Kapłański and Ewa Ernest and her sister are mentioned. They were ordered to serve the diners in the nude, and at the end of the meal were raped. The following day they were all executed. Bela Hercberg-Goldman, who had initially been selected but was saved, was also later murdered together

---

[5] "Theodor Eicke", Wspomnienia Rudolfa Hoessa, ed. Jan Sehn, (Warszawa, Wydawnictwo Prawnicze, 1960), p. 265.

[6] Jakow Ajzenberg, Skarżysko Book, p. 88.

[7] Sala Warszauer, ib. p. 275.

with her husband.[8] Another incident which sent an even greater shockwave throughout the camp occurred on January 23, 1943. In honor of German guest including Boettcher, Paul Feucht and Schippers, three girls were chosen: Gucia Milchman, a 19-year-old acclaimed for her outstanding beauty, Ruchama Eisenberg, and Mania Silberman. They were all brutally raped and then slaughtered.[9] It is claimed that the wife of the "camp elder" faced a similar fate but was saved thanks to Ipfling's intervention.[10]

Indeed, opinions differ as to Anton Ipfling. He was the only one of the *Werkschutz* officers to stand trial after the war. However, he was never implicated in any acts of piracy or rape. Some of the prisoners testified that he did not allow the Polish overseers to abuse the Jews, enabled families to remain together, and hid children in his office during "selections."[11] Nevertheless, he was found guilty of the murder of 30 prisoners suspected of shirking work or attempting to escape. He was sentenced to life imprisonment, although it was noted that "the defendant did not act out of hatred for the Jews since in his eyes they were not even human beings."[12] Johannes Schneider and Irchal, however, are mentioned as murderers and thieves.[13]

On the whole, there was only a minimal German presence in the camp. Daily supervision was in the hands of non-German guards. In 1946 the Poles demanded that the *Werkschutz* be declared a criminal organization similar to the SS, even though it was impossible to prove specific crimes against its individual members.[14] In response, the German courts argued that the Ukrainians and Poles were not acting on their own initiative, but "were following orders."[15]

---

[8] Testimonies YV: Szlomo Grinszpan, op. cit.; Awraham Kristal, 0-16/1955; Berek Szafranski, M-21/1-22, p. 7.

[9] Chaim Milchman, Testimony, YV, M-1/E/1972/1793, cf. Staerkemeldung 23.1.1943, see n. 1.

[10] Srul Najman, Akta w sprawie Franz Schippers, YV, JM/3786, nr. 602, Guta Najman, ib.

[11] E. Erlich, Sefer Staszów, p. 370; Eugenia Różycka, Testimony, YV, TR-11/61159.

[12] Urteil gegen Ipfling Anton, Nuernberg, 20.11.1967, YV, TR-10/604, p. 24.

[13] Szmuel Herling, Rywka Fruchtman, Szmelcman Berek, YV, M-21/Mappe 358, pp. 10–19.

[14] Rada Zakładowa P.F.A. w Skar.-Kam., 2.4.1946, YV JM/3700, p. 19.

[15] Urteil gegen Ipfling, see n. 12, ib., p. 47.

The Jewish camp regarded the *Werkschutz* as a band of avenging angels heralding "selections" and the death pit. The following examples illustrate the behavior of its individual members.

Representing the intelligentsia was Iwan Romanko, a Ukrainian Volksdeutsch who commanded "Ekonomia" in mid-1942. There he beat and plundered both men and women at his own initiative, and was involved in incidents of rape.[16] A fellow soldier, Teodor Sawczak, who was an informer working for the Germans, was thought to be Ukrainian although he declared himself a Pole. For him, the Jews were targets of extortion, like Mosze Najman whom he threatened with death if he did not turn over to him a diamond ring. Sawczak was notorious throughout the camp for his brutality.[17]

Jewish money reached the pockets of the *Werkschutz* guards in other ways as well. Periodic raids on the camp turned up money that was seized and transferred to the SS account in the Radom bank. Some of this wealth inevitably stuck to the searchers' hands. There were guards who offered, for a price, to help prisoners attempting to escape. Once he received his fee, the guard would shoot the escaping prisoner near the perimeter fence, thus doubling his earnings since he received a reward for preventing the escape. Moreover, without bribing a guard, a prisoner's chances of getting food into the camp during the search at the gate were almost nil.

The *Werkschutz* was therefore a good way to make a small fortune while releasing one's frustrations through acts of violence. On one occasion two prisoners were waiting by the fence for a Pole who was to throw them bread he had purchased for them. Unfortunately, they were discovered by a guard whose palm had not been greased and were beaten to an inch of their lives; the guard did not wait for any orders.[18] In the plant, the guards were in charge of carrying out "official" beatings. In response to a foreman's complaint, a prisoner would be sent to the guard room where he (or she – even if only a child) would receive from 10 to 35 lashings, depending on the severity of the "offense."[19] It came as no

---

[16] Akta w sprawie Romanko Iwan, YV, 0-53/65; cf. YV, M-21/3-61, pp. 18–23.

[17] Mosze Najman, Akta przeciwko Teodorowi Sawczakowi, YV, JM/3991, sygn. 4204.

[18] Jechiel Granatstein, Hod vegvura, (Hebrew), (Jerusalem: "Zeher Naftali", 1986) p. 78.

[19] Anklageschrift, p. 5; cf. Sitzungen, pp. 28–29, 81.

surprise that when the court published its verdict against Sawczak, it described the *Werkschutz* as "devoid of all human feelings." [20]

The third branch of authority within the camp was the Jewish internal administration. We know that in the concentration camps the SS created a cadre of collaborationist functionaries by taking advantage of internal conflicts, such as religious and national differences, the tension between veteran prisoners and newcomers, etc. They thereby sought also to induce the "prominente" to identify with the ideological goals of the occupiers, thus gaining their cooperation in the repression of other prisoners. This psychological manipulation earned the SS the title of "human behavior technicians." [21]

At Skarżysko, the Hasag management had the problem of forcing thousands of prisoners to obey a small group of Jewish functionaries and ensuring that the camp functioned properly without the need for large numbers of *Werkschutz*. The disturbing question is whether in the forced labor camp, where the only "rulers" were not SS officers but Jewish functionaries, Hasag succeeded in manipulating them so that they identified with its goals: the maximum exploitation of the prisoners at minimum cost and the physical annihilation of the "unproductive".

In seeking an answer we must first examine the structure and nature of the Jewish administration. From October 1942 it consisted of three operational branches:

1. **The "camp elder"** *(Lageraelteste)*, the camp's official representative before the authorities;
2. **The Police** *(Polizei)*, headed by a commander and second-in-command;
3. **Functionaries**, working in the various services.

The number of members of the internal administration varied, ranging between 30 and 40 individuals during the Radom Period.[22]

It was the "camp elder's" job to handle the "Jew file" it the camp, submitting a daily report of the number of those fit for work, ill, dead, escaped, etc. He also appointed several of the camp functionaries and

---

[20] Akta T. Sawczaka, Wyrok, Kielce, 19.2.1952, see n. 17.

[21] Andrea Devoto, "Aspekty socjo-psychologiczne i socjo-psychiatryczne obozów koncentracyjnych", BGKBZH, 18, (1968), p. 120.

[22] M. Strigler, In di fabrikn, op. cit., p. 19.

passed on to them and to the Jewish police the authorities' directives. He
was entitled to separate living quarters with his family and had free access
to the camp's storerooms. The first "camp elder" was Zalcman, with
Eljasz (Pinie) Albirt of Kielce as his deputy. While still in the Skarżysko
ghetto, he had organized groups of youngsters for work at Hasag, thus
gaining the respect of the Germans. He became *Lageraelteste* in 1942.[23]
His second wife, Hana, and his daughter were also in the camp with him.

The police, whose members were known in Yiddish as *Policjanten*, was
in charge of order and security in the camp, and never numbered more
than 15 to 20 men. They conducted the morning roll call, supervised the
prisoners as they left for work and returned to the camp, and guarded the
camp gate and fence from within. During a "selection" they were all on
station. When the number of prisoners increased, some of the Jewish
police would accompany groups to work. Their symbols of office included
a round cap and rubber truncheon. They were exempt from work and
enjoyed freedom of movement between the plant and the camp, a larger
food ration, clothes, and quarters in the family huts together with their
wives. The policemen were responsible to Lejzer Teperman, the police
commander from Radom, and his second-in-command, Josef Krzepicki
from Radomsko. They appointed new policemen and had the authority to
sentence prisoners to lashings or to hold them in detention.

The jobs of the functionaries were diverse, and the turnover among
them was great. Available testimony contains very limited information
as to their identity and functions, so that the following description may
not be entirely accurate. Nonetheless,they can be divided into three
categories:

1. **Service Workers**: those responsible for the bread
   stores – Szajber (most likely Elias Szajbe);[24] the clothes
   stores – Ewa Krzepicka; the infirmary – Lola and Mosze
   Finger; and the public bathhouse – Mosze Najman.
2. **Barracks Overseers** *(Blockaelteste, Stubenaelteste)*: responsible for cleanliness and tidiness and the distribution of
   coffee and soup to the night shift who remained in the camp
   during the day. They were issued rubber truncheons and

---

[23] Benjamin Wołowski, Skarżysko Book, p. 85.
[24] Noach Flajszakier, Testimony, YV, 0-33/1823.

green armbands, thus earning them their Yiddish name of *"Grine Lente"*. The following names are among those mentioned as holding this position: Flajszhakier, Wassermann, Ptasznik, Zajfert, Gnat, Smolarz [25] and Simon Wertman. [26]

3. **Work Group Escorts** *(Vorarbeiter)*, known by various names, most often *Komendanten* or *Policjanten*: also issued green arm bands and rubber truncheons, the *Komendanten* (we will henceforth use this name to distinguish them from the police) were responsible for the workers of one of the departments, escorting them back and forth to the plant. They were exempt from work and were in charge of the noon-time distribution of soup, a highly significant privilege in the Skarżysko camp.

The multiple authorities typical of the Nazi system did not interfere with the internal administration of the camp. The following incident illustrates the *modus vivendi* among the various branches of authority. One morning, nine girls arrived at the gate, having missed roll call. The policeman on duty called for Teperman and Krzepicki who ordered the girls to be whipped. Albirt happened to arrivi, and seeing what was going on said: "Maybe they've had enough for one day?" The two officers replied: "It's none of your business. Keep out of this!" [27]

The prisoners held sharply opposing opinions of the different individuals at the head of the internal administration. The two police commanders who literally beat prisoners to death were generally agreed to have sold their souls to the devil in exchange for power and profit, and some considered them indistinguishable from the Germans. Himmler explained their situation most precisely: in the concentration camps capos would be appointed to spur on and oversee their fellow prisoners "and if we are not pleased with them any longer they will cease to be capos and will be forced to rejoin the other prisoners who will beat them to death." [28]

---

[25] Testimonies, YV: Jerachmiel Ginsburg, 0-33/1821; Roza Birnbaum, 0-16/1214; N. Flajszakier, op. cit.

[26] "Akta sprawy p-ko Wertmann Simon", 1947, YV, JM/3712.

[27] Ozer Grundman, Testimony, YV: 0-3/3185.

[28] Falk Pingel, Haeftlinge unter SS-Herrschaft, (Hamburg: Hoffman u. Campe, 1978), p. 164.

Thus Teperman and Krzepicki went too far, burning their bridge back to the society of prisoners. In contrast, Albirt is depicted very positively, and was called "the one ray of light in the camp." He would warn the prisoners before a "selection," and in some instances tried to evade his orders. Children have testified that it was through his help that they survived.[29] Although some accused him of having too great a concern for those close to him and not aiding the others, he remained on the whole untainted by any charges of brutality or extortion.

In principle, all of the functionaries faced the same dilemma: how to maintain good relations with those above them without entirely cutting their links to the other prisoners. During the Radom Period, relations with family members and former neighbors led to highly complex inter-relations between the functionaries and the prisoner population. The same policeman would alternately administer beatings and save lives. On one occasion, Elhanan Erlich was arrested by the *Werkschutz* for shirking work and was convinced his end was near when the policeman Gilek Goldfarb suddenly appeared and asked that the prisoner be turned over to him for punishment. Gilek was known for his ruthlessness, but this incident ended not with a lashing but with a reward. Observing this strange mixture of good and evil, Erlich concludes his story by stating that, "those who were there cannot be judged by ordinary standards." [30]

In the eyes of the prisoners, the most heinous crime was informing. In contrast to the other two werk, there were a plentitude of informers in Werk A since it held many wealthy Jews. Here, too, was the largest concentration of Poles, Germans, and *Werkschutz* members whose shared ambition was to gain control of the Jewish money. The Jewish informers were motivated not only by material benefits, but also by the psychological motive expressed in the idea: "Before I was a nothing; just see how scared they are of me now." The most notorious informers were Sewin,[31] the two policemen Herszkowitz and Zuess,[32] the brothers Mendel

---

[29] Testimonies, YV: Reuwen Weingarten, 0-6/1557; Ozer Grundman, I. Figlarczyk, op. cit.

[30] E. Erlich, Sefer Staszów, p. 382.

[31] Mordchai Śledzik, Skarżysko Book, p. 124; cf. Sewek Szmelcman, Staerkemeldung, Nov. 1942, see n. 1.

[32] Awraham Gastfrojnd, Testimony, YV, M-1/E/1715/1588.

and Chaim Weintraub,[33] Zenek Milsztajn, and Josef Wajcblum.[34] All died in tragic circumstances.

The testimony of the "Radom Tier" is surprising for the sparse information it contains concerning the various *Komendanten*. Many of them survived, and their ties to family members, fellow townsmen, and in some cases partners in business conducted in the camp, seem to have sealed the mouths of the witnesses. Thus, the negative information available relates primarily to those no longer alive. Some are mentioned for their fair treatment of the prisoners, such as Levi Fuks, Awraham Nagel, and Mordchai Judenhertz.[35] On the whole, the prisoners attitude to those in authority over them can be defined as individualistic, a perception of the *Komendanten* as human beings with both good and bad qualities. At this stage, there was no awareness of the issue of the prominent Jews as a social and moral problem.

The hegemony of the "Radom Tier" established in the initial period of the camp remained unquestioned throughout the camp's existence. There was no attempt whatsoever on the part of the "Majdanek Tier" or the "Płaszów Tier" to wrest authority from the hands of Teperman and his cohorts who enjoyed several power bases. First, in terms of the social and psychological make-up of the camp, the "prominent ones" at Skarżysko were part and parcel of the "Radom Tier," formerly from the middle or even the lower classes. The first to reach the camp obtained their posts by virtue of their contact with Polish workers or by bribery. As time passed and new transports arrived, whole families gained control of key positions as those with the authority to do so appointed their own family members as functionaries or policemen. With their deep roots in the community, the administrators knew many of the prisoners and thus also knew who to get rid of and who to make use of – an advantage that undoubtedly facilitated the exercise of their authority.

Secondly, the "veterans" enjoyed the full support of the Hasag management. Since their prisoners were all of the same religion and nationality, the company promoted internal conflicts by manifestly favoring the "Radom Tier" in the assignment of senior positions. This not only demonstrates their satisfaction with the functioning of the Jewish

---

[33] I. Chustecki, Testimony, YV, TR/11/61159; cf. Hans Faerber, Sitzungen, p. 99a–b.

[34] N. Flajszakier, L. Bornes, C. Milchman, op. cit.

[35] Michael Braun, Testimony, YV, M-1/E/990/865.

administration, but also implies a common interest based, in my opinion, on a secret agreement. Within the camp, Hasag granted the prisoners freedom of movement and did not interfere in their internal life. At the same time, instead of choosing unattached prisoners for administrative posts, as was done in the SS camps, here control was placed in the hands of several families, which, although strongly rooted in their community, had not previously been prominent. Handing authority over to people who had never before known the sweet taste of power ensured Hasag of their total cooperation in guarding the working prisoners and eliminating the "unproductive" ones.

In this manner, Hasag found a solution to two problems: how to control thousands of prisoners with only a few Ukrainians and Germans, and how to guarantee the prisoners' obedience to the "prominent" Jews. The Hasag managers revealed themselves to be to guarantee the prisoners' obedience to the "prominent" Jews. The Hasag managers revealed themselves to be "experts in human behavior," in no way inferior to the "students" of Theodor Eicke.

The *Komendanten* were united by their willingness to fulfill their duties, so that their struggle for power acquired the nature of the preservation of the status quo at any price while forestalling any sign of rivalry on the part of other groups. This goal dictated the "internal policy" of the leaders of the Jewish administration, which might be defined as a unique form of the characteristic symbiosis between a paterfamilias, whose power stems from the band of relatives, clients and workers he supports, and the remnants of the foundations of the Jewish community where the beadle ostensibly honored the rabbi and tolerated the rich man for the money he donated. And this was all done by terrorizing the prisoner population which existed in the shadow of starvation and constant "selections".

The Hasag Plants – A Source of Life or Death

The prisoners' thoughts and conversations were dominated by the factory – *die Fabrik*. It was there that they spent 12 hours a day working beside the machines, there that they earned their daily bread allotment, both official and unofficial. Thousands of manifest and covert shackles tethered the camp to the plant, so that for each and every prisoner his place of work was an integral part of the whole experience known as the Skarżysko camp. When on plant grounds, the prisoner was outside the jurisdiction of the camp authorities, subject only to the German and Polish foremen.

In Werk A, Jewish workers were employed in four major departments:

1. Shell and grenade production *(Granatenabteilung – Pociskownia)*
2. Small ammunition production *(Infanterieabteilung – Karabinówka)*
3. Automatic weapons production *(Automatenabteilung)*
4. Instrument production *(Werkzeugbau – Narzędziownia)*

Two days after a prisoner's arrival, he began work in the plant. At 5 a.m. the policemen's whistles ring out through the yard, together with the sound of truncheons striking pallets and heads and shouts of "Get up! Get to work!" The "greenhorn" crowds into the latrine with everyone else and then races over to the "coffee" line. If he is late, he will get nothing to eat until noontime. Luck is with him, and there's still a piece of bread for him. A less fortunate prisoner stares at him enviously. A few manage to throw some cold water on their faces. Cursing and vilifying the prisoners, the *Komendanten* line their people up on the assembly grounds. Roll call is over quickly and the groups start moving towards the gate where the *Werkschutz* is waiting on the other side. The huge column streams out of the camp and flows toward the plant. It is only a short distance, but the mud pulls at the wooden clogs making it very hard to advance. The "Jews Gate" through which they must pass to enter the plant is up ahead.

Over to the side is a large black building clouded with thick pillars of smoke and emitting a deafening noise. It houses the dreaded grenade pressing department *(Granatenpresserei)*. "I had some very hard times during the war," recalls Adam Nowicki, "but none left as deep an impression on me as my first moments at the Hasag plant – enormous production halls, the ear-splitting noise of the presses and huge machines, red-hot shells caught in the air by the prisoners who looked like dwarfs beside the gigantic furnaces." [36]

Karl Procher, the department manager, would choose 20 of the strongest young men from each new transport. They learned the work quickly, since it was Procher's practice to throw any "shirker" onto the glowing shells laid out to cool and to leave him there until he died in

---

[36] Adam Nowicki, Testimony, YV, 0-3/1620.

agony. The task of beating the prisoners was carried out by the engineer Heinrich Hencke and his assistant Leo Rattke, in addition to the Polish overseers "for whom tormenting the prisoners was even more fun than downing a bottle of vodka." [37]

After sealing *(Haerterei)*, the shells went to the polishing department where women worked. During a 10-hour shift, each woman carried 1,800 shells weighing 4 kg each to the polishing machines. Here conditions were a bit more tolerable, with the Polish workers treating the prisoners decently and lending a hand.[38]

The day shift awaited the noon break impatiently. Cauldrons of soup were brought by the department's *Komendanten* and several volunteers who were promised an extra bowl. Doling out the soup was invariably accompanied by curses and beatings, as the starving prisoners crowded around nearly knocking the cauldron over. The clever ones waited for the end to get the thicker soup from the bottom of the pot which might have a piece of potato or even meat in it! But the *Komendanten* saved the very last portions for those under their protection – or those who could pay for them. In no time the prisoners were already herded back to the machines. After the break, time seemed to stand still. The workday was long and monotonous. The shift finally ended at 6:00 in the evening. Each *Komendant* got the manager's signature on a chit bearing the number of his prisoners and had to present it at the entrance to the camp. Exhausted, barely able to drag their feet, the prxisoners moved toward "home". There the most important event of their day awaited them – the distribution of their bread ration and the second bowl of soup. The distribution of bread was once a day.

The *Infanterie* – the division producing ammunition for the infantry – was the source of Hasag's greatest professional pride. It contained two main departments, one producing the bullet itself *(Geschossabteilung)* and the other the casing (Huelsenabteilung) (see Figure 5.2). The mechanized work proceeded along an assembly line manned by two 12-hour shifts. The division was known for the pressure under which it worked, kept up by the manager Bernhard Kremer who threatened his German staff with severe penalties if output dropped. The Polish technical overseers *(Einrichter)* were responsible for quality control, but the work

---

[37] Szlomo Zilberblum, Skarżysko Book, p. 111.

[38] Zofia Horowicz, Testimony, YV, 0-16/1156.

	Lohnburo			26.11.42
	Jüdische Gefolgschaftsmitglieder			Infante(r)ie
	Name und Vorname	–	Geb. Datum	Kontr. Nr.
1	Medaljon	Hela	8.8.16	0142
2	Medaljon	Szajndla	15.6.24	0143
3	Szabas	Tola	29.2.08	0144
4	Lipman	Roza	31.1.25	0145
5	Zylberman	Frajda	26.12.14	0146
6	Awensztern	Chana	10.4.12	0147
7	Fleiszer	Mirla	15.5.14	0148
8	Sierota	Malka	15.5.16	0149
9	Halys	Fajga	2.5.12	0150
10	Lipman	Cypojra	25.12.00	0151
11	Sobol	Perla	16.12.16	0152
12	Plajchman	Lejzor	2.3.23	0153
13	Rychter	Abram	1.1.14	0154
14	Zagdanski	Pejsach	17.4.19	0155
15	Sztark	Majer	10.5.17	0156
16	Brojtman	Nuta	24.4.13	0157
17	Ejzenman	Herszek	15.3.12	0158
18	Drajnudel	Chaskiel	5.9.08	0159
19	Drajnudel	Jankiel	8.5.11	0160
20	Ajzenman	Alter	10.5.18	1061
21	Chustecki	Izrael	2.2.01	0162
22	Grynbaum	Szlama	25.11.02	0163
23	Sznajder	Chil	10.3.21	0164
24	Gryczman	Szaja	10.5.16	0165
25	Zlotowicz	Kiwa	5.6.19	0166
26	Wester	Herszek	10.7.99	0167
27	Zylberman	Jankiel	17.8.19	0168
28	Litwin	Jakob	10.6.18	0169
29	Sztark	Moszek	1.2.23	0170
30	Zlotowicz	Szlama	15.12.21	0171
31	Goldszajder	Abram	16.11.24	0172
32	Broman	Zalman	20.7.16	0173
33	Tober	Chemia	1.2.09	0174
34	Glibman	Jakob	27.12.05	0175
35	Wsta(ż)ka	Abram	21.5.05	0176
36	Cukier	Binem	21.5.09	0177
37	Alter	Szaja	1.2.24	0178
38	Brojtman	Nuta	15.12.16	0179
39	Brojtman	Berek	1.2.22	0180
40	Fiszer	Mosiek	20.12.07	0181
41	Rakowski	Jakob	27.12.25	0182
				Arbeiter Annahme

Figure 5.2 Register of the Jewish workers in one of the Infanterie departments in Werk A (YV, 0-6/37-3)

itself was done largely by Jews, with Kremer instructing his staff to use any means at all to ensure that quotas were met.[39]

The free hand given the German managers allowed for significant differences in their attitudes to the prisoners. Workers in the Bullet Department, both men and women, described the behavior of their manager, Martin Bosch, a Nazi party member, as "quite decent," [40] similar to that of his assistant Fritz Schwinger who had taken a Jewish lover. In the same department, Richard Andress introduced the practice of offering an extra bread ration in reward for exceeding quotas, and the shift manager Rotmund was also lauded.[41]

Only women were employed in the Casing Department, where the processing ended with the pieces being washed in soapy water. Up to Spring 1943, the department was headed by Will Breest "who was okay." [42] He was succeeded by "Morcin" (probably a reference to Walter Knoeffler) who was sometimes helpful but more often abusive.[43]

The figure of Ludwig Krause, the head of the Labor Department where women were employed in quality control of the bullets,[44] seems to pale beside that of his colleague Marianne Tietge who ruled the quality control section of the Casing Department with an iron hand. She regularly beat her victims of both sexes over the head and kicked them in the genitals. Although an ardent Nazi, her political fanaticism did not prevent her from extorting money and valuables from the prisoners. She was sentenced to life imprisonment at the Leipzig trials where the judges, in handing down their ruling, stressed her cruelty.[45]

A prisoner who came under the thumb of Alfred Wagner, a foreman in the department responsible for firing the casings *(Schuhabteilung)* was particularly unlucky. After his transfer to Skarżysko, Wagner, like many others, soon learned that here he could easily swell his own coffers by extorting money from the Jews in exchange for "exemption" from

---

[39] Hans Brandt, Sitzungen, p. 54a.

[40] Anna Warmund, Testimony, YV, 0-33/1840.

[41] Testimonies, YV: Mosze Niechcicki, TR-11/01159; Henryk Greipner, 0-33/1815.

[42] Ktb des Rue Kdo Radom, 18.3.1943, MA, RW 23/17, p. 20; cf. Ester Kohen, Testimony, YV, 0-3/3057.

[43] Testimonies, YV, Ala Neuhaus, 0-33/1833; Tola Chudin, 0-33/1807.

[44] Hana Biedak-Lewkowicz, Testimony, YV, 0-33/1813.

[45] Kamienna Prozess, Urteil, (hereafter Urteil), YV, TR-10/7, pp. 12–14.

beatings. He was in the habit of dunking his victims in vats of ice water and acid and then forcing another prisoner to scrub him down with an iron brush. This "treatment" led to the death of a number of prisoners.[46]

Whatever the department, the night shift was especially difficult, as the prisoners struggled to keep their eyes open, uninvigorated by the meager soup ration doled out at midnight. At Labor, Erich Espenhaym specialized in "rousing sleepyheads" by hitting them on the head, earning him the nickname of *"Krimineller"*.[47] He shared the dock at Leipzig with Walter Knoeffler, Erich Greichen, Ernst Voigtlaender, Kurt Burzlaff, and Walter Gleisberg, all *Infanterie* managers. An examination of the political record of this group reveals that some had formerly been Communists and had never even joined the Nazi party. The judges found this somewhat embarrassing since, representing East Germany, they sought to lay the blame at the feet of National Socialist indoctrination. Reluctantly, they were compelled in several cases to conclude that the defendants' brutality derived from "pure sadistic pleasure." [48]

The Automatic Weapons Department had a fairly good reputation among the prisoners and it was not by chance that many of the "favored" prisoners and those who offered bribes worked here. The workday in this department ended at 5:00 in the afternoon and most Sundays were free. A newcomer soon learned that if he produced too many *schmelz* (rejects) he would earn himself only five lashings. The manager, Kurt Frietsche, promoted a relaxed atmosphere, and on one occasion when informers revealed that Poles in the department were selling food to the Jews, he ordered them to "keep their mouths shut." [49]

The second largest plant in Werk A was the Instrument Division *(Werkzeugbau)* whose many departments produced dies, installations, instruments, machine parts, etc. It was manned by hundreds of Poles, some 800 Jews, both men and women, and around 40 German foremen. They all answered to Willi Seidel, whose Alma Mater was the French Foreign Legion and who was not a member of the Nazi party. The charges against him filled more pages than those of any of the other defendants at the Leipzig trials. Amongst the brutality, extortion and murders, one of the

---

[46] Urteil, ib., p. 23; Karl Herold, YV, M-21/2-49, p. 9.

[47] Akta w sprawie Espenhayn Erich, YV, JM/3700.

[48] Anklageschrift, pp. 7, 34; Urteil, pp. 8, 34.

[49] Jakow Scherman, Testimony, YV, M-9/15(4).

charges related to the "death lists" which struck fear in the heart of every prisoner.

Until the end of 1942, the Hasag management required the directors of each of the plants to draw up a weekly list of prisoners who had become debilitated and should thus be put to death. The department managers openly prepared their lists of "dismissed" workers *(Entlassene Juden)* and submitted them to the acting camp commander. The resulting "selection" and murder of victims would take place two days later, since as a rule they were not taken directly from the work place. Seidel's lists often included the names of prisoners whose relatively good appearance indicated that they had money or valuables for barter, and he would then offer them the chance to ransom back their lives, replacing their names with those of indigent prisoners. The victim had two days to get the ransom together.

Other Germans also borrowed Seidel's idea: Emil Kalinowski extorted dollars in exchange for removal from the "death lists" and turned the Jewish policeman Josek Patac over to the *Werkschutz* because he knew too much about his operation. He sent 12-year-old Frida Ostojowski to her death, but the manager Oskar Zipfel intervened and saved her life.[50] When the wife of the prisoner Ginsburg was included on the list of "dismissed workers," he offered his manager, Richard Pawlowski, a gold watch for her release. The deal was closed.[51] Pawlowski and his wife Dora, manager of the Polishing Department *(Polerki)* were notorious throughout the plant for their physical abuse and extortion practices.

Another man who stood accused at the Leipzig trials was Hans Faerber, known as "Boxer," who endeavored to justify his actions by invoking the need to punish the prisoners for producing damaged goods. When asked by the prosecutor whether the Jews had done this on purpose in order to hurt the German war effort, he replied "absolutely not," explaining, "any attempt at sabotage on the part of a Jewish prisoner would have been unthinkable." [52]

On the subject of sabotage, the camp prisoners' accounts must be viewed with a great deal of caution since, as the German scholar Falk Pingel notes, a large number of rejects can not be taken as proof of the

---

[50] Frida Ostojowski-Amit, Testimony, YV, 0-33/2575.

[51] J. Ginsburg, op. cit.

[52] H. Faerber, Sitzungen, pp. 98–99a; Gustaw Leipnitz, ib.

intent to commit sabotage.[53] It must be remembered that in principle there was a significant difference between Jewish and non-Jewish prisoners regarding the decision to take such a risk. The Frenchmen or Russians knew that they belonged to viable nations that were fighting the Nazis, so that sabotage had both a psychological and national value for them. This was not true for the Jews, however, whose nation was being wiped off the face of the earth. On the one hand, they were well aware that any attempt to interfere with German war production meant cutting off the branch they were sitting on, and on the other it was clear that victory for the Reich would bring an immediate end to the last of the Jews in Europe. They were caught in a trap, one that made even the Germans stop and think.[54] The only options a Jewish prisoner had were immediate death for sabotage, or death at some later date, that might, with a great deal of luck, be put off indefinitely. It is not surprising that the available testimony from the Radom Period makes no mention of attempts to sabotage production.

It thus follows that since sabotage was not involved, the only motive for the German abuse of the prisoners was extortion. They needed money to maintain la dolce vita, the most obvious example of this being Seidel who was always well supplied with good drink and pretty women. Indeed, women were very much on the minds of the German staff and all of them sought clever ways to meet this need. On one occasion when Karl Genthe was grotesquely drunk, he decided to visit the women prisoners' barracks in the middle of the night, but this was too much even for his Hasag masters who were not known for their excessive morality, and he was sent back to Leipzig.[55] Other Germans found Polish girlfriends, as Seidel testified: "It was the same for us as for everyone else, the women from the plant came to our hotel." [56]

Jewish girls were at a much greater risk. The Germans did not consider the many cases in which rape ended in murder as instances of "racial impurity" *(Rassenschande)*, but for the Jews the rape was a more heinous crime than the murder itself. The various German managers and commanders chose for themselves the prettiest girls to clean their rooms,

---

[53] F. Pingel, op. cit., pp. 205–206.

[54] A. Speer, Der Sklavenstaat, op. cit., p. 426; cf. Seyss-Inquart, in: R. Hilberg, op. cit., p. 343.

[55] Adolf Stelzner, Sitzungen, p. 130b, 78b; Anklageschrift, p. 14.

[56] W. Seidel, Sitzungen, p. 15; Herbert Koch, ib., p. 22.

and the precise nature of their relationship was never openly displayed. In all three werks there were rumors of affairs of this sort, the overwhelming majority of which ended with the men murdering their Jewish lovers, particularly if they should become pregnant. The prisoners' attitude to "mixed couples" was ambivalent. Although they understood the girls were merely looking for a way to survive, there was nevertheless a note of reproof. Heated arguments raged in the Bullet Department over Schwinger's lover, but on the whole the more tolerant attitude won out since he was not considered an anti-Semite.

One love affair that sent shockwaves throughout the German staff took place in the Autumn of 1943. Hugo Ruebesamen's colleagues in the *Werkzeugbau* began to whisper among themselves that he had succeeded in "becoming friendly" with the most beautiful Jewish girl in the department. Hellmut Porzig was especially envious, as he too had dreamed of getting his hands on one of the women. One day, when the girl was not at her machine, Porzig decided to play the detective and discovered that she was in the manager's office with the door closed, and that Ruebesamen had also disappeared. He rushed to tell the others about "that pig Ruebesamen," and the rumor finally reached Seidel. In order to get the girl to confess that she had had sexual relations with Ruebesamen, Seidel beat her until she lost consciousness. He promised Ruebesamen immunity from prosecution if he confessed his guilt. The girl was taken to the Radom Gestapo. Ruebesamen was arrested and despite his professions of innocence was sentenced to prison. Typically, even at the Leipzig trials where he appeared for the prosecution, Ruebesamen continued to maintain that he had never had sexual relations with a Jew.[57] The girl's fate is unknown.

Given the inhumane conditions which prevailed at Skarżysko, two *Werkzeugbau* managers, Karl Herold and Martin Giesel, deserve to be commended for their courage. One of the women prisoners who found herself pregnant and knew this meant she would be sent to her death at the next "selection," appealed to Herold for help. Herold and Giesel managed to get her to a local doctor who performed an abortion. They were informed on to Dalski by a Werkschutz guard and both were called up before the management. They received a severe reprimand and were

---

[57] Zeugenaussagen, Tschenstochau-Prozess, YV, TR-10/8, pp. 51, 78, 80, 267; Hugo Ruebesamen, Sitzungen, p. 63.

warned that an SS court would send them to a concentration camp for ten years. However, in view of production requirements, the management decided to let the matter end there. The two "offenders" were stripped of all privileges and were ostracized by the other staff members because they "were not worthy to be called Germans or to stand on German soil." [58]

The witnesses for the prosecution at the Leipzig trials included those Germans against whom the prisoners voiced no grievances: Herold, Giesel, Zipfel, Voigt, Brandt, Brellendin, and others. Heinrich Stelzner admitted that he was appalled to hear of the crimes committed by his colleagues.[59] It must thus be said that not all of the Germans lost all vestiges of their humanity or were infected by the unnatural atmosphere at the Skarżysko plants.

What was unnatural about this atmosphere? Erich Dechant, sentenced to 15 years in prison, stated in his defense that "everything that happened in Kamienna was like in a madhouse." [60] The prisoners called it "Kamienna hell" *(die Hoelle von Kamienna)*. The common denominator behind these two terms was the unique form of terror tactics devised by Seidel, Dalski and their cohorts. Their primary aim was thievery and not extermination as such, so that their methods took on the nature of business negotiations. In this sense, the Skarżysko camp was essentially different from a concentration camp. As a result, as long as a Jewish prisoner had the strength to work or the money to buy his life, he had a chance to survive. Each new prisoner lucky enough to be sent to Werk A had to devise a way to fight for his survival, ensuring that for him Hasag-Skarżysko might be a life-giving production plant and not a death factory.

---

[58] Die Hoelle, op. cit., p. 13.

[59] Heinrich Stelzner, Sitzungen, p. 60a.

[60] Erich Dechant, Urteil, p. 31.

Chapter 6

The Struggle to Survive

To Submit or Resist

Examination of the Skarżysko prisoners' struggle for survival reveals that it had its own dynamics, methods and strategies, some of which were unalterable, while others changed with the period in the camp's history or the nature of the prisoner's "tier". The "Radom Tier" is of particular interest in this context, since, unlike the prisoners from Majdanek and Płaszów, for most of them Skarżysko was their first camp experience. Thus, the stratagems and artifices developed by the Radomites became models of survival techniques later learned and copied by prisoners of other transports.

The first three months in the camp determined the prisoner's fate: either he became apathetic, thereby condemning himself to die, or he learned to adjust and to fight for his life. The longer a prisoner remained in the camp, the better were his chances of survival.[1] Being young or female were considered the greatest advantages since women suffered less from hunger, kept themselves as clean and adequately clothed as possible, and were more likely to be able to get along with those in authority at whatever

---

[1] Aleksander Teutsch, Próba analizy procesu przystosowania do warunków obozowych osób osadzonych w czasie II wojny światowej w hitlerowskich obozach koncentracyjnych, Przegląd Lekarski, nr. 1a (Kraków: Wydawnictwo Lekarskie, 1962), p. 91.

level. Social and cultural background were of secondary importance and did not influence the prisoner's place in the "pecking order" which consisted of five classes:

1. **The "prominente"** – the heads of the internal administration and police commanders and their families;
2. **The "courtiers"**– lower-level functionaries, including rank and file police;
3. **The "money barons"** – a small group of wealthy prisoners who controlled the market in valuables and foreign currency;
4. **The "proletariat"** – the large majority of the prisoner population, including the equivalent of laborers, craftsmen, small tradesmen, servants, etc.;
5. **The "mussulmen"** – those doomed to die.

It was very rare for a prisoner to move upwards on this social ladder, and impossible for him to enter the closed circle of the "prominente".

These distinctions were still unknown to Chaim Singer when he was brought to Skarżysko from the town of Błędów-Mogelnica in December 1942 together with his two brothers. To his great fortune, he managed to smuggle 100 dollars into the camp, but his elation was short-lived as he soon got his first sight of what awaited him: "I saw thousands of people in rags, filthy ... at roll call a short man with yellowish skin stood beside me dressed in a paper bag for a jacket. I asked if he was an African Jew and he replied: 'a month from now you'll look just like me.' " [2]

He took the warning to heart, and within a few days had found several friends from his hometown who explained to him how things were in Werk A. This made him more optimistic, for he was told that if he had a bit of money he could survive. Indeed, he started off in much better shape than, say, a prisoner at Auschwitz: he was young, had money, and had his brothers and friends around him, whereas one entered a concentration camp naked and alone and thus had no hope whatsoever of leaving it alive. Singer had high hopes, and so his eventual despair was that much deeper.

In late 1942, a fierce winter swept through Werk A, which in November held 2,450 prisoners, 1,203 of them women.[3] The camp suffered the

---

[2] Chaim Singer, *Sefer Mogelnica*, p. 513.

[3] Staerkemeldung, 6.11.1942, YV, 0-6/37-3.

greatest blow of all: a typhoid epidemic. The two small huts housing the infirmary were quickly filled. The patients lay on wooden pallets with no mattresses or blankets, no extra food rations, no doctors, and no medicines. Mosze Finger, known as "the gravedigger," commanded the infirmary. He and his wife Lola were later charged with theft of property and cruelty to the patients. In early 1943, Dr Sachs was appointed head doctor. He was greatly hated by the prisoners for refusing to treat them without payment.[4]

The epidemic spread, claiming the lives of Chaim Singer's two brothers. The infirmary could not hold all the sick, and every day corpses were taken out and thrown into a nearby crate. It was not unusual to hear the wretched moans of those not yet dead echoing from within that crate. A "selection" was conducted every Sunday. The weakest prisoners were herded onto trucks and taken to Werk C where trenches awaited them, dug and readied by a group of gravediggers headed by Finger.

Usually a general "selection" was also conducted in the camp yard on the same day. As all the prisoners stood silently in long rows, the camp commander, escorted by several functionaries, passed among them looking for "mussulmen". Meanwhile, *Werkschutz* guards encircled the prisoners, their rifles cocked and pointed at the crowd. When the whistle finally blew, the thousands of terrorized people fled back to their barracks, seeking a moment of peace until the next "selection". There were no attempts at collective resistance and little is known of any individual acts of defiance. The prisoner knew that if he tried anything he would immediately pay with his life. Nonetheless, mention is made of an unnamed prisoner who refused to dig trenches for those sentenced to death and in response was himself shot by the *Werkschutz*.[5] The policeman Pfefferman was killed by Bartenschlager for his unwillingness to beat the prisoners.[6] And perhaps when a condemned man, as he walked to the truck that would take him to his death, secretly handed another prisoner the bread ration he would no longer need, this could also be seen as an act of resistance.

Many of the younger prisoners regarded escape as their only hope of survival. The possibility of success was enhanced by the small number of

---

[4] Testimonies, YV: Regina Finger, 0-16/161; Izak Zajdentreger, 0-16/1323.
[5] Stanisław Lis, 20.1.1950, Akta T. Sawczaka, see Chapter 5, n. 17.
[6] Szulim Gottlieb, Testimony, YV, 0-16/1346.

Werkschutz guards, the location of the camp within the forest, and the fact that the fence was not electrified. The prisoners' clothing had no identifying marks nor was there any tatoo on their body. Most escapes were attempted in the twilight hours on the way back to camp, or by leaping over the fence. In November 1942, an average of two Jews a day escaped from the camp. On November 29, 1942, seven escaped. On the following day, ten prisoners were executed in retaliation. Between December 1, 1942 and late January 1943, 135 prisoners escaped from Werk A alone.[7] These figures provide an answer for those who like to ask: "Why didn't they try to escape" ?

Some of the escapees became trapped in the Szydłowiec ghetto and were sent to Treblinka. There is no evidence from this period of Jews being concealed by Poles. The overwhelming majority of the escapees were caught in the vicinity of the camp where *Werkschutz* guards, hungry for reward, lay in wait. Some of the managers, such as Henryk Laskowski, also joined in the hunt, turning their catch over to Ipfling in exchange for vodka and sugar.[8]

In December 1942, Henryk Szaniawski and a friend managed to escape with the help of transit passes supplied by the Polish foreman Wincenty Wójcik. Constantly on the move ever after, Szaniawski encountered Poles who were helpful and others who were heartless, and eventually survived the war, although his friend was caught and killed. Benjamin Zweig suffered a particularly ironic fate. Thanks to a 4,000 zloty bribe, he escaped and reached the ghetto of Sandomierz. Two weeks later, in January, 1943, the last Jews in the ghetto were deported and Zweig found himself on a transport – headed for Skarżysko! The "ransom" he paid the German manager Brest enabled him to reclaim the very same work assignment from which he had fled.[9]

Those who remained in the camp fell victim by the hundreds to illness or "selections". "Jew exchanges" were performed in Werk A with amazing exactness. For example, the 620 Jews who arrived in the camp on January 18, 1943 replaced precisely 620 who were "dismissed". A total of 1,119

---

[7] Staerkemeldungen, Dezember 1942, Januar 1943; ib. 30.11.1942, see n. 3.

[8] Akta w sprawie Laskowski Henryk, YV, 0-53/65, p. 338.

[9] Testimonies, YV: Henryk Szaniawski, 0-16/5482, B. Zweig, op. cit.

prisoners perished in that month of January, fully 26.4% of the camp population. Nevertheless, the number of prisoners remained virtually unchanged: 3,211 at the start of the month and 3,214 at its close.[10] This state of affairs contributed to the continued internal stability of the "Radom Tier". All the new transports were brought from nearby towns, those preserving the social and cultural composition of this group. Some two-thirds of the original prisoner population remained alive, including the great majority of members of the internal administration. It was riddled, however, by deep scars. The typhoid epidemic had claimed family members and friends, and the social gap between the *prominente* who had consolidated their position and the many prisoners who had lost everything in the wake of disease grew wider.

How did the individual fare? Chaim Singer was left stunned and grieving when he lost his brothers and friends to the epidemic. His money was running out. Forced to face the bald realities, he no longer saw the camp as a place where one could survive. The annihilation of the surrounding ghettos deepened his despair, for there was now nowhere to run to. Who could he look to for help? The fortunate ones still had family members around them. A healthy prisoner could bring an ailing relative a piece of bread, could spirit him out of the infirmary before a "selection," could share his soup with him. For those left entirely alone, the *Landmannschaft* served as a substitute for the family. Thus a band of youngsters from Staszow managed to organize an "emergency committee" and to turn the internees of the "Staszower Barracks" into a united group. Elchanan Erlich relates that his friends collected money to buy medicines for him and that the committee even succeeded in getting some of the cruellest the heads of the Jewish police to contribute.

Another way to increase one's chances of survival was to become involved in the camp's underground economy which evolved thanks to the existence of an internal administration and class of prominente on the one hand, and the prisoners' freedom of movement within the camp on the other. Added to this was the fact that the prisoners had free time, that men and women were interred together, and that all branches of authority cooperated. As in any normal social unit, the camp's economy was based on three "production factors": raw materials, manpower, and capital.

---

[10] Staerkemeldungen, 1-31.1.1943, see n. 3.

The source of raw materials was *"organizacja"* – a term used in all the camps to mean "pilfering." In the words of Ozer Grundman: "Anyone who could steal something from the factory did; he had no other means of ensuring his survival." Pilfered items included tin scraps, sacks, bits of wood or iron, empty tins, rubber belts off machines, rags, crate handles, and more. Naturally, Hasag considered any pilfering an act of sabotage, punishable by death. Several shoemakers caught at the gate with leather scraps were shot on the spot. In one shocking incident, a prisoner caught stealing a rubber belt was given a public hanging.[11] But even this did not deter the starving prisoners.

The primary source of manpower were the craftsmen in the camp and other prisoners with initiative. With their skillful hands and makeshift tools, they created a wealth of useful items, such as knives, scissors, thimbles, combs, bowls, and spoons. fashioned from scraps of tin. The shoemakers developed a whole "industry" on their pallets, fixing soles with bits of rubber and manufacturing new shoes from wooden clogs and leather scraps they got from the Poles.[12] The tailors worked for the *prominente* and the Poles and even the Germans took advantage of this source of free labor to have them sew clothes for themselves and their wives.[13] Some imaginative women stole red chalk (used to mark the shells) and added machine oil to produce a red ointment which served as make-up. With the rags employed in the plant to clean machines, seamstresses mended clothes or sewed small items of apparel, dolls and baby clothes. Those who knew how knitted sweaters for the *prominente* and the Poles, while others made belts from rope. Prisoners employed in the Instrument Division unravelled the cotton gloves they were given for sorting bullets and used the threads to knit lacy collars and cuffs. Jute aprons were found to be an excellent material from which to sew wallets embroidered with threads pulled from colored rags.[14]

These skills gave rise to small trade of three types, with bread or zlotys as the means of payment:

1. barter between "ordinary" prisoners inside the camp;

---

[11] Testimonies, YV: Awraham Lewkowicz, 0-33/1816, N. Flajszakier, op. cit.

[12] Testimonies, YV: Chaja Szapira, 0-3/3375; M. Braun op. cit.

[13] Natan Wencland, Testimony, YV, M-1/E/1806/1664.

[14] Testimonies, YV: Ala Erder, 0-33/1817; Ester Kerżner, 0-33/1826.

2. the supply of goods to the "internal market", i.e. to the prominente and whoever had money, by "retailers";
3. the supply of goods to the "external market", i.e. the Poles employed in the plant.

The camp economy consisted not only of this "production sector", but also of a "service branch" providing a variety of services. Women did cooking and laundering for the *prominente*, who, along with the Poles, also commissioned work from watchmakers. Some prisoners had a primus stove whose use they rented out. Those with money bought foodstuffs from the Poles and sold them in the camp or cooked and sold them by the portion: soup, barley, noodles, potatoes, or even meatballs. The two official camp barbers, Melech Sobol and Szmuel Herling,[15] sometimes earned a few pennies by taking someone out of turn.

The third factor in the "economy" – capital – came from a variety of sources. Some of the prisoners had left their property with Polish neighbors, and, using the Polish plant workers as go-betweens, had money smuggled into the camp for them. Moreover, each new transport brought property into the camp: dollars concealed in the soles of shoes, diamonds hidden inside fillings in teeth, gold made into a dental bridge or swallowed, jewelry in a bar of soap or a ball of wool. Hunger and disease gradually compelled each newcomer to sell off whatever he possessed. The potential buyers were again the *prominente*, who also served as middlemen for sales to the Germans, Ukrainians, and Poles. Since even the Germans feared the eagle eye of the SIPO, such deals were closed in utter confidentiality. The experts in the "gold market" were the goldsmiths, one of whom, Zucker, worked for the Germans in the plant, and the dental technicians, such as the Perel brothers.[16] They received their fee for removing gold dental bridges after the sale of the precious metal. When the German Hans Faerber punched the prisoner Zinna in the mouth causing two of his teeth to fall out, the latter was very pleased that he would not now have to pay the technician's fee.[17]

One highly profitable venture was the "wholesale" smuggling of bread into the camp. A considerable number of accounts reveal that prisoners

---

[15] Testimonies, YV: Szmuel Herling, Melech Sobol, M-21/358, p. 13.

[16] E. Kerżner, N. Flajszakier, op. cit.

[17] Chaskiel Miller, Sitzungen, p. 101b.

purchased bread, apparently without knowing its source. Noach Fla-jszakier describes the methods of smuggling in detail. One of these involved the group of prisoners sent to the kitchen in Werk B each morning to fetch coffee for Werk A. The Polish cook would fill two vats with bread in place of coffee. Another method was to have Poles toss sacks of bread over the fence into the camp.

There was also a "cooperative" strategy. At the bakery, the Poles would hide several dozen loaves of smuggled bread under a pile of "Hasag bread". When the illegal shipment reached the camp storehouse, it was quickly transferred to the women's barracks where it was cut into portions and handed over to the "wholesalers". The workers at the saw mill, managed by Commandante Staszek Frajdenrajch, also became bread smugglers.[18] Since anyone caught smuggling would pay with his life, the members of the internal administration turned a blind eye to this activity, and undoubtedly earned a tithe for doing so.

"Luxury" items for the wealthy prisoners were supplied by the workers with the choicest jobs, such as in Konsum, the German commissary which also supplied shoemaking and tailoring services; the supply room, visited by foremen from all departments bringing goods and news; the yard brigade responsible for cleaning the plant grounds; the carpentry shop; or the central heating department. Within the camp itself, the work place reserved for those with "friends in high places" was the bread storehouse which also held jam and sugar. These "privileged ones," however, were only a tiny proportion of the thousands of starving prisoners who sold even their clothes to survive. Krzepicka, in charge of the camp clothes store, did not distribute her wares for free. An indigent prisoner could only get something to wear if he had a chit from the "camp elder" or a German plant manager. When Tola Chudin's only dress was stolen, she went to the clothes store where she was given a paper apron in its stead. Only with the help of a friendly policeman was it exchanged for a dress.[19]

Yet no matter how hard a prisoner fought the war for survival, he would inevitably lose if he did not take advantage of the complex web of relations between the camp and the Poles employed in the Hasag plants.

---

[18] N. Flajszakier, op. cit.

[19] T. Chudin, C. Szapira, op. cit.

Was There Help to Be Found in the Shadow of the Gallows?

Although labor relations at the Hasag plants were dictated by directives from above, the "Jewish–Polish" problem had rules of its own. The Jews saw the Germans as evil foreign rulers who would one day be gone. But the same did not go for the Poles. The overseer looking over a prisoner's shoulder often turned out to be a former neighbor or long-time business associate. This situation also gave rise to the ambivalent attitude of the average Pole to the Jews. Although he considered their collective fate to be thoroughly justified, he frequently found common ground with "his own" Jews.

The case of the foreman Wincenty Wójcik demonstrates the complexity of the problem. After the war he was tried for his sadistic conduct toward the prisoners. Nevertheless, several members of the "Radom Tier" testified that he and his wife had assisted them to transfer money and letters (and it will be recalled that he also helped Henryk Szaniawski to escape). Much was said at the trial of the severe beatings inflicted on the Jewish prisoners, particularly the men, by their Polish overseers. No management directive whatsoever could be found ordering this behavior. The Poles themselves admitted that "such things were a matter of routine." [20] It was rare for a woman to be beaten, perhaps because of courtly traditions or in accord with the oft-heard slogan: "Jewish men out – Jewish women with us!" *(Precz z Żydami – Żydówki z nami !)*.

If the shell department, where "the good" (Tadeusz Sikorski), "the bad" (Paweł Ciekierski) and "the ugly" (Przybyszewski) Pole could all be found, is any indication, then a similar situation prevailed in all departments.[21] Henryk Greipner relates that during one night shift several drunken overseers were about to pour out a vat of "Polish soup", but the decent Polish manager Bolesław Bielski convinced them to sell it to the prisoners in exchange for two bottles of vodka. On another occasion, when the overseer Serek hit Greipner and the prisoner hit him back, the Poles threatened him with a beating until the German department manager intervened and tempers cooled.

---

[20] Ryszard Koterka, Akta w sprawie Wincentego Wójcika, 1948, AKGBZH, sygn. SORd-200, p. 117.

[21] Pola Strażyńska, AGKBZH, SWK, sygn. 219, p. 150; H. Greipner, op. cit.

There were also moments of grace. The prisoner Goldszajder who was injured at his work, tells of a young Pole who helped him, stating: "It was an act of human kindness and he risked his own life without getting anything in return. To my regret, I have forgotten his name, but I would like to take this opportunity to thank him, an anonymous righteous gentile who saved my life." [22] With unconcealed emotion, the members of the yard brigade recall the overseer Tatarski, who despised the Germans and helped the Jews.[23] Jews often found themselves caught between a rock and a hard place, like the prisoner Ginsburg who took over for a Polish overseer when he left his post to arrange some business affairs of his own. At that very moment the German Pawlowski entered the department and, seeing what was going on, dismissed the Pole and appointed the Jew in his stead.[24]

From the very start of the camp's existence, mutual economic ties developed, with the Poles serving as buyers, middlemen, and suppliers for the isolated Jews. The Hasag management soon became aware of the situation, and as early as September 22, 1942 issued a notice (see Figure 6.1) stating: "We hereby absolutely forbid any Polish workers from purchasing food for Jews or sending any sort of letters for them. Anyone caught disregarding this prohibition will receive the severest of punishments." [25]

How did the Poles react to this prohibition? The Polish version appears in the plant newspaper from 1967: "At that time we worked together with Jews.... The Poles, who also suffered from hunger, shared whatever they had, like brothers. Moreover, sometimes we could buy bread.... We would smuggle it into the department.... We didn't take any money for it, although some people did sell bread." [26] Jewish testimony claims that the Poles sold bread at very high prices, on the average four times its value on the black market.[27] A similar price was demanded for medicines and other goods.

---

[22] Jechezkiel Goldszajder, Sefer Mogelnica, p. 510.

[23] M. Horowicz, op. cit.

[24] J. Ginzburg, op. cit.

[25] Bekanntmachung, Skarżysko-Kamienna, 22.9.1942, AGKBZH, SWK, sygn. 237, p. 33.

[26] "Na szubienicę kata robotników hitlerowca Adryanowicza", "Nasze Słowo", Skar.-Kam., 20.2.1967, nr. 6, AGKBZH, SWK, sygn. 234, p. 100.

[27] M. Strigler, In di fabrikn, op. cit., p. 188.

Bekanntmachung

Es ist jedem hier arbeitenden Polen strengst verboten, für Juden

Lebensmittel zu besorgen, noch irgendwelche Briefe zu befördern.

Wer dabei gefasst wird, hat strengste Bestrafung zu erwarten.

Die DIREKTION

Skarżysko-Kamienna, dnia 22 września 1942 r.

OGŁOSZENIE

Niniejszym   najsurowiej   zabraniamy   polskim   pracownikom

kupowania artykułów żywnościowych dla żydów, względnie

wysyłania jakichkolwiek listów dla nich.

Kto jednak zostanie na takiej czynności przyłapany, zostanie jaknaj-

surowiej ukarany.

DYREKCJA

Figure 6.1   Notice of the Workers of Skarżysko-Kamienna from 22.12.1942.

In 1967, a Polish court addressed itself to Hasag's prohibition, stating that the primary aim of the camp was the physical annihilation of the prisoners and the maximum exploitation of their remaining strength "since, while the backbreaking work and starvation rations can be explained by Hasag's desire to obtain maximal production at minimal expense... the ban on supplying food to Jewish prisoners and the diabolical punishments meted out to those disobeying this ban could only have been dictated by the explicit intent to starve the prisoners..."[28] To illustrate, the arrest of two(!) Poles by the *Werkschutz* is mentioned. It would appear that the diabolical punishments were not in fact applied, and they are mentioned only to justify the very limited succor given the Jews by the Poles. Where it did exist, it consisted only of a little extra plant soup and an occasional piece of bread.

In actuality, the Hasag management gave *de facto* recognition to the illegal import of food for the Jews, but did not wish to give its *de jure* approval for two reasons, one political and the other economic. In political terms, Hasag wanted to preserve the basic distinction between the Poles and the Jews so that the Poles would feel themselves to hold a privileged status and would cooperate with the Germans. Economically, any improvement in conditions for the Jews made it necessary to improve conditions for the Poles, an added production expense that Hasag sought to avoid. Moreover, the Poles were well aware that free import of food into the camp would result in competition, thus bringing prices down, so that they too preferred the status quo despite the risks they incurred by the need to smuggle. The plant management was not unduly concerned by the fact that the Poles were asking inflated prices since this padded their low salaries with no cost to Hasag. The Poles also had another source of income. For bringing a prisoner money or valuables held for him outside the camp, a Pole received a commission of 20–50%, depending on the value of the "shipment" and the degree of risk involved. A commission of 25% was considered fair.[29] Thus, the Jewish camp, by becoming a link in the black market, not only paid for itself but also largely maintained the Polish staff, a situation very much in Hasag's interest. The Spring of 1943 saw a shift in this "liberal" policy resulting from the increased activity of

---

[28] "Sentencja wyroku w sprawie Jerzego Adryanowicza", Sąd Wojewódzki w Kielcach, 2.10.1967, AOKBZH w Kielcach, sygn. IV.K.3/67, p. 37.

[29] M. Horowicz, H. Greipner, A. Lewkowicz, op. cit.

the local underground and the renewed wave of escape attempts. In February, some 20 prisoners escaped,[30] making their way to the ghettos of Kielce, Piotrków and Częstochowa. In March, five youngsters from Jędrzejów escaped.[31] Money which arrived from Jews in Piotrków helped Halina Zajączkowska and Tadeusz Głogowski, who joined the Polish partisans, to flee the camp.[32] In view of this state of affairs, the Hasag management issued a warning on March 31, 1943 imposing the death penalty on any Pole caught aiding a Jew to escape by supplying him with food or money.[33]

In April, the Pole Tadeusz Nowak was arrested while giving bread to Jews and money for the prisoners was found in his pocket. The rumor that he was to be hanged spread through the plant. Although serious offenders were handed over to the Gestapo in Radom, this time the management decided to carry out Nowak's sentence on factory grounds. On April 21, 1943, the entire Polish staff was assembled and Nowak was hanged before their eyes.[34] The following day a notice was issued to the Poles stating: "The SS and Police Commander hereby grants amnesty to all current offenders, but those caught in the future committing a crime similar to Nowak's can expect the same fate. Workers! The management appeals to your conscience. Remember when the Jews exploited you and sucked your blood. Remember the Bolshevik barbarians in Katyń: twelve thousand Polish officers murdered. Everyone knows this was the work of the Jews. Anyone helping the Jews, the murderers of his brothers and comrades, is a traitor.[35] (original emphasis) (see Figure 6.2).

This notice clearly reveals the motive behind the change of policy: leftist propaganda, accusing the Germans of responsibility for the Katyń affair, fomented unrest among the Polish workers. At this time, too, news of the uprising in the Warsaw ghetto reached the area, arousing the admiration of all factions in the Polish underground. Painting Poles who helped Jews as traitors to the common German–Polish cause is further

---

[30] Shmuel Krakowski, Jewish armed resistance in Poland 1942–1944, (Hebrew), (Tel-Aviv: Sifriat Poalim, 1977), p. 291.

[31] Wolf Brener, Jendrzewer Buch, p. 183; L. Fajgenbojm, ib., p. 191

[32] Ben Giladi, Testimony, YV, 0-33/1810.

[33] "Ogłoszenie", Skar.-Kamienna, 22.4.1943, AGKBZH, SWK, sygn. 218, p. 53.

[34] Teodor Sawczak, AGKBZH, SWK, sygn. 212, p. 76.

[35] "Ogłoszenie", see n. 33, ib.

Skarżysko-Kamienna, dnia 22.4.1943 r.

OGŁOSZENIE

Mimo zakazu kierownika Policji SS i naszego ogłoszenia z dnia 31.3.43 r. w którym wyraźnie zaznaczyliśmy, że <u>kara śmierci czeka każdego</u>, kto w jakikolwiek sposób pomoże <u>żydom do ucieczki</u>, czy to przez donoszenie wiadomości, podawanie artykułów żywnościowych lub też tranzakcji pienię żnych.

<u>Pracownik</u> TADEUSZ NOWAK

nie zważając na rozporządzenie policyjne i nasze ostrzeżenie dopuścił się tego przestępstwa kilkakrotnie i to jak sam zeznał załatwiał tranzakcje pieniężne dla żydów na okrągłą sumę

<u>20.000 - dwudziestu tysięcy złotych.</u>

Niniejszym ogłoszeniem kierownik Policji SS w Radomiu udziela amnestji dla wszystkich dotychczasowych przestępców. W przyszłości jednak każdego, któremu zostanie udowodnione podobne przestępstwo <u>czeka los NOWAKA</u>

PRACOWNICY!

Dyrekcja apeluje do waszego sumienia. Popatrzcie wstecz, wspomnijcie czasy, kiedy żydzi was wyzyskiwali i wyssali do szpiku kości, pomyślcie o bolszewickim barbarzyństwie <u>w lesie Katyńskim</u>

<u>dwanaście tysięcy polskich oficerów zamordowanych.</u>

Jest przecież dla każdego całkiem jasne, że sprawcami są żydzi.

Kto pomaga żydom, mordercom swych braci i kolegów, jest zdrajcą.

DYREKCJA

Figure 6.2   Notice of Tadeusz Nowak's arrest and death sentence (AGKBZH, SWK, sygn. 218, p. 53)

proof that the Jewish camp became an effective political weapon in the German authorities' war on the Poles.

Following the events of April, the Poles smuggled less bread in, and hunger in the camp grew worse. The Jews continued to fight their struggle to survive with extraordinary tenacity. How did the Radomites manage to survive?

The answer lies in their strong ties to their surroundings. They were not removed from the environment where they had lived their whole lives and where they had developed wide-ranging contacts with the local population. Furthermore, the vast majority did not have to undergo a process of "proletarianization." In other words, those who had previously been small tradesmen or craftsmen did not have to "re-invent" themselves in order to adjust to life in the camp. Many were even able to go on working in their former occupation. The continued existence of family cells and *Landsmannschafts*, even if only shadows of their former selves, also played a considerable role by enabling this group to maintain a united social unit which produced its own patterns of behavior and became deeply rooted in Werk A. Hence, since the Radomites succeeded in bringing with them part of their past reality into the camp, they did not feel the need to attempt to pull back from their present reality and thus were intensely involved in it. This attitude was their primary source of strength.

New People – New Problems

With the arrival of hundreds of men and women from Majdanek in the Summer of 1943, a new stage in the history of the Skarżysko camp began. Exhausted and frightened, they looked about them at the dense green forest: what sort of strange camp could this be? Quickly, they were divided into three groups, two of which were soon marched off towards the forest. No one knew where they were being taken. The others were lined up anew – spent men and women dressed in weird clothes given them just before they left Majdanek. They walked together: Ala with her mother, Ewa, thrilled that her husband was with her, Janina and Miriam, both all alone, and beside them 15-year-old Flora, who had found herself on the transport by some unfathomed miracle. Row by row they marched toward their new future.

At the camp gate dozens of Radomites stared curiously at the new-comers. They were only summarily checked as they passed through the gate; the *Werkschutz* knew they were penniless. In that first "selection," some 60 men were sent to their death. Several hundred of the fortunate ones were crammed into "Ekonomia," others into the old rat-infested huts. When the newcomers fell ravenously on their first soup ration, the veteran prisoners looked on with contempt, mocking them with: "Barefoot and bare-assed! What are those letters painted on their back? K.L.? What's that? Oh, *Konzentrationslager* (concentration camp)! What do we need them here for, the *kaelniks*!" Thus, on their very first day at Skarżysko, the prisoners from Majdanek earned the name they would continue to be known by in the camp – *kaelnik* (for a man) and *kaelanka* (for a woman).

So their new life began. Some of the women, many of whom arrived clad in rags, managed with the help of a foreman to get hold of a dress or smock from the storeroom. The men were given nothing. They dragged themselves around the camp in search of an extra morsel of bread and bitterly remembered the rumors of the "good camp" they were being sent to that had accompanied their departure from Majdanek. During their free time, the *kaelniks* tried to acquaint themselves with their new surroundings. Compared to the iron discipline of Majdanek, Skarżysko seemed to be neglected and filthy, yet the veteran prisoners "looked a lot better than us." They were particularly impressed by the family barracks – whole families still together! Sure, they had come with property straight from their homes, so "their life was not bad at all! They laugh at us, at what we look like .... those simple craftsmen look down on us as if we were inferior beings." [36] The *kaelniks*, of course, had brought no money or valuables to sell.

The newcomers had plenty to say, too. "The camp elder, Albirt, '– writes Regina Finger –' and the policemen Krzepicki and Teperman, hated the people from Majdanek, and as a result their condition rapidly deteriorated. Here informing and fawning to the authorities were the order of the day, together with violence, and the helpless were mercilessly destroyed.... There were no moral scruples or ethics. Beside the living corpses one saw the members of the administration who lacked for nothing. They hated us because we were culturally superior to them. At every 'selection', our people were the first to go." [37]

---

[36] Noemi Konik, Testimony, YV, 0-33/1830; Ewa Bornes, op. cit.
[37] Regina Finger, Dokumenty i materiały, op. cit., p. 39.

Indeed, the basic conflict between the two groups derived from the difference in their social background. Among the prisoners from Majdanek were many people from Warsaw, doctors, engineers, public officials, and so on, who, although brought up in traditional families, were non-religious and preferred Polish to Yiddish. To the Radomites they appeared alien, especially the women, most of whom were assimilated Jews. At the same time, however, with no interest in anyone aiding the "Warsaw bandits," the Hasag management sought to intensify the conflict. Not one of the newcomers ever reached the status of major functionary in the camp.

At first, the *kaelniks* kept only to themselves, but in time, as they worked side by side with the veteran prisoners, they grew closer to them and learned the secrets of *"organizacja"*. The first friendships developed among the women. At the plant, the *kaelniks* were helped by the Poles, and the names of Ponikowski and Stępinski from the Instrument Division are mentioned in this regard. Young Flora relates that "the Poles were nicer to me than the people in the barracks. My overseer often gave me bread, or even a sandwich." [38] Adjustment was much harder for the men. Some apprenticed themselves to the craftsmen; the bolder ones stole potatoes off the carts. Several of the more charitable veterans helped with anonymous gifts. There were also some well-known figures from Warsaw whose barracks-mates did as much as they could for them. [39]

Several new doctors were put to work in the infirmary, thus improving their working conditions, although the patients continued to die from lack of food or medicines. Those stricken with dysentery were given a powder made from burnt bread, and rags or toilet paper served as bandages. Every now and then, drugs were smuggled in. The doctors did their best, some of them without demanding money. Among them, Dr Nikielberg and Dr Seidenbeutel are lauded in testimony [40], and little Flora's life was saved by the dedicated ministrations of a doctor and nurse whose names she could not recall. The nurses Zosia and Genia and male nurses Sobkowski

---

[38] Flora Merder-Kwintner, Hayiti sham begil nehaday, (Hebrew), (Tel-Aviv, "Moreshet", 1985), pp. 41–43.

[39] Efraim Rotenberg, Testimony, YV, 0-33/2803.

[40] Ewa Zucker, Testimony, YV, 0-3/166; A. Erder, op. cit.

and Szaweslajn also helped ailing prisoners and even protected them during 'selections.'[41]

A good many of the *prominente* began to show an interest in the younger and more attractive *kaelankas*, taking no pains to hide their intentions. When a policeman appeared in the barracks in the evening bearing bread in place of flowers for a young girl, it was obvious that he was asking: "Do you want to be my cousin?" The term "cousin" (*kuzyn or kuzynka in Polish*) was used for an unmarried couple living together. Sex was forbidden by the authorities and was in fact of little interest to people who were starving. Nevertheless, the *prominente* or ordinary prisoners who had not yet lost all trace of their manhood often visited the women's barracks and vice versa while the Jewish administration turned a blind eye. Although during the Radom Period there had also been married and unmarried couples in the camp, "free love" never became common in that conservative society.

The groundwork was laid for the greater popularity of the practice by the social changes which took place after the Winter of 1942–43. The men began to feel the hardship of their solitary life, while many of the veteran women prisoners had gotten old before their time. Thus a void was created in the social structure of the "Radom Tier," and it was filled by the young women from Majdanek. The first steps were taken by the prominente. Menasze Hollender describes what he saw in the family barracks:

> "Here lived the select married couples who had paid a high price to be allotted quarters in these barracks. In most cases they were fictitious couples. Young girls, alone and attractive, brought from Majdanek barefoot and in rags, became an object to be purchased, "cousins" of the camp elite. For a piece of bread and a pair of shoes, they would do anything their patrons wanted. Most of the girls had no other choice. If they didn't give in to the will of a *prominente* they could expect only hunger, hardship, and often death. The people in the family barracks lived a life of luxury. The barracks had its own kitchen. They each cooked their own meals with food purchased from the Poles. They traded in foreign currency, gold, favors from the foremen, and anything else they could get their hands on. Shouting matches among the women for kitchen space or a better place in the barracks were a matter of

---

[41] Izak Kajzer, Jendrzewer Buch, p. 254; H. Greipner, op. cit.

routine. Sometimes the men would intervene, and then there would be fistfights and people would inform on each other." [42]

Second rank functionaries who lived in the "privileged barracks" (officially for men only) devised their own solutions. If a girl came to spend the night with her "cousin," his pallet- mate slept on a table. The policemen often shattered the bulb in the women's barracks when they came to visit their girlfriends. Modesty was accommodated by means of "walls" erected around the pallets with blankets or paper sacks. In some cases the girls became pregnant. Rumors in the camp spoke of abortions performed by a doctor from the town. Some women even gave birth secretly. The babies were immediately taken from their mothers.

When in the Autumn of 1943 new barracks were built (see Figure 6.3) with double-decker pallets for two, "cousins" became an integral part of camp life. Even "proletarians" with a penny to spare set out to find themselves a girlfriend. And some of the youngsters simply paired off, producing the normal run of love affairs, unfaithfulness, and midnight rendezvous on a narrow pallet. The whole camp knew who was sleeping with whom and who had several "cousins". This clandestine sex life no longer raised any eyebrows, but it did supply the meat of the inevitable gossip which added a bit of spice to the harsh life in the camp. On the whole, the existence of "cousins" played a positive role both for the individual and for camp society at large by easing the pain of loneliness, facilitating the adjustment of new prisoners, and blurring class distinctions. Some of these *ad hoc* relationships even developed into true love, with many of the couples marrying after the war.

Shattered Hopes

Autumn 1943 brought news from the front which raised the hopes of the tormented prisoners. Seemingly, in view of the shared anticipation of imminent German defeat, a change might have been expected in the Polish attitude to the most problematic subject: political and military cooperation. Such cooperation could have included the theft of ammunition for the local underground, aid in escape attempts, cooperation with the partisans, and help in organizing resistance in the camp at the proper time.

---

[42] Menasze Hollender, Testimony, YV, 0-3/1012, p. 23.

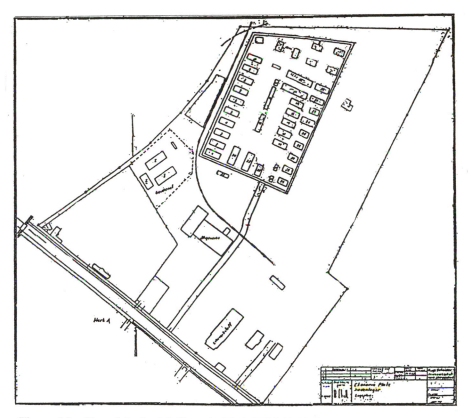

Figure 6.3   Plan of the Jewish Camp in Werk A (20.11.1943)

The first signs of cooperation had appeared in the Spring of 1943. German terror tactics restricted the Poles' freedom of movement within the plant, and it appears that as a result they began to recruit Jews to help in the theft of ammunition. There is much testimony to this effect, including that of Mosze Niechcicki who agreed to help his foreman, Stanisław Szwed, to get crates of bullets to the partisans in the forest. Szwed provided Niechcicki with food and underground newspapers from which the prisoners learned of the uprising in the Warsaw ghetto.[43] Szlomo Rosenzweig also speaks of helping to steal ammunition, and

---

[43] Mosze Niechcicki, Sefer Piotrków, p. 891.

bullets were smuggled out of Bosch's department by Poles, with the prisoner Hersz Rozenbaum supplying the explosives.[44]

Close cooperation developed in the supply room between the manager Nowicki, a member of the Polish underground Armia Krajowa (AK), and the prisoner Menachem Horowicz. Ammunition was smuggled out in carts under the coal allotted to the Poles by the plant management. Ammunition for the partisans was made from rags, and they seem to have been the beneficiaries of the sale of jewelry which Nowicki bought from the camp Jews. When the Poles came to the supply room, they brought with them newspapers smuggled into the camp in pieces for the prisoners to wrap their bread rations in.[45] The Poles did not always make the Jews privy to their secrets, and several disasters occurred as a result. In the Summer of 1943, two trucks arrived at the supply room bearing Wehrmacht soldiers, and the Jews loaded them with munitions. When it was later discovered that the soldiers had in fact been partisans in disguise, the Jewish supply clerk was executed. Bullets were found in the pocket of the prisoner Jechiel Kinel, and it was suspected that they had been placed there by a Pole who was afraid to be caught carrying stolen ammunition. Despite his pleas of innocence, Kinel was hanged before the eyes of the entire camp.[46]

In late Summer 1943, hardship in the camp grew worse while news from outside raised new hopes. There was again a wave of escape attempts. In the Autumn, some 30 to 40 prisoners escaped. They had three options: to get hold of Aryan papers, to find a hiding place among the Poles, or to join the partisans in the vicinity. The partisans were the subject of conflicting stories in the camp. Adam Nowicki states that AK partisans he ran into after his escape took a passive stance to the Jews hiding in the forest and in only a few cases murdered them or turned them in to the Germans.[47] Others claim that Dr Seidenbeutel and his friend Stern managed to escape without a trace with the help of the partisans.[48] An odd

---

[44] Hersz Rozenbaum, AGKBZH, SWK, sygn. 218, p. 55; cf. S. Rozenzweig, see Chapter 3, n. 12, ib. p. 120.

[45] M. Horowicz, op. cit.

[46] Abram Wolfowicz, SWK, AGKBZH, sygn. 211, p. 78.

[47] A. Nowicki, op. cit.

[48] A. Erder, op. cit.

incident is reported by Stefan Sendłak, a member of the Council for Aid to Jews (*Rada Pomocy Żydom, "Żegota"* – RPŻ), who states that on the night of September 17, 1943 a band of partisans infiltrated the camp and took 20 young prisoners back with them to the forest.[49] No other source has yet been found to corroborate this story.

The cooperative efforts represented by the connections between the Jews and the Polish underground, their participation in the theft of ammunition, the chance of escape and possibility of joining the partisans came to a tragic head in the case of Lola Mendelewicz. While employed in the bullet control department, she agreed to hand over stolen amm-unition to her boyfriend Edek. Edek, who worked outside the camp, made contact with the Polish partisans and passed the bullets on to them. Edek was eventually forced to escape, and could not carry out their plan to take Lola with him. Betrayed by a bribed *Werkschutz* officer, Edek was caught redhanded with the ammunition and, after being shot at, was arrested. Although the Germans attempted in vain to extract from him information about his co-conspirators, SS investigators brought from Radom with bloodhounds sniffed out Lola and arrested her as well. Handcuffed, the two were marched from one end of the camp to the other "for all to see and fear." Testimony has it that as they were led to their death they called out "Long live the Jewish people! Vengeance!"[50]

A few prisoners succeeded in escaping without being caught, among them Dr Czaplicki who was aided by Stanisław Szwed, and Hana Lewkowicz who obtained Aryan papers and was hidden by Poles.[51] Others fell into the hands of local farmers who turned them over to the *Werkschutz*. Under such circumstances, there was no chance of organizing a mass escape. In the Autumn of 1943, Niechcicki heard from Szwed of an underground plan to attack the camp in order to effect the release of hundreds of Jews who would then join the partisans, but such a raid was never carried out. The fact of the matter is that the Polish partisans, as an official organization, took no steps whatsoever to aid the Jews to escape and did not admit them to their ranks.

The lack of action on the part of the Polish underground can be

---

[49] Raport **Stefana** Sendłaka do RPŻ, 22.9.1943, M. Arczyński, Kryptonim "Żegota", z dziejów pomocy Żydom w Polsce 1939–1945, (Warszawa: Czytelnik, 1979), p. 223.

[50] Fride Mape-Zonszajn, Pinkas Chmielnik, p. 847.

[51] Jan Czaplicki, AGKBZH, SWK, sygn. 217, p. 142; Hana Lewkowicz, op. cit.

explained by political reasons. As early as February, 1943, when the supreme command of the AK ordered weapons to be conveyed to ghettoes willing to fight, the AK members in the field did not agree to do so. The problem arose anew in regard to the Jewishforced labor camps. In the Summer of 1943, initial contact was established between the underground directorate of the Bund in Warsaw and their members interred in nine camps, including Skarżysko. In the Autumn, talks were held between delegates of the Jewish underground organization *Komisja Koordy-nacyjna* (KK), and the military organs of Underground Poland *(Polska Podziemna)*. The Poles responded to the suggestion that arms be smuggled into Jewish camps with considerable reservations. The Bund report from November 15, 1943 notes the failure of the talks and states that in addition to the money and letters *Komisja Koordynacyjna* was attempting to convey to the camps, the organization was also seeking to get weapons in.[52]

Available sources reveal that in late 1943 the aid provided the camp prisoners by the various organizations was still nil. In Spring, 1943, the Jewish Social Relief (JUS) headed by Dr Weichert was re-established in Kraków. It was resolved that the JUS would send drugs and food directly to the forced labor camps in the future.[53] For the meantime, this remained a directive on paper only. As for the RPŻ, Sendłak's report from September 1943 makes no mention of any contact with the Skarżysko camp, contrary to the version put forward by one of the heads of the organization, Marek Arczyński, who claims that a local cell was established in the city and had the cooperation of activists of the underground parties who made every sacrifice to extend help to the suffering Jews.[54]

In the Summer of 1943, more help arrived from the Jews of Piotrków for their relatives at Skarżysko which an RPŻ source describes as a monthly grant of 12,000 zlotys.[55] This, however, was a private contribution not made on behalf of the RPŻ or the Bund. A Bund official,

---

[52] List do Przedstawiciela Bundu w Londynie, 22.6.1943, Bund – Pisma do Londynu, YV, 0-25/97; Sprawozdanie za czas od 1.7.1943 do 15.11.1943, ib.

[53] Oświadczenie dr. Weicherta, Kraków, 8.3.1945, YV, 0-21/7.

[54] M. Arczyński, Kryptonim " Żegota", op. cit., p. 120.

[55] Teresa Prekerowa, Konspiracyjna Rada Pomocy Żydom w Warszawie, 1942–1954, (Warszawa, Państwowy Instytut Wydawniczy, 1982), p. 236.

Kotkowski, claims that 20,000 zlotys arrived in the Summer from the central office in Warsaw. They were to be distributed among the Bund members in the camps, but no way was found to get the money into Skarżysko.[56] Beginning in the Autumn 1943, the contribution of Jewish organizations abroad to the RPŻ budget grew larger, and according to a report from October of that year, "Jewish organizations sent considerable sums to eight camps, including Skarżysko, amounting to several hundred zlotys each."[57]

Meanwhile, mortality in the camp remained extraordinarily high, with the men from Majdanek being the most vulnerable. It is estimated that only about one-third of those sent to Werk A were still alive. In view of production needs, the Radom SS command promised to provide medicines for the prisoners.[58] With hunger still rampant, the *kaelniks* sought their own ways to get food. In August 1943, Lejb Bornes sent a letter to a friend in Warsaw and three months later received money from him, smuggled into the camp in a soup vat with a false bottom. Hana Zajdenwerg wrote to a family friend, Zdzisław Szparkowski (who won the title of Righteous Gentile), who got money to her.[59]

It is thus clear that before 1944, most of the aid reaching the camp came from private sources, and only little, if any, came from underground welfare organizations, whether Polish or Jewish. Without any help from outside, the hope of organizing an escape and joining the ranks of the partisans was also dashed. The camp prisoners had no choice but to obstinately continue the struggle for survival alone and to go on believing that a new day would soon dawn.

---

[56] Charles Kotowsky, "Remnants", manuscript, p. 94.

[57] Sprawozdanie RPŻ z 23.10.1943, see n. 55, ib., p. 398.

[58] G. Kuhne, Sitzungen, pp. 112b, 113a.

[59] Chana Zajdenwerg, Testimony, YV, 0-33/1820; cf. M. Arczyński, Kryptonim " Żegota", op. cit., p. 164.

Chapter 7

The Kuehnemann–Pollmer Partnership

The Arrivals from Płaszów and the Start of a New Era

November 1943 brought freezing temperatures and a new regime to the Jews in the camp. Rumors that Ipfling was leaving to be replaced by Paul Kuehnemann had started in October. As soon as the prisoners caught sight of their new commandant – short, chubby and hunchbacked – they immediately labeled him "der Hojker"(the hunchback) and knew they were in for trouble. Not only did he speak fluent Yiddish, but he constantly toured the camp. Ipfling might have been a murderer, but at least they saw very little of him. What was this new one up to? Those in the know reported that before the war Kuehnemann had been a nightwatchman in a Jewish factory where he had learned their language and customs.[1]

This was the man who welcomed the transport from Płaszów in mid-November 1943. Some 1,000 men and women streamed through the gate of Werk A. As they advanced, they heard from the policemen escorting them that they had been brought to the best camp! Yet compared to Płaszów, it seemed small and shoddy. They soon received their first surprise: Amon Goeth, commandant of Płaszów, had kept his word and the

---

[1] Paul Kuehnemann, "Stand der reichsdeutschen Gefolgschaft am 31.5.1942", Werkschutz, YV, JM/3700, p. 15.

newcomers were handed the parcels containing blankets and pillows that had been loaded on the train at Płaszów at the very last minute.

In a routine search at the gate, the *Werkschutz* checked mainly their bags, confiscating any money or jewels they found. Madzia Ofir managed to smuggle in a gold chain hidden in the false bottom of a sewing kit, and she was not the only one to do so. Again the veteran prisoners crowded around near the gate, this time joined by the people from Majdanek. Curiously, they looked the "greenhorns" over. Those with a good nose for business immediately sensed that these people were not like the wretched *kaelniks*. As soon as the newcomers were herded into the barracks, they were bombarded by questions by the camp prisoners: "Who are you? Where do you come from? What did you bring with you? What do you have to sell? What's this – you don't understand Yiddish!"

If the "Majdanek Tier" had included people from two cultures – Jewish and Polish – this new transport brought Jews who were totally foreign to the autochthonous camp population: Kraków Jews, among them numerous academics and graduates of public schools who spoke only Polish. They had long since abandoned tradition and viewed the typical Jewish town as a center of fanatical and ludicrous conservatism. But now the shoe was on the other foot. The newcomers looked with disbelief mixed with pity and scorn on both the provincial Jews who barely knew a word of Polish and the *kaelniks* in their bizarre rags.

Amongst the new prisoners were Jews who had brought some of their money with them to Płaszów and up to August 1943 had maintained close ties with the Aryan side. Thus, at Płaszów the prisoners had suffered relatively little from severe hunger and had been the first to receive aid from the JUS and from Dr Weichert. These advantages were obvious from the appearance of the Plaszowites who arrived in Skarżysko and, in fact, determined the nature of their adjustment to their new camp.

The veteran prisoners stared enviously at the fine clothes and real shoes of the newcomers, at the faces of the well-bred girls who had not yet lost their youthful charm, at the self-assurance of the well-to-do. There were married couples, mothers and daughters, sisters, and "elite" cliques. They soon settled in the older and newer barracks, and somehow found themselves straw mattresses and blankets.

The new arrivals did not undergo any "selection". The men were sent to do construction work within the camp (where new barracks were still going up) or to Werk B where another production hall for shells was being erected.[2] Others were sent to the Automatic Weapons Department. To the amazement of the veterans, the newcomers learned at astounding speed just who and when to bribe in order to get a good job assignment. This was a sure sign that these were people it was worth getting along well with. When the Germans came to choose girls for work, the veterans advised them to pretty themselves up so they might attract the eye of Kalinowski and be chosen for his department, known for its special privileges. The less fortunate were sent to work on shell casings or to the backbreaking grenade section.

The *Werkschutz* also sensed that this transport was a "fat cow," and so conducted frequent searches, confiscating some 8,000 zlotys between November and December alone.[3] Even when their money was gone, the Plaszowites did not apprentice themselves to the local craftsmen. On the whole, they helped each other out, but only within their own "tier," operating in the framework of the decimated families or newly formed "bands" of girls, such as the "Hasag Five" who lived and cooked together and shared their bread rations, money and clothes.[4] The men preferred to fight their struggle for survival alone or with one close friend, the choice, for example, of Jeszajahu Rechter and his son who joined forces with Peterseil.

Relations between the Jewish administration and the Płaszów prisoners were based on the principle of "respect and suspect". Krzepicki and his cohorts were not at all pleased by the influx of intellectuals, among them many who spoke fluent German, yet, perhaps even subconsciously, they seemed to refrain from physically disciplining the numerous "professors". In point of fact, the Krakowites did not constitute a threat to their authority, and only a small number of men from Płaszów were recruited for the police, whose ranks had to be padded because of the now larger camp population. The veteran Jewish administrators found an ally in Paul Kuehnemann, with whom they were able to share a bottle of vodka and do business. The Plaszowites were not unaware of this situation, and had a very low opinion of the administrators in general, to wit: "All of those in charge were scum and parasites, drunk with power, greedy and

---

[2] Schaja Jurista, Testimony, Moreshet Archives, A.600.3.

[3] Werkschutz-Hasag, Skar.-Kam., Meldungen, see Chapter 3, n. 32.

[4] Madzia Ofir, Testimony, YV, 0-33/1822.

informants";[5] "They were illiterate people with power and money in their hands"; "The camp clique amassed a fortune from stealing the prisoners' rations." [6]

Opinions of the local police were no better. They are characterized unequivocally as money-hungry, cruel and vengeful, "garbage that rose to the top as a result of the upheavals of war, but would sink back down to the bottom as soon as it was over." [7] The policemen were especially put out by the proud "Kraków girls", who were not tempted by the status of "cousin". It may be inferred from their guarded comments that it was not the institution of "cousins" they disapproved of, but the prospect of an intimate relationship with "that sort of person." In point of fact, the camp's "love life" became more complicated under Kuehnemann, who insisted on strict separation between the sexes. Gossips whispered that this gave "the hunchback of Skarżysko" a chance to "patrol" the women's barracks and spy on the pretty girls. On one occasion, Kuehnemann caught a couple in *flagrante* and ordered them to perform the act again before an audience of prisoners, an incident that shocked the whole camp.[8]

In the Winter of 1943–44, another typhoid epidemic broke out, although this time claiming fewer victims due to the natural immunity of the Płaszów prisoners who had already been exposed to the disease. Taking swift action, the camp authorities put to death all those who fell ill. The "new era" in the camp's history, however, really began with the appointment of a new *Werkschutz* commander, Walter Pollmer. At the same time, a large portion of the guards were replaced and most of the *Stossstruppe* officers dismissed. Pollmer brought with him his own stormtroopers who were quartered not in Werk C like their predecessors, but in Werk A.[9]

What led to the change in policy? It will be recalled that in the Spring of 1944, faced with the impossibility of obtaining further transports of Jews, the authorities decided to improve the prisoners' living conditions in the camp. This was not the only factor involved. There can be no doubt

---

[5] R. Aptowicz, op. cit.

[6] Irma Laksberger, Testimony, YV, 0-16/251; M. Hollender, op. cit.

[7] Rena Taubenblatt-Fradkin, Testimony, YV, 0016/249.

[8] N. Flajszakier, op. cit.; C. Singer, see Chapter 6, n. 2, ib.

[9] Sentencja wyroku w sprawie Jerzego Adryanowicza, 20.10.1967, AOKBZH w Kielcach, sygn. IV.K.3/67, p. 37.

that in view of the *Wehrmacht's* defeats at the front, there was a fear of growing unrest among the German staff and therefore a need to increase supervision of them. Who did Pollmer choose for his ally in this task? The loyalty of the Ukrainian *Werkschutz* officers was catastrophically undermined. As for the Polish collaborators, their suitability for the job was now seriously in question, both because of their fear of the Polish underground and because of the danger that they were double agents.

In light of this state of affairs, the Jews seemed the most appropriate candidates for potential ally, and this intent dictated Pollmer's declarations that "he sees the prisoners not as Jews but as workers." [10] He himself was not involved in executions, leaving the "dirty work" to his assistant Reinhard Neumerkel. [11] Under Pollmer's orders, the searches of prisoners returning from work were almost totally eliminated. What is more, he set up his own spy network of and to this end "planted" several Jewish policemen in the various factory departments, instructing them to gather information on all staff members, including the Germans.

In Spring, 1944, the policeman Hayim Weintraub was murdered by a group of German foremen, among them Dechant, Pawlowski, Koch, Faerber and Laskowski, who beat him to death with their fists and clubs. His wife claimed that Weintraub was killed because he had threatened to report one of the foremen to a "higher authority". [12] At the Leipzig trials it was found that Weintraub was an "SS informant" who passed on information about Hans Faerber and his business dealings with Jews. [13] Pollmer, preferring to keep the whole matter quiet, never ordered an investigation of the murder. This was also a warning to other Jewish informants not to expect any help if they were found out. The incident sent shock waves through the camp and was never forgotten by the prisoners.

These tragic events paled before Pollmer's "miracles": the daily bread ration was raised to 500 grams; the soup ration was increased and its quality improved; workers in the more onerous departments were given sausage; sugar and margarine were distributed before holidays; in the camp the barracks and yard were cleaned up and sanitary conditions

---

[10] L. Bornes, op. cit.

[11] Anklageschrift, p. 18, 40; Sitzungen, p. 102a.

[12] Fela Weintraub, Akta w sprawie Henryk Laskowski, see Chapter 6, n. 8, p. 339; cf. Abram Edelstein, Testimony, YV, M-1/E/2499/2615.

[13] H. Faerber, Sitzungen, pp. 99a–b, 115a.

improved; some 35 barracks with heating stoves were built. Many of the "prettified" huts were now given names such as the "Krakower Barak" where the Płaszów men lived or the women's "Eleganter Barak," and one was even known as the "Fleisch (meat) Barak." This was Barracks no. 6, which, thanks to Hinda Ginsburg, stood out for its cleanliness. A visiting German commission was so impressed that the barracks was awarded the prize of a meat ration which was used to make meatballs and earned it its odd soubriquet.[14] In the Spring of 1944, the prisoners were given clothing and shoes originally belonging to Jews murdered at Majdanek. The transports from Łódź and Płaszów that arrived in March were amazed at the prisoners' freedom of movement and the superficial searches at the gate.[15]

How did the children fare in this "paradise"? Among the Radomites, some 15–20 children had been brought to the camp with their parents. The older ones were put to work in the plant departments; the more privileged – that is, the children of the *prominente* – stayed in the camp. On the whole, the Germans and Poles left them alone, but this was not always true. When a collective punishment of 20 lashes was meted out to the workers in the Automatic Weapons department, 12-year-old Natan Śledzik was not exempt.[16] Girls suffered the same fate. Lili Wermus, aged 14, arrived in Skarżysko alone on a transport from Majdanek and worked first in the Instrument Division and then in the Polishing Department. For no apparent reason she was accused of stealing ammunition and, fortunately, received "only" a severe beating.[17]

Fearing a possible "selection", the parents of young children tried not to leave them alone in the camp during working hours. The shoemaker Ajzenberg's 5-year-old son spent the day near his father in the workshop; 6-year-old Perla Lewkowicz "worked" in the Polishing Department while her 8-year-old brother kept himself occupied in the office of the elderly German Urban. The Płaszów transport also included a number of children who were given various "work assignments."[18] According to Amalia Bertgram, who arrived on this transport with her young son, in the wake

---

[14] J. Ginsburg, op. cit.

[15] Testimonies, YV: Tola Szajak, 0-33/1824; Pola Goldminc, 0-33/1831.

[16] Yoram Simoni (Natan Śledzik), Jendrzewer Buch, p. 189.

[17] Lili Wermus-Sznycer, Testimony, YV, 0-33/9414.

[18] A. Lewkowicz, I. Laksberger, op. cit.

of one "selection" conducted in the camp, several children were taken by truck to some unknown destination. This story is confirmed by Fela Kojfman-Sznitlich who was brought to Skarżysko together with her young daughter.[19]

From these testimonies, it is not entirely clear when this "selection" took place. In fact, all "selections" ceased in the Spring of 1944. The new "euphoric" mood was not even ruined by the inspections of Kuehnemann, who periodically shot Jews he decided were loafing. To his credit it must be said that he did not interfere with the outside aid sent to improve the prisoners' conditions, as long as it was provided legally.

Aid from Outside and Its Effect on Camp Life

In January 1944 the WVHA informed the local SS commanders that the central SS warehouse would no longer distribute medical supplies to the smaller work camps and it was now up to them to provide this service themselves.[20] As a result, several prisoners from Płaszów received the camp commandant's permission to visit the JUS offices in Kraków, escorted by the *Werkschutz*. They brought back medicines, food and other supplies for the ill.[21] Following official procedure, the JUS would send medicines and food in accordance with a list prepared in advance by the camp's head doctor. The German authorities would then acknowledge receipt.[22] After the war, charges were leveled against Weichert since, compared to the vast quantities of aid sent to the JUS from abroad, assistance to the camps was almost nil and only a small part of the shipments to the camps ever reached the prisoners.[23]

Whatever the extent of official aid, it must be acknowledged that Weichert helped to develop parallel channels of illegal aid as well. One of the contacts in Kraków was the Polish pharmacist Tadeusz Pankiewicz. Through him, even prisoners at Płaszów managed to send money and

---

[19] Fela Kojfman-Sznitlich, Pinkas Chmielnik, p. 251; cf. Amalia Bertgram, Testimony, YV, 0-16/209.

[20] Mieczysław Pemper, "Protokoły przesłuchań świadków z ramienia Specjalnego Sądu Karnego w Krakowie", maj 1945, YV, 0-21/7, p. 108.

[21] Szymon Szlachet, przesłuchanie 25.6.1947, YV, 0-21/8.

[22] JUS, Juedische Unterstuetzungsstelle fuer das GG, Taetigkeitsbericht Nr. V, fuer die Monate April-Juni 1944, YV, 0-21.

[23] Stanisław Smreczynski, przesłuchanie 17.5.1945, see n. 20, p. 53.

letters to their relatives at Skarżysko. In Werk A their contact was Lucia – Ludwika Stolarska – who was recruited by Rosa Horn whose job it was to distribute the money in the camp together with Gelberowa and Langer. The Council for Jewish Aid (RPŻ) in Kraków refused to cooperate with Weichert, regarding him a Nazi collaborator.[24] Stolarska admitted that it was only in early Summer 1944 that she received a proposal from the RPŻ in Warsaw to organize the transfer of money to the prisoners at Skarżysko. The RPŻ contact, Tadeusz Bilewicz, brought her 88,000 zlotys for this purpose which she doled out to the various prisoners, partly as she herself saw fit, since the go-betweens were afraid of local informants.[25] Available testimony does not contain the names of the prisoners who enjoyed this aid.

The books of the Polish researchers Marek Arczyński and Teresa Prekerowa, who studied the activities of the RPŻ, contain no reference to Lucia. As RPŻ contacts in Skarżysko, Prekerowa mentions Bilewicz, Wanda Bodalska and Ewa Sarnecka. The latter arranged the escape of Rachel Żak Summer 1944.[26] The RPŻ agent Józefa Rysińska testified that in 1943 she travelled to Skarżysko bringing false Aryan papers for prisoners planning to escape, but she never had any direct contact with the camp itself.[27]

There are also conflicting versions concerning the aid provided by Jewish organizations in 1944. The general report of the National Jewish Committee (*Żydowski Komitet Narodowy* – ŻKN) from May 24, 1944 lists 13 camps in the *Generalgouvernement* with which the ŻKN maintained regular contact.[28] These include Skarżysko to which 50,000 zlotys were sent in March 1944.[29] Since delegates of the Bund (Leon Feiner) and Poalei Zion (Adolf Berman) increased the ŻKN coffers with

---

[24] Dr. Michał Weichert, przesłuchanie 8.9.1949; Tadeusz Pankiewicz, 16.3.1949, YV, 0-21/8.

[25] Ludwika Stolarska, przesłuchanie 14.3.1949, Feliks Rogowski, Róża Horn ib.

[26] T. Prekerowa, Konspiracyjna Rada, op. cit., pp. 241, 309.

[27] Józefa Rysińska ("Ziutka"), Testimony, YV, 0-33/1804.

[28] Sprawozdanie ŻKN 24.5.1944; List M. Weicherta do B. Kobrynera, 18.10.1949, YV, 0-21/7.

[29] "List Zygmunta Lasockiego do Pełnomocnika Rządu w Kraju, Warszawa, 11.3.1944", S. Wroński, M. Zwolakowa, Polacy i Żydzi 1939–1945, (Warszawa, Książka i Wiedza, 1971), p. 284.

party funds, they demanded that the money be distributed to their party members in the camps in proportion to their contributions. The RPŻ agents objected in principle and refused to obey these instructions, claiming that under surreptitious conditions it was impossible to search out specific party members within the camps.[30]

Prisoners' testimonies also refer to this assistance. Meir Weissblum from Opatów, a member of the religious Zionist youth movement Bnei Akiva, and the engineer David Efrat, allied with Poalei Zion, received letters from Warsaw in early 1944 whose authors identified themselves as Jewish Fighting Organisation(ŻOB) members, among them "Antek". Both prisoners were asked to convey information concerning the condition of the Jews in the camp, and particularly that of members of the Zionist movement. They were later asked to organize a public committee of Zionist movement and Bund members in the camp. Its primary function was to distribute aid money received from Warsaw. Weissblum and Efrat chose several individuals for the committee, among them Felicja Comber, Perlow, Brenner, Maniszewicz and Machtinger. On instructions from Warsaw, the committee members were to select agents to hand out the money. For reasons of security, none of the contacts knew of the existence of any other. Within the camp it was generally believed that the money was coming from Opatow, a rumor encouraged for fear of informants.[31]

According to Weissblum, the committee members were asked to ensure that the aid money went to Zionist and socialist youth. Opinion was divided in regard to this principle of distribution. Elhanan Ehrlich relates: "At that time I heard from Yehiel Weinstock [apparently one of the contacts – F.K.] of financial aid entering the camp from Jewish sources outside Poland, and that the money was intended for those who were known for their Zionist activities before the war.... Since I objected to this absurd distinction between one Jew and another, I refused to accept any support ... I could not accept the idea that while ... people were literally starving to death ... the situation justified checking someone's Zionist credentials! Among those who received aid were people who were managing without it, but the group led by the engineer Efrat ... didn't

---

[30] T. Prekerowa, Konspiracyjna Rada, op. cit., p. 45.
[31] Meir Weissblum, Testimony, YV, 0-33/2804; cf. Itzhak (Antek) Zuckerman, Sheva shanim hahen, (Hebrew), (Beit Lohamey Hagetaot, 1990), pp. 346, 419.

care." [32] Several Majdanek women who were not the lucky recipients of healthy grants voiced similar opinions.[33] In response to these charges, Weissblum maintains that after the war the ŻOB agents accused Efrat of distributing money to the members of non-Zionist parties and to unaffiliated prisoners as well.

The picture which emerges of the activities of the various aid organizations is not gratifying. Partisan interests, matters of prestige, and political considerations seem to have carried more weight than concern for the prisoners' welfare. Not only did each organization operate individually without any awareness of the activities of the others, but in certain cases they deliberately withheld vital information from each other.[34] The appalling lack of accuracy in Polish studies leads us to assume that the aid from the RPŻ reached the camp as a result of Weichert's connections, and not the other way round. A comparison of the reports of the various organizations with prisoner testimony creates the obvious impression that – with no exceptions – the reports embellished the facts and exaggerated in describing the organizations' achievements, both "for the sake of history" and to demonstrate the need to increase support from institutions abroad. We must therefore conclude that the prisoners were not saved from starvation thanks to the aid they received, since it arrived too late and reached too few. The primary factor accounting for improved living conditions in the camp was the shift in Hasag management policy which affected all of the prisoners.

Notwithstanding these reservations, outside aid, both legal and illegal, was a great boon. Overall conditions improved and a new hospital, infirmary and kitchen were built for the ill. Moreover, the prisoners' dependence on the Poles employed in the plant decreased. Hope for an imminent end to the war improved mutual relations. Cooperation between the Poles and Jews now focussed on reducing production and the theft of ammunition. In the Polishing Department, Etla Ajzenman and her friends attempted to limit daily production, encouraged in their efforts by their Polish overseer Lepiasz. In the Small Ammunition Division, Malka Finkler passed defective items and Moniek Szajbe, together with the

---

[32] E. Erlich, Sefer Staszów, p. 383.

[33] Flora Kwintner, Noemi Konik, op. cit.

[34] Michał Weichert, przesłuchanie 8.9.1949, Warszawa, YV, 0-21/8, p. 7–8.

Poles, arranged for the "disappearance" of crates of ammunition.[35] During this period, only two prisoners are known to have escaped: Rachel Żak and Bezalel Szajger.[36]

The paucity of escape attempts can undoubtedly be attributed to the improved conditions. Not only did the *kaelniks* breathe a sigh of relief, but the "ladies from Kraków" as well now felt quite at home in the camp. Nobody knew, however, whether this was merely the lull before the storm. One day, probably in Summer 1944, the aid committee received a letter from Warsaw reading something like this: "Your end is near. None of the Jews in the camp will survive because the Germans desire to exterminate all Jews. Your only chance is to rebel. We are ready to help you. We will send you arms and Polish identity papers to be distributed to the Zionist youth.... Consider this and let us know what you have decided." [37]

Meir Weissblum, who relates the story of the letter, claims that the committee did not regard itself as a branch of the ŻOB, but the organizations in Warsaw seem to have thought differently. The committee, which meanwhile had made contact with Bund and Zionist movement members in the other two *werks*, managed to arrange a meeting during the prisoners' visit to the common washroom in Werk A. Agreement was reached regarding identity papers, but the question of arms aroused harsh debate. When a vote was taken, only two were in favor, with the majority opposing on the grounds that they would immediately be discovered and would bring disaster down on the entire camp. Neither arms nor the promised identity papers were ever received from Warsaw. Thus the dreams of mass uprising and escape were dashed.

Singing and Card Games – The "Cultural Life" of Werk A

Life in Werk A had many faces. Although all its inmates lived within the same reality, each viewed it through his or her own eyes. The Radomites particularly remember "Ekonomia," the prisoners from Majdanek the family huts, and the Kraków "intelligentsia" the Jewish shtetl.

---

[35] Testimonies, YV: Etla Ajzenman, 0-33/1829; Malka Granatstein, 0-3/3323; Moniek Szajbe, oral information.

[36] Bezalel Szajger, Testimony, YV, M-1/E/549; Lili Sznycer, op. cit.

[37] M. Weissblum, op. cit.

"When [the prisoners] returned from the plant, the camp became one great marketplace. In certain barracks the pallets were turned into stalls. Men and women sold their goods. There was shouting and hawking just like in the shtetl stalls. On the pallets ... bread, rolls, butter, cheese and meat were stored under dreadfully insanitary conditions.... There cosmetics and clothes were produced, and stalls selling the goods were set up in front of the barracks. There were also vats with camp soup sold here for good money, and vats with homemade soup. The cries of the vendors hawking their wares filled the camp. This is one of the songs praising the quality of the homemade soup:[38]

Come on Jews, this is the spot
To get your soup – thick and hot!
The spoon stands up, it is so thick
Thick like porridge, just the same
It wouldn't put your Mama to shame!

Come and buy it – everything's there,
Beans and beets, and not too dear!
Dumplings, noodles, potatoes
What could be better for you?
Even salt is in it too!

Come on Jews, here to my vat
To get your soup swimming in fat!
Homemade soup! To get a bowl –
Pay one little coin, that's all!
For two zuzim the whole pot's yours!
Just feast your eyes, how thick, how thick
And cheap – before it's sold come get it quick!

The spoon stands up – so please don't wait
Tomorrow it will be too late!
This is soup for the elite,
Even the great! The komendanten
Krzepicki, Gilek, Teperman
And the dog of Kuehnemann!

The spoon stands up, the clock is ticking,
Tomorrow you'll be in your grave!
So get it now – for heaven's sake!

---

[38] M. Hollender, op. cit., pp. 24–25.

Get it now while it's still hot!
What's in your belly is what you've got!
Come on Jews, this is the spot
A bowl of soup – homemade and hot!"

(Translation from the Yiddish)

Did a Jew live on soup alone in Werk A? Did social life center solely around barter and haggling? Surprisingly, despite improved living conditions and the presence of a large number of intellectuals, only very few sources report any sort of cultural activity in the camp. Lack of sources, however, is not proof that none such existed. In point of fact, any prisoner who wished to preserve his sanity had need to express the heavy burden under which he suffered at some time or other. Even the "soup song" tells it all: the dumplings and noodles that Mama used to cook symbolize the prisoner's longings for the home and family which are no more, so what point is there to life? The songwriter ridicules himself and the other prisoners buying, selling, and rushing about although "the clock is ticking", a constant reminder that his time is near. The song even contains a protest against those in authority whose bellies are always full, and a sweet dream of vengeance. But for the moment he is here, in despair, for everything has been taken from him, even his soul. So he shouts: "Eat, tomorrow you'll be in your grave!" This macabre humor was the only defense mechanism available with which to combat the constant fear of death.

Thus, even the prisoners in Werk A became poets. An infinite variety of verse was composed, forgotten and lost over the years. The fact that it is not mentioned in testimony derives from the misplaced fear of former prisoners that tales of community singing might blunt perception of the horrors of daily life in the camp. It all began spontaneously. Huddled together in their dark barracks during the freezing night of that worst of winters, the girls would sing the dismal "Treblinka Song" known in many of the camps:[39]

Treblinka, there
A grave for Jews from everywhere
You never leave it once you're there
For that's your end...

---

[39] Erna Nessel, Testimony, YV, 0-33/650.

Yiddish was the language of choice in which to sing, but Polish folk songs recalled from schooldays were also heard. Virtually every women's barracks had its songstress who would start off on her own and then voices from all corners of the barracks would join in, one by one, to form a melancholy choir:

> The tyrant Hitler rose to strike
> With his band of murderers
> Hunting us down like woodland beasts
> Leaving us homeless,
> Leaving us with nothing.[40]

Each prisoner sought comfort in his or her own way. During the work week, the day and night shifts never met, and exhaustion left no strength for any "social life". Only on Sundays were all the prisoners together in the barracks. This was the day for visiting family members or former neighbors. The conversation, along with the cup of tea that might be offered the visitor, generated a sense of togetherness that was so lacking in the life of the camp where everyone was primarily occupied in ensuring his or her own survival. The youngsters sought out another form of "amusement" as well. When the weather was fine and all was quiet, couples could be seen walking along the camp paths. Small groups gathered in the barracks shadows to read the newspapers smuggled into the camp or simply to reminisce, while others argued loudly over the latest news from the front.

Many of the men took the opportunity to visit the "Rabiner Barak" of Rabbi Yitzhak Finkler from Radoszyce who arrived in March 1943. They asked his advice on whether to risk an escape attempt, debated the distribution of aid, sought arbitration on financial disputes, and lamented the death of loved ones. On the Sabbath eve his pallet was always surrounded by hassids who came to hear his stories of the righteous and sing Sabbath hymns. Here Chaim Singer found comfort and company. Some of the Jewish police harassed the rabbi, but on one occasion, when the police commander entered the barracks to find a group of raucous boys playing cards while across the way other Jews were singing hassidic melodies, he chewed out the card players and ordered them to join the worshippers.

---

[40] E. Kerżner, op. cit.

Even Kuehnemann treated the rabbi with a degree of respect. When the latter refused to obey an order to eat non-kosher *kaszanka*, Kuehnemann did not insist. The "hunchback's" restraint in the matter amazed the other prisoners. Neither did the commandant interfere with the rabbi's performance of his religious duties. In fact, when he found Jews asleep in their barracks on Yom Kippur, he was angry with them for not attending prayers.[41]

There was always electricity in the air before Jewish holidays, whose dates the observant prisoners kept careful track of. For Rosh Hashanah, Rabbi Finkler's followers even managed to get hold of a shofar. The rabbi led the prayers in his barracks which overflowed with worshippers. One of those present, Rabbi Abraham Altman, writes that "for me and for many who took part, it was like the giving of the Torah on Mount Sinai.... Such heartfelt prayers could only have been offered there. That was the year in which all the members of our family were killed, and we felt as if they were there with us." [42] Many of the prisoners fasted on Yom Kippur, regarding it as a day of mourning for their families.

As Passover neared, there was again a heightened atmosphere in the camp. This led Jeszajahu Rechter to organize a Seder for the inmates in his barracks on Passover eve, 1944. With everyone doing his part, they managed to obtain flour, beets and potatoes. On the Seder night, they covered the windows with blankets and posted two lookouts outside the barracks. "We baked matzos on the stove in the barracks ... and used coffee for wine, pouring it into tins. Potatoes and beets served in place of all the holiday dishes ... Thirty prisoners were seated around the table ... There was utter silence and then my son got up and began to sing "How is this night different from all other nights?"... We never heard the rest. After those words, everyone burst out crying. That was the Haggadah we Jews recited at that Seder in the camp."

Spring 1944 brought a new era and new songs to the camp. Several young talents were discovered among the "Majdanek girls" who got the idea of organizing an entertainment troupe. Performances were held in the barracks with every now and then a Sunday show held on the "stage" near the camp fence. The program was in both Yiddish and Polish, and

---

[41] Jeszajahu Rechter, Testimony, YV, 0-3/3530; see n. 32, ib. p. 385.

[42] J. Granatstein, Hod v'gvura, op. cit., pp. 97–100.

included songs, improvisations and recitations. Maryla Tyrmand and her friends performed the popular music sung in Warsaw cafes in the 1930s and verses by Julian Tuwim.[43] Testimonies rarely mention these shows, although they do speak of Chaim Albert "the singer," who, together with his girlfriend Hana, was very popular with the officials. They also appeared in the barracks of the "simple prisoners," singing familiar Yiddish songs which won them numerous fans. Even the camp barber, Melech Sobol, revealed himself to be an amateur actor, organizing "plays" and singing for the *Werkschutz* with the approval of Kuehnemann himself.[44]

Another artistic product worthy of attention were the "couplets," – short verses in Polish or Yiddish composed *ad hoc* to familiar melodies. Although lacking in literary quality and often somewhat vulgar, they fulfilled the important function of a "daily press" in the camp, "covering" the latest news, criticizing the internal administration, conveying information on perilous foremen, highlighting various social phenomena, and even providing a "gossip column." Because of their popularity, they became a means of collective protest in two ways. First, they constituted the only context in which the prisoners enjoyed freedom of expression, although they naturally took care not to provoke the authorities openly. Secondly, they provided a social pressure valve through which internal tension among groups of prisoners and hostility between the prisoner population and the Jewish officials could be released and thus attenuated.

Madzia Tyras-Ofir recalls how Heidi Reisler succeeded in "covering" all of the daily news in her verses, whether a rhyme on an unmatched pair of boots she was allotted or an "Anthem to the Lice" who bothered her sleep at night. Each day when they returned from work, the girls were greeted with a new verse which inevitably generated waves of laughter. In each plant, anonymous lyrics passed from one prisoner to the next, immortalizing the various overseers. Thus, for example, the girls mouthed the following lines on Balewski, notorious for beating prisoners:[45]

"Mr. Balewski has a whip he hefts –
striking out to right and left – ay, ay, ay!

---

[43] H. Greipner, A. Lewkowicz, op. cit.

[44] Hana Albert, Testimony, YV, 0-33/1832; B. Zweig, op. cit.

[45] Bronia Ofir, Testimony, YV, 0-33/1799.

The souls already tormented so –
there receive another blow – ay, ay, ay!"

Sharp-tongued criticism of the internal administration and "camp elder" was ced in the following "couplet": [46]

Albert to nasz ojciec,
Albert to nasz tata,
Albert nam umila nasze młode lata.
Daje nam Gnata i Tepermana
I kompania jest dobrana...

Bo Albert pragnie,
By Żyd wyglądał ładnie,
By uspokoił nerwy,
Nim pójdzie na konserwy...

(Albert is like a father, like our dad,
A pleasant youth for us is his only desire:
Gnat and Teperman he gave us
A bunch for everyone to admire.

For Albert wants a Jew to be a handsome man,
To calm his nerves, before he becomes
Another tin can.)

(Translated from the Polish)

The lyric reveals that those prisoners who understood the workings of internal politics were well-aware that the coalition between "good" Albirt and "bad" Teperman made it easier for both to wield their authority in the camp.

Neither did social criticism spare the "pallet lovers" who had by now become a routine part of camp life. The author of the following verse aimed his or her barbs at the girls who "went too far": [47]

Za zupę, za zupę
I za kawałek chleba,
Dają panienki d...
Czy trzeba, czy nie trzeba...

---

[46] E. Ajzenman, op. cit.

[47] R. Taubenblatt-Fradkin, op. cit.

For soup, for soup
For a piece of bread
Girls will spread their...
Just between you and me,
They'll do it even
When there's no need.

(Translated from the Polish)

In sum, any depiction of the social and cultural life in Werk A must relate more to what was lacking than to what was present. The meagerness of cultural activity seems to have stemmed from the attitude of the administrators who came from a relatively impoverished cultural background. Thus they enjoyed what was offered, but did little to encourage any further initiatives. The spiritual world of the Radomites, expressed in prayer and Yiddish music, prevailed over the two other sectors of the prisoner population as well. There do not seem to have been any independent works of quality produced by the prisoners from Majdanek or Płaszów, so that it would appear that "the muses were silent in the marketplace."

* * *

In the Summer of 1944, the cries of the hawkers in the camp marketplace were joined by the roar of the cannons on the Russian front now drawing near. In the plant there was a sense that it was time "to pull up stakes", and the jittery German masters started hitting out at everyone. The Jewish prisoners noted the sudden disappearance of certain Poles, while others walked around with mysterious grins on their faces. Everywhere people were poised for something that would finally have to happen. Rumors ran wild throughout the camp: the Russians had already reached Radom or Kielce; they're going to blow up the whole plant with us in it; we're being sent to Auschwitz; they're going to kill us on the spot.

In no time at all, the camp lost its calm appearance of a daily routine occupied only by the business at hand. The doors of the administration offices were constantly swinging open as any friends of the "men in high places" came with their questions, trying to garner any crumb of information as to the fate of the camp. But even Teperman and Albirt knew little. Up to the last moment, the Germans did not reveal their plans to them. Did the Jewish administrators try to organize a last minute escape? Available sources make no mention of such an intention. What is certain is that when the prisoners saw that their leaders were not getting out despite their connections and money, they concluded that any escape they themselves attempted could not possibly succeed.

On Tisha B'Av the bomb fell: the camp was being evacuated! The prisoners were thrown into panic. Men and women tore around the barracks in a frenzy, gathering up their meager belongings, their worldly possessions. The entire camp was thrown into confusion. No one trusted the Germans. At the camp gates, the first groups returning from work were already being stopped. Here and there a victim was yanked out of line, the others were raced to the assembly yard. The *Werkschutz* were out in force and the day of judgement began – the "great selection." Kuehnemann and his aides ran between the rows of prisoners pulling out anyone who appeared exhausted, pale, dirty – some 140 people. A group of *Werkschutz* officers headed for the hospital where they turned out around 60 patients along with the doctors. Thus Dr Roman Glasner and Dr Grinberg, who refused to leave her ailing mother, were marched to their death.[48] The unfortunate ones were quickly herded into trucks waiting in the road. The curses and screams of the doomed rose heavenward as the trucks moved off toward the "firing range" in Werk C. The trenches had already been dug.

Within one week, practically all the Jewish prisoners had been evacuated in stages. Some 4,000 prisoners were taken by truck or train to one of three destinations: Buchenwald, Częstochowa, or Sulejów. Frightened, hungry and crowded together, they again found themselves on their way to the unknown. Behind them, the barracks and pallets, infirmary and kitchen were left deserted. That had been their home, the camp at Werk A.

---

[48] "Likwidacja obozu w Skarżysku-Kamiennej i przyjazd do Buchenwaldu", Maximilian (Menasze) Hollender, YV, 0-16/787.

Chapter 8

The History of Werk B

Werk B was located about half a kilometer from the southern border of Werk A, to which it was attached administratively and economically. In late 1941, the first groups of Jews were brought here from the Skarżysko ghetto, and every evening were returned to their homes. In the Summer of 1942, work on the camp began, and two large groups arrived, one from the town of Włoszczowa and the other from Szydłowiec. By July, internal reports of Hasag's "Labor Acquisition Department" already bore the names of Jews "dismissed" from Werk B.[1]

Close contact with the Skarżysko ghetto was still maintained. Every Friday, a cart arrived in the camp with parcels and pots filled with food sent by worried parents to their children in the camp. The pots were later returned to the ghetto. The optimists were convinced this arrangement would be allowed to go on indefinitely, but, as one of the young girls tells it: "On the eve of Shemini Atzeret someone came from the town and told us that deportations had begun.... That was a terrible night of fear and dread.... The next day the cart came with the pots as usual, but this time the pots were empty."[2]

Several of the ghetto families, among them the Friedmann's,

---

[1] Mitteilung, 21.7.1942, Skar.-Kamienna, YV, 0-6/37-3.
[2] Sala Kuperman, Testimony, YV, 0-33/1842.

Warschauer's and others, managed to enter the camp before the final deportation. Others tried to save their children by finding them work at the plant. One of those for whom an "arrangement" was found in Werk B was Rywka Lewin, who worked on the Hasag farm as a shepherdess. She relates:

> I was 13, spoiled, and very attached to my mother. The idea was very hard for me to accept, but my mother, who believed this was the only way for me to stay alive, prevailed on me to agree. One day my mother left the ghetto to come and say good-bye to me. She brought me jewelry which I could exchange for food if I was really in need. 'Be strong,' she said, 'this is our fate. We're dividing up our inheritance: you and your sister will survive while your father and I and your youngest sister have to go.' This parting was so painful that I stood there, frozen in place... I couldn't cry or look back. For hours I stared at the sky and suddenly it grew dark and large drops began to fall. It was the sky who cried for my bitter fate." [3]

In the "Dance Halls" of Werk B

On October 15, 1942, Werk B held 774 inmates constituting 17.3% of the total Skarżysko prisoner population.[4] Transports continued to arrive regularly, bringing people from places like Stopnica, Staszów, Końskie and Radomsko. The fearful winter of 1943 claimed fewer victims here than in the other camps: by January 1, 1943 "only" 11.4% of the prisoners had died. As for escape attempts, up to the end of December 1942, 12 Jews had escaped, with no attempts in January. The roll-call in October 1942, in which four prisoners caught trying to escape, including 13-year-old Henryk Zukerman, were publicly executed, was still fresh in the inmates' minds.[5]

The most compelling reason for the small number of escape attempts, however, was disagreement among the prisoners as to the nature of Werk B. Some held that it was the worst camp, even worse than the infamous Werk C, while others insisted that "their" camp had advantages even over Werk A. The primary reason for these diametrically opposed views was

---

[3] Rywka Lewin-Abramowicz, Testimony, YV, 0-33/1847.

[4] Staerkemeldung, Skar.-Kam., 15.10.1942, YV, 0-6/37-3.

[5] Fride Zonszajn, Pinkas Chmielnik, pp. 843–848.

the huge difference between the working conditions of those assigned to the industrial sector and those employed in food production in Werk B.

The industrial sector consisted of two main plants. The larger one, to which the great majority of prisoners was assigned, produced ammunition for anti-aircraft guns and was known as the "2 cm Department" (*2 cm Abteilung*). The workers toiled on two 12-hour shifts. The shells and casings passed from one section to another, undergoing the various stages of mechanical processing. The press section, where hot oil splattered everywhere, scorching the prisoners' faces and clothes, had a particularly bad reputation. Both men and women worked in the "500 section" *(Pięćsetki)* which got its name from the daily quota of 500 shells, and women were employed in the quality control sections. The smaller plant produced blanks *(Platzpatronen)* for the training of Wehrmacht soldiers, and this became a specialty of Werk B.

The prisoners took a dim view of the entire industrial sector, both because of the backbreaking labor required and because of the German managers. The general manager was Walter Glaue, aged around 40, whose name appears infrequently in testimony. In contrast, a great deal of attention is paid to the "three big shots" of Werk B: Wilhelm Leidig, manager of the "2 cm Department", Georg Hering, in charge of the casings for the blanks, and Richard Pawlowski, already familiar to us from Werk A.

New workers were absorbed into Leidig's domain in a swift and convincing manner. He would show each of them a shell and ask "Do you know what this is?" If the prisoner did not supply the correct answer immediately, he was beaten savagely on the spot. Leidig instituted a "law" whereby any prisoner not fulfilling his daily quota received thrashings in a number equal to the number of missing shells. He meted out this punishment in a room adjacent to the department, after tying his victim's feet and head to a chair. Even women were not exempt.[6] To his credit, it must be said that he demanded good quality soup for his workers and supervised its fair distribution.[7]

Leidig was, in fact, a boss who ruled by means of his rod, from which he was never parted. He was known as a sadist who was unjustifiably

---

[6] Mordchai Goldwasser, Testimony, YV, M-1/E/1349/1295.

[7] Jehuda Wittenberg, Testimony, YV, 0-33/2805.

cruel. He was aided by his mistress, the Polish woman Janina Półtorak, who, arrayed in fine clothes, would appear unannounced in the women's sections and rain harsh blows down on them. This atmosphere of terror was carried on down to the Polish overseers as well, including the infamous Wojciechowski and Suligowski, both from Skarżysko. Their colleague Roter, constantly declaring that "all Jews are Communists," gladly lent a hand in the collective punishments.[8]

It is hard to judge who looms larger in the prisoners' testimonies, Leidig or Georg Hering. The Jews who had been abducted from the ghetto for work in Werk B even then spoke of the "doctor" whose specialty was blows to the ears and nose. Mordchai Goldwasser, one of the most veteran prisoners in the camp, states that Hering had six crippled youngsters with broken limbs whom he regularly marched through the plant to demonstrate to the Jews what they could expect if their work was not up to scratch.

As a believer in collective terror, Hering was credited as the founder of Werk B's famous Dance Hall *(Tanzsaal)*, situated in Hall no. 163 and known by the prisoners as the Music Hall *(Musiksaal)*. It held a collection of instruments of torture: wooden boards, rubber stanchions, whips, etc. The offender would be forced to lie half naked on a bench where he was beaten by several foremen at once. He was forbidden to cry out or he would be beaten on the head. If the prisoner fainted, a bucket of water was thrown over him and the beating continued. Meir Guza, who survived such an experience in the Dance Hall, relates that the Pawlowski's were also among Hering's cohorts.[9] At least one voice, however, is raised in Richard Pawlowski's defense. On one occasion, Genia Briks, who was assigned to his section, was ordered to report to the *Musiksaal* for not fulfilling her quota. When she stood before Pawlowski, trembling in fear, he commanded her to tell (!) the others that she had received 5 lashings, although he never laid a hand on her.[10]

Amongst those who graduated from Hering's "penal academy" was Kurt Moerschner. At the Leipzig trials it was revealed that he had never been a member of the Nazi party.[11] Moerschner was in charge of the

---

[8] Testimonies, YV: Rut Deutscher, 0-3/3287; Genia Gola, 0-33/1856.

[9] Testimonies, YV: Meir Guza, M-1/E/2433/2506; Hana Żychlińska, M-21/1-16, p. 8.

[10] Zahawa Briks-Kompiański, Testimony, YV, 0-33/1849.

[11] Anklageschrift, p. 14, 38; Urteil, p. 10.

quality control section for the blanks, managing a mixed staff of 160. To his credit, he did not victimize his workers and was even considered a decent person. When the girls in his section surprised him for Christmas with a mouse tied to the lamp in his office, he joined in the joke with the others.[12]

A notice was sometimes placed on the door of the *Musiksaal* announcing the "program": thrashing, whipping, or some other sort of torture. The victims who lost consciousness were carried out to the camp on stretchers by their fellow inmates, and there displayed in a general assembly. A sign pinned to their chests read: "I look like this because I did not obey the boss." Chil Bałanowski and Baruch Gorlicki, an official of Poalei Zion from Chmielnik, both died from this "treatment". Other victims included Leib Ogniewicz and several women.[13] Werk B's inquisition chambers were even mentioned in the Polish and Jewish post-war press as a symbol of the tortures undergone by the Skarżysko prisoners.[14]

Special procedures for those condemned to death were also devised here. Their numbers were recorded at a "selection" and two days later the list was handed over to the Jewish police together with orders to remove them from their barracks and deliver them to the *Werkschutz*. Ester Krueger, then 13, relates that the prisoners often refused to go with the policemen, resisting forcefully.[15] Tragic scenes, etched forever on the memories of family members and friends, ensued. Neomi Apelzweig pleaded with the policemen to allow her to eat her soup before being taken away. Fride Zonszajn states that sixteen-year-old Bela Perlstein managed to cry out before her death: "Brothers, if you survive, take revenge on the murderers!"

Even youngsters were not exempt from this tragic fate. Wolf Friedman was not saved by his youth or his strong body when he became exhausted from the brutal labor and constant beatings. On July 3, 1943, the *Werkschutz* arrived in the camp with a list of 10 names, including his. Zelig Friedman painfully records his slaughtered brother's

---

[12] S. Kuperman, op. cit.

[13] Towa Kozakowa, Testimony, YV, 0-33/1828; M. Guza, op. cit.

[14] Jerzy Wirgiliusz Krawczyk, Kamienna łez potokiem spłynęła, Folks-Sztyme, Warszawa, Maj 1987.

[15] 'The story of Ester Krueger", YV, 0-36/11, p. 1958.

last words: "If you live, you must never forget and must tell it all! " [16] It is not surprising that during these months Werk B earned the reputation of a cemetery for the Jewish youth of the nearby towns.

The condemned prisoners were executed in the adjacent forest. There was not even a "burial brigade." In most cases, several people were chosen at random to bury the bodies. Ben Zion Rosenberg, recruited for this task, distressingly recalls how he recognized several friends among the victims: "This work devastated me. I couldn't sleep or eat, I had nightmares, and I walked around in a daze." [17] On one occasion the bored Werk-schutz organized a "dance macabre" before the burial. Each of the gravediggers was ordered to grab a body and dance around the pit with it while singing in Yiddish. At the signal, they all flung the bodies into the ground at the same time. In reward, each of the "dancers" received 100 grams of bread.[18]

The industrial sector periodically underwent temporary crises. In early 1943, production was drastically reduced and groups of prisoners sent to Werk A and Werk C. In the Spring, work in Moerschner's section ceased almost entirely. Although a group of prisoners from the Piotrków transport was assigned to the "2 cm Department" in March 1943, within a month 36 men were transferred to the Grenade Department in Werk C.[19] Those who remained preferred to suffer the cruelty of Leidig and his assistant Willi Stein, who earned a name for himself by devising a clever method of raising quotas. More productive workers were promised a slice of bread and coupons for an extra soup ration which were hung above the clock in the hall. As a result, the prisoners sabotaged the machines of the most industrious among them for fear that the quota for the entire department would be raised.[20]

It was, however, only in Werk B that educated girls were also given clerical jobs. Raca Jedwab, Lunia and Dora Rosenzweig are mentioned as the secretaries of German managers.[21] Although the prisoners in the repair shop suffered the ruthless reign of Leon Stanko, Rut Deutscher was

---

[16] Zelig Fridman, Pinkas Chmielnik, p. 745.

[17] Ben Zion Rosenberg, Szydlowcer Book, op. cit., p. 455.

[18] M. Goldwasser, op. cit.

[19] Pesej Rotenberg, Sitzungen, ib. p. 85a.

[20] Irena Bronner, Testimonies, YV: 0-33/1656, p. 28; 0-16/4601.

[21] Lunia Rosenzweig-Lipszyc, Testimony, YV, 0-33/1844; R. Deutscher, op. cit.

fortunate enough to be chosen for a clerical position. But this time the Poles would not agree to the promoting of a Jew, and Deutscher was soon returned to the shop floor.

In the Camp of the Unknown Commander

The attempt to discover the names of the German commanders of Werk B unearthed a strange phenomenon in the testimonies – the nearly total absence of names. Indeed, researchers have widely adopted the view that "it is now an impossible task to determine with any certainty which German in which period filled the post of commander of each of the three camps." [22] Nevertheless, while Ipfling's name is mentioned by the large majority of prisoners from Werk A, only extensive digging enables us to state that the camp commander of Werk B for two years was Leonard Haas.

Of all the German commanders known to us, Haas was the most mysterious. Like two-faced Janus, he appeared to be a typically cruel SS officer, while underneath he was sensitive to the suffering of others. In the role of the former, he issued orders, conducted "selections", and condemned the debilitated to death. He is described as the latter by Lunia Rosenzweig-Lipszyc, in whose opinion Haas sought a haven from conscription and was, in fact, repulsed by the Nazi system. He once said that if his comrades in the SS heard him speaking amicably with Jews, as he did when there were no witnesses about, he would have been sent to a concentration camp long before.

Haas saved Lunia's sister during the deportations from the Skarżysko ghetto, and according to Genia Gola, at her request he erased the names of her girlfriends who had been marked for death at a "selection." In no testimony is Haas's name mentioned in connection with any acts of brutality or murder. It would appear that, to compensate, Haas surrounded himself with a band of corrupt aides only interested in obtaining for themselves both money and women. One of the most successful in this endeavor was August Badura who regularly invited girls to "work" in his office and was known to be a rapist. [23] For a while, Kurt Schumann was

---

[22] Wyrok Sądu Wojewódzkiego w Kielcach w sprawie J. Adryanowicza, 12.3.1973, AGKBZH, SWK, sygn. 244, p. 105.

[23] August Badura, Werkschutz, YV, JM/3700, p. 15; L. Lipszyc, op. cit.

assigned to the camp. He was the only one brought to trial after the war for the murder of Jews, among them the Jewish policeman Chęciński and his wife.[24] In the eyes of the prisoners, however, the man actually in charge was Gustav Schmidtke, a tough, cruel character who amassed a fortune for himself by stealing from the Jews.[25]

Some 30 Ukrainian *Werkschutz* were attached to the camp commandant. The small size of the camp enabled them to keep watch over every corner. They knew every beautiful girl and every wealthy man. There were, however, also several humane men among them, such as Kokoć and "Jankale", who helped the prisoners. Irena Bronner, who worked alongside them and heard their songs, relates: "When I looked at them and heard them singing 'Dumka' with such longing, it was hard for me to believe that these cheerful lads were the same ones who carried out the terrible executions in the forest."

The Jewish administration was headed by the camp elder Jacob Milgram from Skarżysko, his second-in-command Zygmunt Nirenberg from Końskie, and Jermelow, known as "Jeremia", the commander of the Jewish police from Radom. They were assisted by Renia Baumgarten, the head of the *sanitarka* (infirmary). The Radomites' attitude to the Jewish administration in this camp differed somewhat from that in Werk A. Werk B held many noted families from Skarżysko and the neighboring towns and they all knew each other. Thus, there is a clear polarization in the testimonies: either they make no mention of anything incriminating or they speak of such things in great detail.

A typical example of this uneven treatment is the case of Milgram who married the daughter of a prominent Skarżysko family in the camp. In consequence, his name does not appear in the testimony of any family members. Others, however, are sharply critical of him, stating, for instance, that "this capo, who always carried a stick in his hand, behaved like a supreme ruler, persecuting the prisoners and treating them like slaves and he took every opportunity to profit from them, particularly by extortion." One of the girls once asked a friend to hide an expensive watch during a search in exchange for a percentage of its value, and then did not honor her part of the bargain. When the cheated girl complained to

---

[24] Akta w sprawie Schumanna Kurta, YV, JM/3991, sygn. 131; Lejbusz Czaryski, Testimony, ibid.

[25] Gustaw Schmidtke, Volksdeutschen, YV, IM/3700, p. 16.

Milgram, he demanded the watch for himself, threatening to turn the whole matter over to the Werkschutz if he did not get it.[26] In fairness, it must be said that there were also instances in which he helped those condemned to death in a "selection" to escape their fate.[27]

Milgram was apparently transferred to Werk A, and later Jermelow, who had the worst reputation of all, was removed from his post. In contrast, Rena Baumgarten is mentioned approvingly by many former prisoners. She was transferred to Werk C under unclear circumstances. These changes indicate that the Jewish administration in Werk B was not as stable as it was in Werk A.

In Autumn 1943, Zygmunt Nirenberg became the camp elder and seems to have been the police commander as well. The picture painted of him is more favorable despite the beatings and his lust for money.

Among the 12–16 members of the Jewish police, the most celebrated, and not for his kindness, was Reismann, in charge of supplies. As for the others, "there were several bad and less bad Jewish policemen, but relative to the times, they were fairly humane." [28] They had very limited sources of income here since most of the transports arrived after being searched in Werk A. There was nothing to take from the camp indigents, and the wealthy preferred to bribe the higher authorities rather than the lowly functionaries. There was a much worse opinion of the *commandenten* in the plant, among them Szapszewski, who was brought to trial after the war.[29] Other overseers are described in better or worse terms. Hering chose the most "suitable": Abraham Berliński and Chaim Zilberberg left bitter memories in the minds of the prisoners. Of the latter it is said that "he wore boots like Hering and delivered beatings like him too." [30]

In terms of living conditions, there was no difference between Werk B and the other two camps. The prisoners were given the same soup and their barracks were rife with the same fleas. The more privileged among them set up "family rooms" in the corners of the barracks and the members of the Jewish administration settled into the local "White

---

[26] Lea Lęczycki, Testimony, YV, 0-33/1846.

[27] M. Guza, op. cit.

[28] Rafael Einav, Testimony, YV. 0-33/1805.

[29] Jerachmiel Barkai, Testimony, YV, 0-33/1850.

[30] R. Abramowicz, op. cit.; Erita Troppa, YV, 0-16/48; Regina Kalman, YV, M-1/E/2370/2445.

house." Unique to Werk B, however, was the *Steinhaus*, formerly an office building which the Germans turned into family rooms, selling the right to live in them for large sums of money or handing them over to prisoners under their protection. The building was outside the camp and boasted running water and bathrooms. It is not surprising that the *"hoi polloi"* looked with envy on the "aristocrats" and gave this residence the name of *Lordenhaus*.[31]

Another unique phenomenon in Werk B was the hot water in the barracks attached to the kitchen to which prisoners were taken in groups escorted by a policeman. There is no doubt that it was thanks to this facility that the morbidity rate in the camp was relatively low. Those who fell ill were taken to the "hospital" in Werk A. Others were treated at the local infirmary. Until the arrival of the transport from Majdanek, there was no doctor here. The first was Dr Rosenblatt from Warsaw who is described as "a marvelous person, a friend of Korczak, who barely survived himself yet helped the others." [32]

Most characteristic of Werk B was the lack of an "underground economy" of the type found in Werk A. There was little opportunity for pilfering from the plant, and the extent of barter with the few Poles was very limited. The craftsmen worked only for the Germans and *prominente*. This state of affairs raises speculation as to the circumstances which enabled the inmates to survive and which won Werk B the reputation of being the "privileged camp".

Between the Lifegiving Flakes and the "Furrows of Passion"

Alongside the infamous industrial sector of Werk B was a second economic branch unique to this camp. It centered around the food plant comprising a mill and kitchen on the camp grounds and a nearby farm. If the "economic life" of Werk A might be described as a system of parallel lines linking each of the outside plants to a group of prisoners in the camp, in Werk B the system was one of concentric circles spreading out from a central point, the food plant. Some 120 Jews and 80 Poles were employed

---

[31] Rina Potasz, Testimony, 0-33/1848.

[32] Josef Liebermann, Testimony, YV, 0-3/1391.

here and it was run by the Hasag Department of Supplies and Economics (BEWI) whose local office was inside Werk B itself.

The man in charge of the entire food plant was Jan Laskowski, who had worked in the munitions factory for many years and was well-known to the Jews of Skarżysko. When Hasag arrived, Laskowski suddenly became Volksdeutsch.[33] Without exception, all Jewish testimony lauds him as a friend and savior. Ben Zion Rosenberg writes: "In this hell he was an angel, and saved my life more than once." Laskowski forbade the beating of Jews, and all his Polish workers were well-aware of this prohibition.

The most important part of the food plant was the potato mill. Transport workers carted the potatoes from the train to the storerooms and they then underwent the various stages of processing: washing in water troughs, cooking in huge vats, mashing by presses, drying, flaking, and automatic packing. Not only were the finished flakes sent to all the labor camps in the Radom district, but they even found their way into the Wehrmacht soldiers' soup on the Eastern front. Some 50 Jews were assigned to the mill. The more privileged among them were clerical workers and a group from Chmielnik from which the manager chose one girl as his housekeeper.[34] Jews from Skarżysko worked in the packing department. According to Rosenberg, one of them, Weizhendler, was made "commandant" of the transport workers whom he abused and beat until they managed to get rid of him.

In all stages of processing, the prisoners had their hands on potatoes, some of which they naturally smuggled into the camp. Not surprisingly, the munitions workers yearned to be transferred to Laskowski's food plant. Lea Lęczycki, who could take no more of the beatings in Leidig's department, bribed her Polish overseer with a bottle of vodka and he advised her to short circuit her control instruments. Fortunately for her, after being slapped around a bit, she was sent to the mill for "incompetence."

The farm was used to supplement the austere diet of the Germans in the plant. Fruits and vegetables were grown, and cows, sheep, chickens, etc. raised. It was run by Wilhelm Ronnenberger and his wife, of whom it was whispered that they despised the Nazi regime. Indeed, their

---

[33] Jan Laskowski, Hasag-Volksdeutschen, Stand Dezember 1942, YV, JM/3700, p. 16.

[34] Giza Leinkram-Szmulewicz, Testimony, YV, 0-33/1841; F. Zonszajn, op. cit.

treatment of the prisoners seems to bear out these rumors. The farm was the most sought-after work assignment. It employed some 20 Jews under Golda Scharfherz. In Lunia Lipszyc's opinion, there was a gentlemen's agreement between Laskowski and the farm manager to use the farm as a haven for the young girls. Frania Pomeranzblum, for example, was in charge of the geese.[35] With the arrival of the transport from Płaszów, Marylka Monderer was sent to the farm as a shepherdess who daily led the sheep to the no-man's-land between the camp's two fences.

Another familiar figure on the farm was the Jewish wagon driver Ostrowiecki who brought vegetables to the German hotels in the vicinity. He feared no one and was regarded as a hero by the Jewish prisoners. He was very popular and always willing to help. When one of Marylka's sheep drowned in the pond, the shepherdess was terrified of the punishment she could expect. Without a moment's hesitation, Ostrowiecki pulled the sheep out of the water and informed the manager that it was all his fault![36]

Under Ronnenberger's watchful eye, the Polish overseers did not dare abuse the prisoners. It was harder to see everything that was going on in the vegetable garden which was at some distance from the farm. Here the overseer was the Pole Dziewięcki, a kind and decent man. The garden manager, Gałczyński, however, did his best to turn the vegetable plots into "furrows of passion." From time to time, particularly in the winter when the weather was freezing, he would select an attractive girl to "work with him" in the greenhouse. Even those who were disgusted by the insistent manager's advances were afraid to refuse. These adventures lost their flavor when one of the girls showed signs of pregnancy, as dangerous here as it was in Werk A.

The affair of the "furrows of passion" came to a head when Gałczyński began to go after Gizela, whose husband was also in the camp. At first, Dziewięcki came to her aid, always entering the greenhouse at the critical moment, but when things began to get out of hand, Gizela complained to her husband. He made sure the Germans heard of Gałczyński's behavior, and the latter was removed from his post.[37] In point of fact, romance flourished more in the plant. Everyone knew of the torrid love affair

---

[35] Frania Pomeranzblum, Testimony, YV, M-1/E/2230/2128; L. Lipszyc, op. cit.

[36] Maryla Liebermann, Testimony, YV, 0-3/1268.

[37] G. Szmulewicz, op. cit.

between the manager Walter Glaue and a Jewish girl. Stanko, too, periodically invited a pretty worker to a "tête á tête" in his office. The name of the Volksdeutsch Cholewa appears in the War Criminal Register for acts of brutality to male prisoners, but this did not keep him from chasing after the women.[38]

The kitchen was ruled by Laskowska's young daughter-in-law, known as a vicious and greedy woman. Here the food for the Jews and the Poles was cooked in separate vats. Sala Friedmann, famed for her beauty, was in charge of the Jewish kitchen. She paid a tidy sum for the position and held onto it stubbornly. Because assignment to the kitchen could only be achieved through bribery, there was a constant turnover. Mrs Warschauer from Skarżysko, Fischlewiczowa from Radomsko, and Fela Koza worked here, amongst others.[39] There were separate mess halls for the Germans and Ukrainians in which Jewish girls, also considered the more privileged, served the food.

The many inmates employed in the food plant could not directly affect the diet of the hundreds of other prisoners.

Nevertheless, potato flakes and extra bread and soup rations smuggled into the camp saved the others from total starvation. A bit of soup cooked by a farm worker would also reach the lips of her pallet-mate who worked for Leidig. The leftover bread and soup gathered up by the waitresses in the Ukrainian mess hall found their way to the girls with whom they shared their barracks. Women who worked as maids for the Germans helped family members assigned to the industrial plants. Thus the food that was plentiful in the "first circle" also saved the lives of the impoverished Radomites.

In the Summer of 1943, some 150 people from the Majdanek transports arrived in Werk B. They were absorbed in much the same way as in Werk A. Virtually all the men were sent to Leidig's department and it showed in their condition. As one of the daughters of the camp *prominente* describes: "They looked terrible, dressed in rags. We called them "kaelniks" like in the other camps. A few of the girls were lucky enough to be sent to work for Laskowski.... The other managers chose the prettiest ones. But here

---

[38] Chowelo (Cholewa), War Criminal Register, YV, m-9/12-8; Nuta Wolfowicz, Sitzungen, pp. 45a–46a,b.

[39] Wolf Monderer, Testimony, YV, 0-3/1614; R. Abramowicz, op. cit.

people didn't starve to death, because from time to time they'd get thrown a few potatoes or flakes." [40]

The Pseudo Revolution of the Plaszowites

In the Autumn of 1943, life was following its normal routine and there were no signs of a new era in the making. The Jews arriving from Płaszów in November 1943 heard that Werk B was the best of the camps. Some two hundred of them were eventually sent here.

This time, the *Werkschutz* and Germans carried out a thorough search. The camp elder, Nirenberg, stood by, closely watching what was going on. What would they find on whom? On the basis of their outward appearance – fine clothes and packages – the newcomers had money. What did they find on one? Dental instruments – interesting! Straw mattresses, old blankets, a spoon and tin were handed out, and the new prisoners were taken to the barracks where they were greeted by swarms of fleas. Everyone fled - this was supposed to be the "best" camp?

The initial shock was devastating: "The camp Jews made a particularly depressing impression on us.... They plodded about in wooden clogs, the soup tins hanging from their belts clanging somberly with each step. They spoke among themselves in a strange jargon, a mixture of Yiddish, Polish peasant dialect and camp slang. When the soup was brought, they fought viciously for a place near the vat.... The Germans often photographed these scenes." [41] A few of the veteran prisoners dared to come a little closer, looking for someone they knew, asking for news of the outside world, wanting to know where Jews were still living. They did not ask what the newcomers had to sell, for they had nothing to pay with.

The large majority of the new prisoners were inevitably sent to the "2 cm Department" where they were received with the shocking news that the vile Leidig had been murdered! Rumor had it that he had been killed by the Polish partisans on his way to town. Willi Stein assembled the plant workers and told them that Leidig had fallen ill and died. "We honored his memory with several minutes of silence, and did so with great pleasure of course." [42] The fact is that from that time Stein ceased to beat

---

[40] R. Potasz, op. cit.

[41] I. Bronner, YV, 0-33/1656, op. cit., p. 26.

[42] R. Einav, G. Gola, op. cit.

the prisoners. Apparently he preferred to make surprise inspections of the women's barracks where he enjoyed the sight of the half-naked women. He was especially on the lookout for embracing couples and would chase the terrified men back to their barracks.

The Plaszowites tried more than their predecessors to develop relationships with the Poles. Among those employed at that time in the "2 cm Department", the names of three are mentioned. They serve to exemplify the range of treatment towards the Jews. Tomaszewski was a devout anti-Semite who, to his great misfortune, fell in love with one of the new prisoners and so did not display his hatred of the Jews. Jastrzębski was offensive to the workers, while the overseer Loza was exceptional for his fair treatment. According to Irena Bronner, he was apleasant, cultured man "who often shared his breakfast with one of us."

There were very few escape attempts during this period, and most of those who tried were caught on the spot and executed.[43] No evidence of Polish aid in these attempts has been found. As to cooperation between the partisans and the prisoners, testimony offers more rumor than fact. One example is a story of partisans disguised as Wehrmacht soldiers who stole crates of ammunition from the warehouse. As they were leaving, the *Werkschutz* spotted two prisoners hiding among the crates. As shots were fired from both sides, the partisans managed to flee. There were also rumors of stolen ammunition transferred to the partisans in milk jugs by the prisoner Kanarek.[44]

It is difficult to tell to what extent underground activities were involved in the tragic story of Bela Sperling from Skarżysko, an affair which had a profound effect on the entire camp. Bela, an attractive girl, was transferred to the "2 cm Department" by Glaue. When crates of cracked shells were discovered, she was charged with sabotage and executed. Camp gossip added a romantic element to the story, whereby Glaue had taken revenge on Bela because she refused his advances. "It was a frightful and unforgettable scene. As they led her to her death, Bela's screams pleading for her life could be heard from the forest beyond the camp." It was said that she still showed signs of life when they buried her.[45]

---

[43] Rachel Berger, Testimony, YV, 0-33/1845.

[44] R. Potasz, L. Lęczycki, op. cit.

[45] R. Abramowicz, op. cit.

Not only the Jews were shocked by this incident. Laskowski, who did not like Glaue, sent a report of the affair to SS headquarters in Radom in which he charged Glaue with impeding production and with "*Rassenschande.*" The *Werkschutz* commander Pollmer then took it upon himself to remove Glaue from his post.[46]

Irena Bronner, who for a time was employed in painting shells, relates a unique tale of sabotage. The shells had to be immersed in a vat of red lacquer of fixed consistency. During one inspection, Jastrzębski ordered the girls to change the composition of the lacquer. Several days later, Irena and her workmate were summoned to the control center where they were informed by a furious German officer that all of the shells had been junked. The girls were accused of sabotage and were severely beaten in the Ukrainian guardroom.

That autumn, a new German, Herman Klemm, arrived in the camp as second-in-command,[47] and instituted a "*Neue Ordnung*" (new order). Four of the 17 policemen were dismissed and sent back to the plant.[48] Several of the "cleaning women," who moved freely about the camp in exchange for bribes, suffered the same fate. These two measures, reversing the decisions of the "camp elder", occasion questions as to the nature of the relations between the Jewish administration and the German command.

It will be recalled that in Werk A the administration had a free hand in appointing functionaries and enjoyed the support of Kuehnemann. In Werk B, however, things were different. Haas did not interfere in the running of the camp, and this had a two-fold effect on camp life: his subordinates had a great deal of freedom in this area, and in contrast, the status of the Jewish administration was weakened.

Without the manifest support of the camp commander, the Jewish functionaries each had to fight their own battle to preserve their status and thus had to alter their policies to suit the changing circumstances. As a result, with the arrival of the Plaszowites, Zygmunt Nirenberg was faced with a decision. Should he apply a system of extortion and punishment or should he recruit them as allies to strengthen his position?

---

[46] R. Potasz, op. cit.

[47] Benjamin Orenstein, Churban Czenstochow, (Central Farwaltung fun der Czenstochower landsmanszaft in der amerikaner Zone in Dajczland, 1948), pp. 261, 269, 626, cf. Klemm Hermann, SS-Oberscharfuehrer, YV, M-21/3-55.

[48] Leon Rosenzweig, Erklaerung, 28.6.1949, YV, M-21/3-55.

Krzepicki and his cohorts preferred the first method, and hence the Plaszowites in Werk A learned to sidestep the Jewish administration and manage for themselves. This looked to Nirenberg and his confederates to be a very risky proposition, since they understood that if the Plaszowites began to "make their own arrangements" and negotiate directly with the Germans, the members of the administration might be summarily dismissed and replacements found. In consequence, Nirenberg was forced to adopt a conciliatory policy toward the newcomers out of his awareness that the only advantage the members of the Jewish administration had was their familiarity with the constellation of the camp and that this could be sold in order to ensure their role as middlemen and decisionmakers.

One excellent example of this policy was the deal Nirenberg struck with the dentist he had spotted during the search of the new prisoners. The doctor was allowed to work solely in his profession, his fiancée was assigned to the farm, her father was made a cook and her mother a waitress in the German mess hall. In return for these favors, the diamond smuggled into the camp in a filling in the mother's tooth found its way into Nirenberg's pocket.[49] The two formed a "pact", under whose influence even the policemen refrained from beating the newcomers excessively.

It was obvious to all the prisoners that the arrival of the Plaszowites improved conditions in the camp to a certain degree. One of them was Dr Stanisław Strasser, who became head doctor and at whose initiative supplies for the infirmary and food and drugs for its patients were received from the JUS.[50] Here and there, with the help of Polish middlemen, money and food parcels arrived in the camp. "In unknown ways, a very small bit of help would reach us from time to time. Some said it came from the Jews of America and others that the Jewish underground was responsible.... Several times real butter and sugar was distributed to us.... There is no need to elaborate on what a boon this was to us, not only physically. It was proof for us that someone in the free world knew of our existence and was trying to help."[51]

Supposedly, the small prisoner population, sources of extra food, and tolerable relations with the internal administration should have aided in

---

[49] J. Liebermann, op. cit.

[50] Oświadczenie dr. Stanisława Strassera, YV,0-21/8.

creating a unified prisoner society. Representatives of three different "classes" in the camp relate to this issue. According to a member of the veteran "aristocracy", Werk B was a snobbish camp with wide social distinctions. The upper class, in her view, were the prominent families from Skarżysko who, due to their property and cultural level, stood above not only the "riff raff" from Majdanek, but also the Jews from the small towns in the vicinity. In a rather apologetic tone, she describes the Jewish camp officers, fellow Skarżyskoans, who were compelled to beat the "masses" so as to maintain order. She depicts the low ranking policemen as *"Untermenschen"*, and does not mention the Plaszowites at all.

A representative of the Krakowite "intelligentsia" also claims that no unified prisoner society developed in Werk B. He sees the primary source of the class distinction in the prisoners' work assignments. His remarks also reveal an ambivalent attitude toward the local *prominente*: on the one hand there was a desire to form friendships with them because of the benefits that could be derived, and on the other one wished to keep apart from them because of their different mentality and intellectual level. At the same time, this gentleman notes that the members of the intelligentsia sought to help one another and in time formed a mixed circle of people from various towns.

A representative of the "industrial proletariat" who worked together with Jews from Majdanek and Płaszów claims that "there were no big distinctions because the whole camp wasn't big." [52] In his view, there were examples of self-help among the plant workers.

It would thus seem that there was greater solidarity among the "middle class", which here, too, was led by the women. In their common barracks, the women banded together to fight the fleas, sewed dresses out of rags, and gossiped about the *"kuzyns"*. As for that, around 80% of the camp population were partners in such relationships. The most desirable "cousins" were the tailors and shoemakers, rather than the policemen. These affairs also took a unique form in Werk B, since in many cases it was the women who worked in the food plant who chose "cousins" for themselves from among the young men in the camp.

The "cousin" relationships had some rather unusual repercussions. Marylka Monderer's parents wanted to get their pretty daughter out

---

[51] I. Bronner, see n. 41, ib. pp. 21–30.

[52] R. Einav, op. cit.

of the common barracks where the policemen were always after her and decided to marry her to her fiancé, Josef Liebermann. After clandestine arrangements were made, the wedding took place. The wedding contract was prepared by Rabbi Yitzhak Frenkel in Werk A and obtained through middlemen. Friends of the groom made the ring from a copper shell casing. On the appointed night, the guests, including Zygmunt Nirenberg, gathered in the infirmary. The bride's "gown" was a white blouse and blue skirt and she wore a turban made from a white rag on her head. After the ketuba was read and signed by two witnesses, the groom broke a burned out light bulb in place of a glass and someone even provided a bottle of vodka and wine with which drink the young couple's health.[53]

The couple were allotted a corner in the *Steinhaus*, although in the Summer of 1944 they were evicted from it together with all the other residents, some of whom found "rooms" for themselves in the corners of the barracks. Behind the thin walls they erected, tragedies often unfolded, reflecting the agonizing side of "family life" in the shadow of death. Irena Bronner's testimony contains evidence of one such story: [54]

> In the corner of our barracks ... there was a separate room ... where a widow lived with her daughter Hannale, who was somewhat retarded but goodhearted.... Her mother took very good care of her. Once, when Hannale heard we were hungry, she ran to their room and brought us bread with a piece of boiled meat.... Hannale's mother had a young boyfriend, Itzik, who used to visit her. One night we heard Hannale asking her mother: 'Mommy, where's Daddy?' 'Go to sleep, my child.' her mother would answer, 'He's in heaven, protecting you.' The girls who slept near the dividing wall claimed that Hannale always seemed to ask such questions at the most inappropriate moment.... Naturally, we all laughed.... We often heard Itzik shouting angrily at his girlfriend 'Where did the food disappear to?..' We knew no good would come of this for Hannale.... Her mother started to hide the food she saved from her, and Hannale, who wanted to give us something, would scream and cry.... One morning, shortly before the camp was dismantled, several girls were sleeping in the barracks and Hannale was sleeping in her room.... Suddenly two policemen came in, burst into her room and carried her out by force as she resisted and shouted 'Mommy!'....

---

[53] J. Granatstein, op. cit., p. 94; M. Liebermann, op. cit.

[54] I. Bronner, see n. 41.

Hannale's mother didn't show up at noontime with their food. She
came later, went into her room and came back out screaming 'Where's
Hannale?' We answered her with silence. Later people went in to
comfort her, but Itzik wasn't one of them. Not that day and not the
next. A couple of days later we heard that he was transferred to Werk
A at his own request."

Simulated life went on. In an atmosphere of uncertainty and tension,
people tried to find comfort whatever way they could. The religious
prayed in secret; the youngsters organized cultural evenings. Busiek
Waksman remembered all the popular songs and Pawełek Rosenblatt
recited poetry. The "Majdanek Girls" mounted several stage shows in the
barracks with Cesia singing, Warszawska writing an "oral newspaper,"
and Elza surprising everyone with her poems. Janek Leinkram got the idea
of collecting an "entrance fee" from the audience – a little money, a slice
of bread, some rags – and giving them to the most needy.[55]

Under the influence of the liberal "revolution", several of the youngsters saw to the organization of a public "concert" and a number of
rehearsals were held. The performance was never held, however. It was
already too late.

Sober Reality

Shortly before the camp was dismantled, Róża Friedmann and her boyfriend escaped. They were caught and shot at a roll call of all the
prisoners.[56] This incident marked the beginning of the end.

In late July, 1944, the entire camp was assembled for a last "selection".
The commandant marched between the rows examining the bare feet
of each of the prisoners and deciding his or her fate. Irena Bronner and
a girlfriend of hers were saved at the critical moment by Dr Strasser.
When Haas ordered Lilka Goldberg's mother out of line, – relates Maryla
Lieberman – her daughter threw herself at his feet and pleaded for her
mother's life. Haas relented. Giza Leinkram's mother was not so lucky.
When Giza saw her walking toward the trucks she ignored her husband
who was trying to hold her back and started running after her. Her mother
stopped her with the cry "Get away from here!"

---

[55] G. Gola, M. Liebermann, G. Szmulewicz, op. cit.

[56] R. Abramowicz, op. cit.

The condemned prisoners, some 20 in number, were murdered in the adjacent forest. Evacuation of the camp began the following day. Aside from a group of men sent to Sulejów, all the prisoners were transferred to Częstochowa. The potato mill, the pride and joy of Werk B, went with them, in pieces just like the camp itself....

Chapter 9

Under a Cloud of Picric Acid and TNT

Even without the other two camps, the existence of Werk C would have sufficed to convey the bitter taste of Skarżysko to future generations. In the words of Rabbi Israel Fersztendig, one of the witnesses in the trial of Adolf Eichmann: "I heard the opening statement of the attorney general.... When speaking of the concentration camps he listed the very worst, such as Auschwitz, Majdanek, Treblinka.... But he omitted one which I believe should be included among the cruelest of them all: Skarżysko Kamienna, Werk C. Any account of the Nazi brutalities must include this camp." [1]

"It was a place outside human experience. A site of abandonment and madness." [2] "Whoever passed through Werk C will be haunted for the rest of his life by memories of monstrous days and nights, when men envied the lot of the dog who could walk about freely and had food to eat. Transports arrived one after the other, and disappeared.... Within a short time everyone became slaves, each and every person altered beyond recognition.... And today, decades after those atrocities, those people are reappearing and demanding: Remember! Never forget! ... Ghosts appear

---

[1] Israel Fersztendig, Testimony, YV, 0-33/19-33/E/443.

[2] Mordchai Strigler, Werk "Ce", (Yiddish), (Buenos-Aires: Union Central Israelita Polaca en la Argentina, 1950, vol. 1, p. 232.

and sit themselves at your table to talk about those dreadful days.... Today, from a distance of time, they are even more alive, they live in the memory .... in the two short terms: picric acid and TNT." [3]

The Green Corridor to Hell

First there was the forest.

With the first transports in the Spring of 1942, the large majority of men were assigned to the *Waldkommando*, the "forest commando", where they became loggers, road pavers, and construction workers erecting production halls and barracks. By Autumn 1942, these commandos numbered several hundred men. In addition to their work in the forest, they were recruited to dig trenches in the area of the firing range for the condemned prisoners.

The *Waldkommando's* German commandant was Zimmermann, known by the Jews as *"di grine marynarke"* or *"Szawues"* (Shavuoth) for his green jacket.[4] Every day he would leave behind several victims in the woods, killed by his blows to their heads with a heavy block of wood. They were buried by prisoners from a different group who were rewarded with the money and clothes of the dead. The prisoners from Staszów took the news that one of them, Mączyk, had been beaten to death by *Szawues* as a signal for the first wave of escape attempts from Werk C.

Natanel Erlich writes: "In November 1942, more Jews died from murderous blows than from starvation or the backbreaking work. But danger awaited outside as well. When my friend Mendel and I decided to escape, we planned to reach the "Amler " work camp at Staszów. We leapt over the wire fence and ran.... We arrived at the house of a farmer ... who wanted to turn us over to the gendarmes, and were only saved when I told him that we had been sent by the partisans and if anything happened to us they would burn his house down." [5]

The Jewish youngsters were enthralled by the idea of the partisans, and the *Waldkommando* were convinced they could successfully escape and make contact with these fighting units. During this time, 20 prisoners were

---

[3] I. Friedmann, Bletlech, op. cit., pp. 135, 137.

[4] M. Strigler, In di fabrikn, op. cit., vol. 1, p. 45.

[5] Natanel Erlich, Sefer Staszow, p. 494.

employed on the site of the grounds keeper Lucjan Grzelka, watched over by the Pole Stanisław Ozan and the Jewish capo Leon Kanarek. One of them, Emanuel Kuzimiński, relates that there were already contacts with the partisans in December 1942. Their messenger informed the *Waldko-mmando* that they would be allowed to join their ranks on condition that they first supplied the partisans with ammunition. The prisoners agreed and brought whatever they managed to pilfer to special hiding places in the forest.

This was the backdrop for one of the most dramatic events in the annals of the "forest commandos." In Autumn 1942, when the first Jews were sent to the arduous production departments, the forest became the more desirable work assignment, and those with money bribed their overseers so as not to be included on the lists of workers for the plant. The *Waldkommando* thereby came to be known as a refuge for the wealthy, and accordingly the *Werkschutz* incessantly searched them for money. As a result, on one occasion, the *Werkschutz* officer Iwanejko caught several of the prisoners deep in the woods with stolen ammunition in their pockets. When they realized there was no hope for them, the prisoner Aharon Rygier killed Iwanejko with an axe and fled. (This was on December 10, 1942 according to Ipfling's report.) With the help of the Pole Jan Bielski, Rygier escaped to Germany. There were no consequences to this murder, since the prisoners buried Iwanejko in the forest, and his superiors believed he had deserted.[6]

Another escape attempt ended differently. Two Jews escaping from Werk A were caught by the *Werkschutz* officer Mikolaj Kotula. On the way to the firing range, they jumped Kotula. Although one was shot to death, the other slit Kotula's throat with a knife and fled. In retaliation, the *Werkschutz* murdered several other Jews and all knives were confiscated from Werk A.

At the start of 1943, the "forest commandos" became "construction commandos" *(Baukommando)*. Their ranks steadily thinned out as more and more were sent to the plant. Around this time, *"Szawues"* vanished and was replaced by Stanisław Kotlęga, an ardent *Volksdeutsch*, anti-Semite and sadist. His favorite game was to pour the remains of the soup on the ground so he could watch the starving prisoners crawling about to

---

[6] Emanuel Kuzimiński, Testimony, YV, 0-3/3404, pp. 4–6; cf. Aron Rygier, Staerke-meldung, 11.12.42, YV, 0-6/37-3.

lick up the last drops. His aides were two Polish foremen: Kopernik, an elderly devout Catholic who had never before imagined it was possible to murder Jews indiscriminately. At Skarżysko he became convinced that this was the will of God and abused the prisoners brutally. His colleague Gajda was unconcerned by moral questions. He had come to do business, and had a finger in every pie, even the underground press. In the Autumn of 1943, these three were in charge of overseeing the erection of barracks within the camp (in theory, Poles were forbidden to enter the camp), and became the middlemen for Jews seeking to obtain money from outside.[7]

The importance of the *Baukommando* was reconfirmed in November 1943 when, in the wake of SSuPF Herbert Boettcher's concern over the rising number of escape attempts, the builders began construction of a double fence around the camp and the plant. The Polish foreman Kłosek was very decent to his Jewish workers, unlike the technician Malik who, together with his aides, made sure he had extorted their last cent from them. This was also the basis for the "peaceful co-existence" that developed between the Poles and the Ukrainians, as illustrated by this story related by Jehuda Knobler from Płaszów:

> "During our first month, as we went off to work, we were surrounded by a group of *Werkschutz* men who were plotting something with the foreman Józik. Then Józik came over to us and told us we had to hand over to the *Werkschutz* anything of leather – shoes, boots, and even belts. When my friend Bezalel Guterman heard this, he took out a knife and slashed the boots he was wearing. The *Werkschutz* fell on him and began to beat him. Józik ordered me to hand over my belt, but I refused. I only gave in under the prodding of another prisoner.... who knew Józik well and apparently knew what I could expect if I continued to refuse."[8]

In the Spring of 1944, work began on storehouses on the other side of the firing range where the Germans conducted tests of the ammunition. A "construction commando" there was given the task of carting the "planks" made of double wooden boards. One of the workers suddenly noticed that several of the planks were particularly heavy and discovered

---

[7] M. Strigler, In di fabrikn, vol. 1, pp. 130–136, 140; Peter Sawczak, AGKBZH, SWK, sygn. 214, p. 74.

[8] Jehuda Knobler, Testimony, YV, 0-3/1864.

rifle bullets inside. It became clear that in this manner the Poles were transferring ammunition to the partisans in the vicinity. The Germans accidently came across a suspicious case of ammunition and arrested a Jew who knew nothing about it. The prisoners in the "construction commando" now had a serious dilemma. They could only save the Jew by informing on the guilty Poles. The two groups consulted and it was decided that the secret would be kept and the unfortunate Jew left to face the German wrath. Jehuda Knobler admits that "our primary consideration was the continuation of this anti-German activity and *our commitment to the local Polish underground which could not be jeopardized*" [emphasis mine – F.K]. One would be hard put to find evidence of any desire on the part of the underground to help the prisoners. Nevertheless, Kanarek's men continued to gather information on the munitions trains and to purchase arms with money supplied by the partisans, although Kuzimiński admits they did so out of fear that the partisans would kill them if they refused. In early Summer, 1944, three prisoners from Kanarek's unit escaped, among them Edward Gross, who had obtained a handgun. The three were caught and questioned, and as a consequence ten Jews from the unit were executed. Kanarek and Mosze Gottlieb were among those left alive.[9] At the last minute, Kuzimiński managed to escape and joined the Jews in the Sulejów camp.

Despite the difficulties and dangers of work in the forest, the prisoners preferred to remain in the "construction commandos". The less fortunate were compelled to leave the "green corridor" and enter the hell of Werk C.

The Six Circles of Hell of the Shell Department

Before the war, the industrial complex known as Elaboracja had been afforded special conditions by the Polish authorities. In order to contain the devastating effects of the explosives on the workers' health, shifts were four hours long and the workers were given special food and work clothes. Beds of flowers and greenery were planted around the production halls in the forest. However, when Hasag took over the plant, care of the grounds was neglected and ceased totally when the plants began to absorb

---

[9] Stanisław Ozan, AGKBZH, SWK, sygn. 214, p. 93; cf. R. Bauminger, Przy pikrynie, op. cit., p. 55.

Jewish production workers. The drastic deterioration in work conditions for the Poles and lack of bare necessities for the Jews created a dilemma for Hasag. Who could they place in charge so as to ensure a constant rise in output?

The first candidate, who had already made his appearance in 1940, was Felix Krebs. Despite his youth, he was appointed manager of the Shell Department. He was hoping to be made general manager of the werk when, in May 1941, Dr Artur Rost arrived in Skarżysko with Budin's commission in his pocket. This ugly man, who envied all virile males and was suspected of being homosexual, revealed himself to be a careerist, a businessman and a scrooge. A camp "joke" had it that Rost wept bitterly over every Jew that was shot, because a bullet cost two marks, a lot of money, whereas if you left him to work he would die by himself and you'd come out ahead.[10] Although Rost was an ardent Nazi and an experienced manager with a doctorate in chemistry, his extraordinary achievements in raising production can be attributed to his personal interest. He owned shares in the Skarżysko plants. It was whispered that his assets in valuables and gold teeth (!) totalled 150,000 marks. In Werk C he became master of life and death for his Jewish slaves who, in 1944, numbered 2,400 with another 1,100 Poles, all overseen by only 30 Germans.[11]

Krebs was forced to be satisfied with managing the Shell Department at a salary of 355 marks a month and a safe slot ensuring his exemption from conscription. His department extended over a large number of halls in which three main types of shells were produced:

1. large shells, known by the prisoners as "calves", measuring 15 cm in diameter and weighing 57 kg;
2. medium-sized shells, "nursers", measuring 12 cm in diameter and weighing 38 kg;
3. small shells, "dolls", measuring 10 cm in diameter in weighing 27 kg.

On the average, the work force numbered approximately 500 Jews and 350 Poles with additional transport workers. There were some six German supervisors whose presence was not especially felt, while the actual work

---

[10] Ilona Karmel, An estate of memory, (Boston: Houghton Mifflin, 1969), p. 188.
[11] Anklageschrift, pp. 22–25.

was done by Polish overseers. Special note of their brutal treatment of the Jews was even made at the Leipzig trials, and it was this that turned the department into a living hell.

The first circle of this hell was the rail transport *(Bahntransport)*, directed until 1943 by the German Michael Ernst who was brought to trial after the war.[12] He was followed by Braeutigam and Hoffman. The Poles mentioned in this context are Michał Połynka and his assistant Józef Szewczyk, who marked each minute of the deadly work day with murderous blows.[13] In some instances, an entire train was unloaded during the course of one night by only five men. Salomon Singer has sickening memories of these days when he began work as part of a group of 120 prisoners: "They beat us constantly with clubs, with their fists, on the head, in the stomach.... Every single day we brought the victims of these blows back to the camp without stretchers, one person holding the head and another the legs. We never had a moment's rest since we were often awakened during the day to go back to work." [14] Within only two months, a mere twenty men were left alive! It is easy to see why the job of unloading the trains was known as the "death transport".

The next circle was the internal transport. For reasons of safety, the production halls were set tens and even hundreds of meters apart, with a system of tracks and roads running between them. The group transporting the empty casings from Warehouse 5 to Hall 51 often worked 16 hours a day instead of 12. The prisoners were hard put to decide whether they suffered more at the hands of the Poles or the Jewish commandants.[15] In Hall 51, to which only the privileged prisoners were assigned, the casings were marked with the plant code and then taken to Hall 53 – the central circle of this hell. Here stood two huge vats with boiling TNT. Three "ladlers" *(Giesser)* used buckets to pour the liquid into the shell casings which were placed on tables. In order to fill the daily quota of 5,800 shells, the workers had to run from the vat to the tables with their buckets. The explosive powder which filled the hall not only stained the workers' hair

---

[12] Tschenstochau Prozess, YV, TR-10/8, pp. 16, 48;

[13] Ryszard Mittelberg, Testimony, Archives of Ghetto Fighter's House, (hereafter AHJF), H-1194, p. 24.

[14] R. Bauminger, Przy pikrynie, op. cit., p. 33.

[15] Chaim Szotland, AGKBZH, SWK, sygn. 317, p. 169; Wilhelm Bisam, Testimony, YV, 0-16/1710.

and skin red, but also damaged their hearts and lungs. Of an original 26 "ladlers," 17 died within a few months, several of them at their work place. The death of one in particular is engraved on the memory of witnesses – he was thrown into the boiling vat by the German supervisor Otto Ullmann.[16]

The women were employed in stirring the TNT. Using an automatic motion, they turned a metal rod in a funnel so that the mixture would pour into the shell at an even rate: 2 seconds per turn, 1,800 turns per hour, 12 hours every day.[17]

Three "cells" *(kajuty)* on the sides of the hall were considered a separate circle of this hell. Four Jews worked in each. Here the shells were brought after the liquid had solidified so that a hole could be drilled for the detonator. The daily quota for each cell was 1,600 units. The Polish overseers molested the workers to such a degree that the latter threatened to complain to the German supervisor that the constant beatings were interfering with their work. The prisoners tried to organize a go-slow strike in the hall, but the attempt was quickly put down.[18] The rate at which they worked and the resultant exhaustion led to a decline in the quality of the shells, and in February 1944 a military commission arrived to investigate. Its members were shocked to hear of the quotas from two of the prisoners – who were executed the following day for "squealing".[19]

The *Volksdeutsch* Franciszek Gajowczyk was in charge of the day shift. He got along well with everyone, earning the complete trust of the German management while presenting himself as a man who was only fulfilling orders. He treated the Poles well and it was whispered that he aided the underground. To the Jews he was indifferent, never helping them and, according to M. Strigler who worked in his department, everyone knew that he had the quotas raised in order to advance his own interests. In 1946 he was sentenced in Poland to 4 years imprisonment for treason. No Jews were asked to testify in the three-year trial, and court records

---

[16] M. Strigler, In di fabrikn, op. cit., vol. 1, pp. 9, 207. cf. Edward Sasa, AGKBZH, SWK. sygn. 211, p. 46.

[17] Testimonies, YV: Zahawa Sztok, 0-33/1743; Fryda Immerglück, 0-16/1743.

[18] M. Strigler, In di fabrikn, op. cit., p. 218 ff, 279; J. Knobler, op. cit.

[19] N. Rapaport, Sitzungen, p. 94a.

show they were only mentioned twice.[20] The manager of the night shift
was the *Volksdeutsch* Aleksander Pinno who was closely acquainted with
Jews, spoke Yiddish, and told Jewish jokes. An inveterate coward, he
sought to get along with the Germans and Poles. Although he did not help
the Jews, he was not out to get them either. He showed little interest in the
work, being primarily concerned with seeking out the "fat cats" among the
Jews and offering his services as a middle-man.[21]

The finished shells were brought to Hall 58 – Receiving *(Abnehmerei)*.
Here the work was done at tables. The shells were rolled from one worker
to the next, cleaned, stamped, inspected, and then carted away by the
transport crew. Jewish women were first employed in this section in
Summer, 1943. The quota was changed periodically, eventually reaching
3,500 units a shift. The manager of Hall 58 was the *Volksdeutsch* Walerian
Zieliński, whose cadre of assistants grew as more Jews were assigned to
his section, and included Henryk Sadza, Edward Kowalik, and others.[22]
Hall 58 was the site of the "Polish Soup Affair" in Autumn, 1943.

In order to understand the background of this affair, we must first
explain the extent of the hunger in Werk C which was unlike that in the
other *werks*. Israel Anker testifies: "I wanted to commit suicide. I was
bloated from hunger and I knew I couldn't hold out on the 'transport'
crew." [23] He was rescued by a friend who gave him some money. What did
the other prisoners do who had no friends and no money, who had already
sold their trousers and had no connections among the camp "big shots"?
Without an extra bread ration, the backbreaking work quickly exhausted
all their strength. Even the prisoners from Majdanek, who were no
strangers to suffering, admitted they had never known such hunger. For
the Plaszowites, it was "unnatural hunger." Rafael Zellner, an "alumnus"
of six camps, wrote: "I never saw impoverishment like that at Werk C in
any other camp through which I passed during the war in Europe." [24] Some
prisoners turned to stealing, others to begging. Since there was no chance

---

[20] Akta w sprawie Franciszka Gajowczyka, Sąd Okręgowy w Radomiu, 1946, pp. 25, 20,
38, AGKBZH, SORd 196.

[21] M. Strigler, In di fabrikn, op. cit., pp. 238, 282; R. Mittelberg, S. Engerest, op. cit.

[22] Ewa Zucker, op. cit.; I. Friedmann, Bletlech, op. cit., p. 111.

[23] Israel Anker, Testimony, YV, 0-16/1808.

[24] Testimonies, YV: Rafael Zellner, 0-21/8; Fela Blum, 0-33/1839.

whatsoever of an extra spoonful of soup in the camp, they looked for it at the plant.

The "Polish Soup Affair" began one day when a rumor spread through the camp that now and then some Polish soup was left from the lunch break in Hall 58 and it was returned to the kitchen. The very next day, hundreds of Jewish prisoners were outside the hall hoping to get themselves a few drops. When the overseer Czop, in charge of ladling out the soup to the Poles, saw himself surrounded by this crowd of walking skeletons, he left them the remainder of the vat, and this became a fairly regular occurrence. Some of the prisoners tried to get hold of several portions in order to sell them. A number of Poles who caught on themselves started selling the soup and became increasingly incensed at the Jewish "competitors" who were cheating them out of their profits. Meanwhile, Sadza informed on Czop to Zieliński who was afraid of getting a reputation as a "friend to the Jews" and decided to teach them a lesson. One day a rumor flew about that soup was being doled out for free and hundreds of starving prisoners crowded around Hall 58, pushing and shouting. They were ushered into the hall, the doors were shut behind them, and then the pogrom began. The highly experienced Polish overseers, wielding chairs or rods, rained blows on the heads of the prisoners who fled for their lives in panic.[25]

From that day on, Hall 58 was known as a killing field throughout the camp. Sadza and his cohorts gave his victims no rest until he had extorted money from them all. Sala Fass relates: "When I started to work here I had a daily attack of hysterics because of the fear of being beaten." With dread she recalls the night shifts when the overseers Leśniewski, Szczotka and others would tie prisoners to chairs and beat them, while shouting: "You're waiting for the Bolsheviks, but you'll die before they come!"[26] Every day there were new casualties. These overseers appear in the War Criminals Register, but were never brought to trial. In fairness, let it be said that not all the Poles took part in these atrocities, which were unheard of in the other *werks*. The prisoners were convinced the beatings would end in catastrophe, and indeed, on December 13, 1943, Hall 58 was rocked

---

[25] M. Strigler, Werk "Ce", op. cit., vol. 1, pp. 45–55.
[26] Sala Fass, Testimony, YV, 0-16/1352; cf. H.Sadza, YV, M-9/12-8, nr. 1366.

by a huge explosion which left 25 dead and 25 wounded, most of them Jews. The wounded were then taken out and shot on the firing range.[27])

The final station on the Via Dolorosa of the Shell Department was the transport from Hall 58 to Warehouse 3, known as the "Warehouse of Death". During the course of a single shift, three workers had to transfer 12 carts, each bearing 200 shells for a total weight of 42,000 kg. This they did running all the way along a path marked with the bodies of prisoners who had been beaten to death. Within 4 weeks, only 12 of an original group of 90 men remained alive.[28]

These six circles were only one part of the hell that was Werk C.

"Schmitz" – The Refuge

The word "Schmitz" was a cover term for both the departments revolving around Hall 12 and their mysterious manager, the engineer Hermann Schmitz, Rost's deputy. Although Rost envied the handsome and successful engineer, he avoided conflicts with Schmitz who was said by those in the know to be the protégé of important people in Berlin.[29] Available sources do not reveal who these people were, and only his name might indicate a possible blood relationship with another Hermann Schmitz, the chairman of the board of directors of I.G. Farbenidustrie. The fact of the matter is that Schmitz received generous allocations which he used to expand his department where, among other things, strange experiments with modern weaponry were conducted. The nature of these experiments is unknown, although descriptions of Schmitz's department leave one with the impression that it was all a grand bluff designed to protect the young engineer from conscription.

The "Schmitz" departments were the best work assignment in Werk C. The privileged prisoners were sent here, along with the prettiest girls, chosen by Schmitz himself from each transport. Production work included assembling detonators for anti-aircraft shells, filling anti-tank bullets, and other such jobs. The supervisor was the *Volksdeutsch* Andrzej

---

[27] Kriegstagebuch, Kdo Radom, 13.12.1943, MA, RW 23/17, p. 140.

[28] Testimonies, YV: Mordchai Fass, 0-16/1322; Helena Hochdorf, 0-16/2343; Chaim Wolfman, 0-16/1387.

[29] M. Strigler, Goirolois, op. cit., vol. 1, pp. 83, 114; cf. "SS im Einsatz", Dokumentation (Berlin:Kongress Verlag, 1957), p. 426.

Szarata, who treated the Jews quite decently and forbade the overseers to beat them.[30] The relaxed atmosphere affected everyone there: the Nazi Hellmut Porzig, whom we have already encountered in Werk A, joked with the pretty girl Rina about whether she would welcome him into her home when he came to visit her after the war. In general, the Poles behaved like typical bosses. Even Sobański, a confirmed anti-Semite, treated several of the girls in the department with a modicum of compassion, and Marian (last name unknown) was universally respected.[31] Dr Hornung, the Jewish capo, arranged hot water for "his girls" to wash in! Even the work brigade escort, Rosenblum, is spoken of favorably. It is obvious why the workers here feared transfer to other departments during the periods when production was at a standstill. Schmitz left the job of choosing the candidates for transfer to the overseers, some of whom left the prisoners with money in place and sent the impoverished ones to the Shell Department.[32]

In Summer, 1943 several new workers were assigned to the detonator section and it was their lack of experience which seems to have caused an explosion on September 16, 1943 in which 18 women were injured and several killed. At the insistence of Schmitz, the wounded were taken to the hospital in the city where they were treated and then returned to the camp. Eda Jewin, whose sister was killed in the explosion, received a food package sent by Schmitz through his secretary with the warning that nobody find out since it could be dangerous "for everyone involved." [33]

Ziuta Hartman relates that the systematic theft of ammunition for the underground was organized at "Schmitz." She found this out from the Pole, Kowalik. The Jews Lolek Erlich and Pozner were also involved. Crates of ammunition would be placed outside among the crates of trash, and these would periodically be removed on the "Schmitz" cart. One of the collaborators in this scheme was the transport worker Ickowicz. It was whispered in the department that some of the girls who cleaned up the "litter" on the firing range used the opportunity to hide ammunition in the

---

[30] K. Skrzypek, AGKBZH, SWK, sygn. 213, p. 27; Lea Muskatenblut, Testimony, YV, 0-33/1801.

[31] Rina Cypres, Testimony, YV, 0-33/1857; Erna Nessel, op. cit.

[32] I. Karmel, An estate, op. cit., pp. 233, 382; Felicja Rozenblatt, AGKBZH, SWK, sygn. 217, k. 138.

[33] Eda Jewin (Jakubowicz), Testimony, YV, 0-33/1838.

forest for the partisans. It is not clear whether this was the group involved in the investigation conducted in January 1944 when two crates of ammunition disappeared. A thorough search was made throughout the entire department, but no one was arrested. According to other testimony, a second investigation was conducted in the Summer of 1944 and as a result Kowalik and Pozner were arrested.[34]

As we have seen, an aura of mystery surrounded Schmitz and his strange behavior was often inexplicable. Whenever Krebs and Rost accused him of maintaining too large a work force, he would begin preparations for "a new program." Occasionally he even launched "night raids" on the camp, escorted by the Werkschutz, in which hundreds of prisoners were seized. Accompanied by blows and curses, they were ordered to move crates from one bunker to another. Sometimes when the crates were already loaded onto flatbeds, he would have them taken off again, and several times ordered vast quantities off the production line to be destroyed before embarking on a new experiment whose nature seemed obscure even to the prisoners.[35]

In his attitude to the Jews, Schmitz clearly favored the women. Whenever he walked through the department, all of them would gaze at the handsome gentleman who spoke only French with the more educated among them. Rina Cypres relates, that on one occasion he intervened in the distribution of clothes and when some of the girls complained of a lack of undergarments, ordered them to lift their skirts to prove their contention. When one of them refused, however, he did not insist, and he was never suspected of having an affair with a Jewish girl. His treatment of the men depended on his mood at the time. At one time, the prisoners found aluminum pipes in a warehouse, and cut pieces from them to make pots. When Schmitz caught one of them at his work, he first threatened to turn him in for sabotage, then asked to see how he could make pots with such primitive tools, and finally ordered one for himself, even paying for it in sandwiches.[36]

There were a number of other good work places in Werk C, such as

---

[34] Ziuta Hartmann, Testimony, YV, 0-33/1851; R.Cypres, op. cit.; R. Bauminger, Przy pikrynie, op. cit., pp. 52–53;

[35] M. Strigler, Goirolois, op. cit., vol. 1, pp. 911–913; cf. Fela Rapp, Testimony, YV, 0-33/1803.

[36] M. Strigler, ibid., pp. 114–115.

Friedrich Krosta's Power and Heat Department *(Abt. Kraft u. Waerme)*, or the repair shop *(Reparaturwerkstatt)* supervised by Walter Rudolf.[37] Even the fate of the persecuted prisoner from Werk B, Meir Guza, improved: the Polish cart driver Malik chose him for his assistant and made sure he got a second soup ration. When a German manager once caught Guza and the horse resting, he reprimanded Malik, telling him to beat the Jew rather than the horse "because they're only here to work and die." [38]

Kingdom of the Damned

Here they come...

"From afar you can hear the clack of their wooden clogs with the mechanical movement of the prisoners' feet.... The shouts of the guards and the escorts, stop and count, stop and start again.... Many of the plodders are wrapped in paper shrouds. From time to time a figure moves out of line, dragged aside to kneel by the edge of the road.... They're coming closer, squads of yellow creatures, not of this world, closer to skeletons than human beings, yet as long as the spark of life still flickers, the bitter taste, bitter and embittering, preserves the sense of reality existing in Werk C camp which breathes and chokes on the air filled with yellow picric acid." [39]

When Israel Anker first saw these ghosts, he chose to join the transport crew, for he was told these yellow people were doomed.

The first Jews were sent to the "Pikryna" Department in the Autumn of 1942. They worked there on two 12-hour shifts. Lacking any face masks or protective clothing, their appearance soon underwent a drastic change: their hair, nails and faces took on a greenish-yellow hue. The powder penetrated their skin and dried it. The blistering tools singed their hands. There was neither soap nor hot water, and the powder would not wash off in cold water. It covered their bodies layer upon layer. Everything around the *pikryner* became bitter, including the soup. Sooner or later, everyone fell victim to lung disease, although the Leipzig trials declared that picric

---

[37] Roman Czerny, Sitzungen, p. 37; C. Plutzer, ib., p. 89b.

[38] Tadeusz Malik, AGKBZH, SWK, sygn. 217, p. 37.

[39] Jehuda Knobler, op. cit.

acid and TNT were not dangerous poisons. The average mortality rate in the department was 25 prisoners a week.[40] The men who succumbed to hunger and ceased to wash would rot alive under the layers of filthy paper. Without extra food rations, the average life expectancy in the department was three months! The high mortality rate coupled with production needs forced the plant management to institute additional shifts. In late 1943, a total of between 1,200 and 1,500 men and women – approximately one half of the prisoner population – was assigned to the Picric Acid and TNT Departments.[41]

The picric acid powder was used to produce underwater mines and the TNT powder for land mines. The German Walter Zahn, who beat and shot prisoners with his own hands, was in charge of Halls 13 and 15. He knew every single worker in his department. Hecht arrived in 1943. Known as *"Dziadek"* (Polish for grandfather), he too terrorized the prisoners.[42] The production process began with the preparation of powder cubes in the Pressing Department *(Presserei)*. Four workers toiled beside each press, each performing one of the four parts of the process. The "pourer" *(sypacz)* would pour a cup of picric acid or TNT powder into the mold and transfer it to the "presser" who placed the mold in the press. This was a hydraulic press which applied 2,500 kg of pressure to the powder, turning it into a cube 5×10 cm in size, with a hole in the center for the detonator. The mold was then removed from the press and transferred to the third worker who opened it and removed the cube. The fourth in line cleaned and reassembled the mold, returning it to the "pourer." Before the war, the daily quota was 350 cubes per press. Under Hasag, this was raised to 1,650 cubes.[43]

Because of the high mortality rate of the men, girls were first sent to the presses in late 1943. Such was the fate of Maria Szechter-Lewinger who describes her experience in the following appalling terms:

> "I join a team and the four of us, three men and I, take our places. My job is 'pourer'. 'Pour the powder into the opening, seal the device [the

---

[40] Ludwig Zaendle, Sitzungen, p. 87b ; A. Rost, ib., pp. 114a, 42a.

[41] M. Strigler, In di fabrikn, op. cit., p. 184; cf. Anklageschrift, p. 22.

[42] Hans Brandt, Sitzungen, p. 54b, 122b; Naftali Reh, "Forced labour at Cracow and Skarżysko", YV, 0-2/318.

[43] Testimonies, YV: Lunka Fuss-Kaufmann, 0-33/1819; Izak Jakower, 0-16/1319.

mold] with the plug and push it over to me. What, this is your first time on the press!? Oh no, that's terrible! Hurry up, we have to meet our quota! Do you get it!?' I become nothing but an automaton... Here are the cups of TNT, I have to pour them, pour them constantly... All the time I hear the shouts: 'Hurry up, pour!' – Hand, TNT, opening, device, pour, close, push, hurry, faster, even faster! The devices pass before my eyes at the speed of lightning, the screech of the steel and rumbling of the press are deafening...'Hurry up!' – the nervous workers scream at me. 'We haven't even gotten two crates done!' They're like vultures, I'm afraid to look at them... The quota, the huge omnipresent and omnipotent control, fills the hall and works the presses: eleven crates with 150 cubes in each!... I feel exhausted: the TNT spills on the press, I forget to clean the plug... 'What are you doing?' the presser shrieks, 'You can cause an explosion and they'll accuse you of sabotage! Do you know what that means?... – The gong, a break. Quickly I gulp down a bit of cold sour soup. 'Listen,' the presser whispers, 'Now we're going to work on three devices." We begin... the pace is killing.... We work in utter silence, every nerve focused on the passing devices...'One crate ready!' the presser shouts in joy – we did it at record speed! Now we can slow down just a little." [44]

From the press, the cubes of picric acid were transferred to a table where they were arranged on a metal rack and dipped in a vat of boiling paraffin by one of the workers. In April 1944, a 16-year-old boy was working here. In time he fell mortally ill. He could be seen sitting on a bench beside the barracks, a boy who was now an old man, a dried-out carcass, covered in a yellow rag. He was followed in the job by Szapsia, a 15-year-old from Piotrków, a musical prodigy who knew all the great pieces of classical music by heart.[45] Finally, two girls, whose combined strength could barely move the heavy rack, were assigned to the vat. To their great fortune, they were periodically rotated with the girls who worked in sorting and packaging. Other girls wielded hammers to break up the faulty cubes, egged on by the blows constantly rained on them by their supervisor, Ciok.

In the TNT hall, the chief presser, Ahron Geller, was able to organize

[44] Maria Szechter, "Pikryna działa. Prasa", Dokumenty zbrodni i męczeństwa, (Kraków: Żydowska Komisja Historyczna, 1945), pp. 45–47.

[45] Maria Szechter, "Dzieci przy pikrynie", YV, 0-16/4543.

the rotation of jobs, and with the help of the Jewish capo Shaul the work was bearable.[46] Worst of all was the severe hunger. On Saturday, a two-day ration of bread was distributed, and, as David Schvarzmer relates, "you needed a will of iron not to eat it all up at once. But who could hold out? So Sunday was a fast day." [47]

Izak Jakower adds: "Thus we ate nothing at all until the noon break. We got a spoonful of soup, while the presser who had achieved the largest output got the leftovers in the vat." As a result, 38 of the 40 workers in Hall 13 were listed as unfit for work. It is no surprise, therefore, that the "Pikryna Soup Affair" left a particularly bitter taste. In 1943 a Jewish capo known as "the professor" was assigned here. He offered to arrange thicker soup for the prisoners on condition that each of them give him 10 of the 200 grams of bread he got, since they were going to die soon anyway. Objections to this extortion were raised and word of the affair reached the German manager who removed "the professor" from his post.[48]

Where did relief come from? Once in a while it was a decent policeman, such as Zylbersztajn in Hall 13. The lucky ones who were sent to Hall 24 got soup from the Poles. Or a good friend might offer a small loan which could save a prisoner from starvation.

Strange things happened in the daily life of the "Kingdom of the Damned." The petite Lunka Fuss-Kaufman was sent to Hall 13 where, to the amazement of everyone, she managed to hold up under the draining work load better than most. Walter took note of her, and when she fell ill with pneumonia, he ordered her to rest. Once he grabbed her and, in utter seriousness, took a pair of scissors and trimmed her curly eyebrows. Maria Lewinger also had an odd experience. Stricken with typhus, she hid in the bathroom where Walter found her. In a rage, he ordered the Jewish capo to return her to the camp until she recovered, and on the day she returned he festively handed her a double ration of *kaszanka*.[49] Even the universally feared Hecht at times displayed a humane side. He noticed Helena Szechter's exceptional agility in the weighing department and asked: "Where did you learn to do that, little one?". When she replied that

---

[46] Ahron Geller, AGKBZH, SWK, sygn. 229, p. 2.

[47] David Schvarzmer, Testimony, YV, 0-33/1809.

[48] Mejer Ryzenberg, op. cit.

[49] Maria Szechter-Lewinger, Testimony, YV, 0-33/1802.

she had helped with the weighing in her father's grocery, he was extremely pleased.[50] The one who aroused the greatest wonder was the affable German, Hans, known as *"Pleitzes"*. Szaul Goldhar, who knew him very well, relates that he was an anti-Nazi and passed on information to Goldhar that he had heard on Radio London.[51]

Overall supervision of production was the responsibility of the Pole, Henryk Kopecki, who, in the spirit of the times, served the Germans, looked out for the future in a free Poland, and extorted what he could from the Jews. Although he did not abuse the workers, a Jew with money was liable to find himself on the list of those "unfit for work," and could only have his name erased in exchange for 200 zloty. He appointed Icchak Friedmann overseer and at the same time offered to help him get money conveyed to him for a 30% commission. Out of his concern for the future, Kopecki maintained contact with the underground. He enlisted Towa Kozakowa in the theft of ammunition and she, together with several other girls, spirited cubes of explosives out of the production hall and hid them in the forest. When the rumor spread that escaping Jews had been caught with the aid of the AK partisans, Towa asked Kopecki how this was possible. His reply was that they were not fighting for a Jewish Poland, but for "a Poland without Jews." [52]

Existing testimony provides evidence of diverse military cooperation between Poles and Jews. Henryk Wasserlauf became the assistant to the Polish engine driver, a member of the AK, and helped him to steal ammunition off the train. When he was taken for questioning, he kept his silence despite the 40 lashings he was dealt.[53] Róża Bauminger describes the act of sabotage committed by Roman Gerstel in Hall 53.[54] There were also some disconcerting moments, such as when malfunctions were discovered in the hydraulic machinery and the Jews were accused of sabotage by their Polish overseers who punished them with beatings.

---

[50] Helena Zorska, Testimony, YV, 0-33/1797.

[51] Szaul Goldhar, Testimony, YV, 0-3/3090.

[52] Henryk Kopecki, AGKBZH, SWK, sygn. 213, p. 89; T. Kozakowa, op. cit.; I. Friedman, Bletlech, op. cit., pp. 116, 123.

[53] Henryk Wasserlauf, Testimony, YV, 0-16/1585.

[54] R. Bauminger, Przy pikrynie, op. cit., pp. 53–54; cf. Ida Buszmicz, Testimony, YV, 0-3/2798.

Eventually it was learned that the Poles themselves had sabotaged the machines.[55] This is another example of the tragic dilemma which confronted the camp prisoners. To what end should a starving prisoner collaborate in sabotage? And with whom? With Kopecki who extorted money from them? With Długoszcz who beat them with his club? With Ciok who stunned them with a hammer? They were not even offered an extra slice of bread for their efforts.

In Spring, 1944, a miracle occurred. A "selection" was conducted and 29 of the picric acid workers – Izak Jakower also – were marked for death. However, when the camp doctor, Dr Haendel, intervened, they were sent to work in the *Baukommando* where the overseer Hercke was helpful to them. These men, already bearing the mark of the condemned on their brows, again dragged their feet homeward in the evening:

> "From the halls stretched bands of ash drawn by the prisoners' sandals,
> its color staining the paths through the hell of the daily and nightly to
> and fro of the prisoner's changing shifts.... The powder rose in clouds
> by the sides of the path, changing the color of the leaves on the trees
> lining the road along which they plodded." [56]

Plodding and stumbling, stumbling and falling, the procession of the damned moved on through the darkness until it reached the gate of the camp....

---

[55] Szraga Knobler, Testimony, YV, 0-3/3674, p. 97.

[56] Jehuda Knobler, op. cit.

Chapter 10

The Yellow Kingom of Lady Markowiczowa

Rise to Power and Establishment of the Dynasty

Of the thousands of camps scattered throughout occupied Europe, several have become synonymous in the public mind with acertain figure personifying the atrocities perpetrated there. One such is Dr Mengele, "Mr Rampa" of Auschwitz. When it comes to a barely-known camp such as Skarżysko, it is only the former inmates who remember the Jewish *"commandanta"* of Werk C, Fela Markowiczowa, who became the reigning queen of this kingdom of death. In her life and death, she symbolizes the tragic phenomenon known as "Jewish authorities" during the Holocaust.

The "dynasty" was founded in the city of Skarżysko where the Gutmans accumulated considerable property. The death of the patriarch left only his wife and their three daughters, the youngest of whom, Feigele, future ruler of the camp, became the black sheep of the family. Soon after her marriage to a young yeshiva scholar with whom she moved to Kielce, it became clear that the gentle lad was unsuited to this spirited woman. Rumor had it that she beat him and eventually threw him out of her house. After their divorce, Fela married Markowicz and gave birth to a daughter.

With the German invasion, Markowicz served as a member of the Judenrat until he was arrested by the Gestapo. In her attempts to rescue him, his wife made the acquaintance of numerous functionaries and learned how to gain entrance to German offices. Her efforts failed. When her husband was killed, Fela returned to her family in Skarżysko. Although the events of 1942 convinced her that survival was dependent on the Hasag plants, Markowiczowa had no intention of entering the camp as a simple prisoner. Having learned that it was still possible to secure a "good position" in Werk C, she began to lay the groundwork for taking over control of the camp by ingratiating herself over a long period of time with both German and Polish foremen. Bribes passed from hand to hand, and Markowiczowa was able to enter the camp together with her entire family before the final deportation from the ghetto.

It was clear to her that the Hasag management was not at all interested in who controlled the camp, but only in how many prisoners were available for work. Within a short time she succeeded in unseating the existing Jewish authorities who were unable to keep order in the constantly growing camp, and herself became *"commandanta".*[1] There is no question that she gained control not only by bribes, but also due to her intelligence, dynamism, adaptive skills, and administrative talents. She spoke not only Yiddish, but also fluent Polish and a bit of German. Her lust for power and desire to prove that she was different were combined with extraordinary pride and a thirst to enjoy life at any cost. Her aversion to routine and adventurousness drove her to take the risk: "Every step she took was significant, an indication that there was something out of the ordinary about her."[2] At this time Markowiczowa was around 30 years old and not particularly attractive, but her superb figure and elegant mien were arresting, and she used these feminine qualities to her advantage. She chatted freely with the Werkschutz officers, did not hesitate to invite them, or even Dr Rost and Schmitz, to her barracks for a cup of tea, and behaved totally unlike a typical Jewish woman. This amazed the other prisoners, and they began to treat her as a person of consequence who had entered the camp out of some mad whim.

To Markowiczowa's mind, the bribes that flowed constantly into the hands of those in authority at all levels were a prerequisite of her success. In exchange, the Hasag managers, recognizing her exceptional person-

---

[1] M. Strigler, In di fabrikn, op. cit., p. 364.

[2] Josef Briks, Testimony, YV, 0-19/9-2.

ality, gave her a free hand in the internal administration. The new *"commandanta"*, however, did not aspire to the sort of division of power that characterized the other two camps. She had a more far-reaching concept of power. She was, in fact, the only one who actually implemented the *Fuehrerprinzip* in full by establishing an "absolute monarchy" in which all power was exclusively in her hands. She used the members of her family, whom she knew inside and out, to ensure the invulnerability of her authority, appointing them to all the key posts. One brother-in-law, Henek Eisenberg, was made police commander, and the other, Feldman, was put in charge of supplies. The clothing store was run by the nephew of her late husband, Lolek Markowicz, and the camp office by her niece, Renia Feldman.

Without a doubt, Markowiczowa chose the right person for each job. Eisenberg, a tall, brawny man, was known as an uncultured boor who was enamored of his star-studded cap, his truncheon and the horse which he rode ceremoniously. Unbidden, he conducted disciplinary roll-calls and abused the prisoners. Feldman, a merchant for many years, was interested only in profit, and in addition to the official supplies he smuggled goods for sale into the camp. Along with his whole family he led the life of a "landlord" in the camp and even took part in prayers. The young Lolek Markowicz set up a bed in the clothing store and in the evening invited some attractive young girl to come and chose a dress. Not surprisingly, he earned the sobriquet *"a dasz?"* (Polish for "Will you give out? ") and *"za raz"* (Polish for "for a one-night stand").[3] Young Renia was assisted by Marek (last name unknown) who had his own power base since he was essential to the running of the camp office. Markowiczowa ruled them all and all stood in fear of her.

In accord with "court manners," the *"commandanta"* maintained a degree of distance. Rarely did she appear among the masses, whom she treated with derision and disgust. She walked about the camp with a truncheon in her hand, although she herself did not usually use it. From time to time, supposedly to appease her conscience, she would stop in the courtyard among her starving "subjects" who would crowd around her, kissing her hand and, amidst weeping and wailing, present their petitions to her. Strangely enough, this bizarre behavior was accepted as natural.

---

[3] Henia Strelska, Testimony, YV, 0-33/1836; E. Nessel, op. cit.

Expressions such as "she ruled here like a queen," appear in several testimonies, along with her nickname, which not surprisingly was "Katerina the Second." [4] It was not a simple matter to obtain an audience with her. Eliezer Lewin, who knew her well before the war, writes: "When the policeman brought me to Markowiczowa's room she was seated on a tall chair staring at me with probing eyes, and I stood before her as if I was facing the head of the *Gestapo*" [5] Among the prisoners there were those who both admired and despised her, as Wroclawski, a member of the Warsaw intelligentsia and a picric acid worker explains: "To command (the camp) she had to do things the Germans couldn't know about since it could cost lives... and Markowiczowa was smarter than the others.... She had the head of a commanding general." [6]

The entire "royal family," as they were called by the prisoners, lived in a separate and spacious barracks known as *"Dos Waise Hoiz"* (The White House). No elements of a royal court were missing. The "queen" chose courtiers from among the young policemen, and, to the displeasure of the family's matriarch, the elderly Mrs Gutman, even arranged lovers for her sister who was abandoned by the woman-chasing Eisenberg. In her efforts to endow her family with an aristocratic patina, Markowiczowa married her niece, Renia Feldman, to the medical student Haendel, the son of a professor! The young Haendel, who was not sorry to give up his "job" in the Shell Department, was promoted to camp doctor.[7] The girls in the family were given French lessons(!) and an army of servant men and women cooked, cleaned and laundered in exchange for a piece of bread and an extra soup ration.

The Devious Paths of the "Kingdom of Death"

Lady Markowiczowa's kingdom was sinking in mud and excrement. In the center was the camp in a forest clearing full of mud puddles. Around the edges were the rickety greenish-yellow barracks, new and old. Near the gate was "The White House" with the police barracks adjacent

---

[4] R. Bauminger, Felicja Bannet, "Obóz pracy Hasag", YV, 0-16/828.

[5] Eliezer Lewin, Testimony, YV, 0-19/9-2.

[6] M. Strigler, Goirolois, op. cit., vol. 1, p. 42.

[7] M. Strigler, Werk " Ce", vol. 2, p. 97; H. Hochdorf, op. cit.

to it. At the northern edge stood the doorless communal latrine. The only concession to human sensibilities was an internal wall dividing it into separate sections for men and women. The excrement spilled out in the direction of the barracks creating an overwhelming stench. In the *Waschraum*, the communal bathhouse also divided in two, there was only cold water. The taps froze in the winter and the frosty cold air blew in through the broken windows. The floor was covered with mud and excrement. Nearby was a laundry where the prisoners were supposed to wash their clothes, but it was, in fact, used only by the camp nobility.

Barracks were assigned more or less on the basis of work place. Until new barracks were built, the overcrowding, particularly in the men's quarters, was unbearable. When the day shift left for work, their places on the pallets were taken by the night shift. Hunger and exhaustion soon whittled away at the prisoner population. In October 1942, 14.5% of the prisoners in Werk C died.[8] When the first typhoid epidemic broke out that winter, an infirmary was set up in Barracks Number 7 known as the "*zibele*", taking its name from the Yiddish word for "seven" (*ziben*). In this "corridor to death," the living and the dead, both covered in lice, lay side by side. There were no doctors and no medicines. The "male nurse", Szymon Szapira, formerly a butcher, did what he could, procuring food for his patients in exchange for a commission. When he refused to pay a "tithe" to Markowiczowa, he was sent to work in the plant and was replaced in the infirmary by two "orderlies", Melech and Alek. Their treatment of the ill is described in testimony as inhumane. They were accused of stealing food, brutality, and helping only those who paid them.[9] The charges against Alek are particularly harsh, while Melech is remembered favorably at least by his fellow townsmen whom he aided willingly.[10]

The prisoners did not only die of "natural" causes. Some lost their lives in special operations. In November, 1942, the authorities announced that prisoners could sign up to go to Palestine [apparently claiming they would be part of a prisoner exchange – F.K.]. All those who put their

---

[8] Staerkemeldungen, Oktober 1942, YV, 0-6/37-3.

[9] Testimonies, YV: Bella Grossmitz, M-1/E/1612/1495; Szlomo Kurz, 0-3/1695; Ester Szymkiewicz, M-1/E/1210/1276.

[10] Stefania Heilbrunn, Children of dust and heaven, A collective memoir,(Cape Town: Irgun Yotzey Radomsko *et al.*, 1978), p. 176.

names down were executed on November 9, 1942. Another 58 victims were sacrificed in honor of the New Year. On January 7, 1943, the camp population numbered 683 prisoners.[11] Between mid-October 1942 and late January 1943, 888 prisoners had found their death in Werk C. There were constant escape attempts. In January, 1943, 23 escapees were recorded. Jakow Zając fled one rainy night in February, 1943, and after surviving innumerable dangers in the forest, finally volunteered to be sent to the camp of the "Granat" – Hasag plant in Kielce which seemed to him like paradise on earth after the Shell Department at Skarżysko.[12]

It will be recalled that in Werk C the *Werkschutz* was a special unit whose German commander served also as camp commander. The absence of German records makes it impossible to state with any certainty the name of the first individual to fill this post. Testimony mentions Paul Kiessling in 1942, a man who beat the prisoners and took every opportunity to steal whatever property they had. As was accepted practice among the German officers, he too had a Jewish "servant girl" whom he passed on to Schneider, who then sent her to the firing squad when she became pregnant.[13] This seems to be a reference to Johannes Schneider known in Werk A for his excesses and murders. In Werk C there was at least one person who spoke up for him: Kuzimiński, a member of the "forest brigade," relates that when he was injured he knew it meant his death, but Schneider protected him during a "selection" and sent him to a hospital in town, warning him not to reveal that he was a Jew.[14] In Autumn, 1943, Kurt Schumann reappeared in Werk C, this time in the role of camp commander.

The administrative officer of all the Ukrainians in the *Werkschutz* was Georg *(Jerzy)* Adryanowicz, who was also their commanding officer in Werk C. He was brought before a Polish court in Kielce in 1966 for the murder of Jews and Poles and was sentenced to life imprisonment.[15] His trial lasted six years (!) and became the arena for settling political accounts among former Hasag employees who charged each other with

---

[11] Staerkemeldungen, November–Dezember 1942 -Januar 1943, see n. 8.

[12] Jakow Zając, op. cit.

[13] Testimonies, YV: F. Fragner, 0-53/58, p. 390; Lola Rozenfeld, 0-33/1806.

[14] E. Kuziminski, op. cit.

[15] See chapter 3, n. 25., ibid.

collaborating with the Germans and with the defendant.[16] Following a series of appeals, Adryanowicz was completely exonerated in 1973, generating a scandal in Skarżysko and the surrounding towns.[17] As for the actual charges, there can be no doubt that Adryanowicz issued orders concerning all aspects of the "selections" and mass executions. Any document relating to "selections" and the number of victims that reached his desk was marked "Confidential."

"Selections" were held at irregular intervals and followed a procedure similar to that in Werk A. The orderlies loaded the infirmary patients onto a truck and at the same time a general 'selection' was conducted at which Markowiczowa and Eisenberg were present. The condemned were taken by truck to trenches in the forest that had been dug in advance. Here the Werkschutz, using their clubs, forced the victims into the trenches in small groups and then shot them. Some resisted, as Stanisław Lis relates: "Once I was on the firing range with the German Schneider for ammunition tests when we saw a group of about 60 Jews escorted by six *Werkschutz* men. We hid in a bunker and saw how they started to shoot them one after the other, and then the remaining prisoners began to shout and resist. The Werkschutz ceased firing single shots and mowed them down with automatic fire. Those that did not die on the spot were killed with more machine gun bursts." [18] The Stosstrupp carried out these executions, and a list of their names was turned over to the authorities after the war by one of the "gravediggers," Chaim Szotland.[19]

Little is known of individual acts of resistance since the witnesses were put to death. Strigler recorded the events surrounding the death of Szlomo Griner who was arrested in the Spring, 1944. When he was brought to the firing range with his hands tied, he set on two of his *Werkschutz* escorts and fled, until he was stopped by a fatal bullet.[20] When Awigdor Beker of Staszów was being led to his death, he managed to cry out: "You must

---

[16] Protokól zebrania członków ZBOWiD w Skar.-Kamiennej, 7.6.1967, AGKBZH, SWK, sygn. 234, p. 28.

[17] "Protest", Skarżysko, 26.1973", AGKBZH, SWK, sygn. 244, p. 121.

[18] Stanisław Lis, Akta T. Sawczaka, see chapter 5, n. 17.

[19] List od Chaima Szotlanda do Prokuratora SWK, 19.5.1966, AGKBZH, SWK, sygn, 317, p. 169.

[20] M. Strigler, In di fabrikn, p. 307; "Goirolois", vol. 1, pp. 282–300.

avenge my death!"[21] On one occasion, after 175 victims were caught, it was found that the trench prepared for them was too small. Kiessling ordered that it be enlarged, and when the condemned were taken off the truck, one of them, a rabbi, began praying out loud. Kiessling, unnerved for a moment, shouted at him to finish his prayer quickly, but the rabbi ignored him and continued to pray until he was lowered into his grave.[22]

The "White House" and its Subjects

Numerous wires, both visible and invisible, tied Lady Markowiczowa's reign to her German and Ukrainian masters. The most important of them were their common business dealings, conducted at the prisoners' expense.

One example involves Adryanowicz himself, whom camp gossip included among the *"commandanta's"* many lovers. At his trial, he confessed that he "had dealings with the Jewish functionaries from whom he 'purchased' gold items" [inverted commas in the original].[23] He was supported by a network of "informants" consisting of Poles employed in the plant. Since they were the ones who supplied food to the prisoners, they always knew who had gold or dollars from the goods that were purchased. One Jew who was informed on was murdered when his "boss" found a diamond ring worth a fortune on him.[24] A second network of freelance informants, both Jews and Poles, was kept by the *Werkschutz*. When informed on by one of these people, the prisoner Mosze Najman was forced to hand over a diamond ring to Teodor Sawczak for his fiancée, and barely escaped with his life.[25]

But the most important network was that of "White House" agents ("agents" rather than "informants"!). It was their job to collect information as to who had managed to make contact with the Aryan side and how, who was doing big business with the Poles, who had foreign currency or gold, etc. Some of the agent bought valuables with their own money and then sold them to the "courtiers," while others merely passed on the

---

[21] M. Ryzenberg, op. cit.

[22] David Najmans testimony, see M. Strigler, Werk "Ce", op. cit., vol. 2, p. 15.

[23] See chapter 3, n. 25, ib., pp. 105–106.

[24] Stanisław Lis, Protokół, see n. 16, ib.

[25] Mosze Najman, Akta T. Sawczaka, see chapter 5, n. 17.

information to their superiors in return for a fee.[26] This information was vital to Markowiczowa for her internal politics, which were founded on two immutable principles: firstly) no favors were given for free; secondly, any initiative outside the routine taken by either an individual or a group required her approval.

The testimony of Icchak Friedman provides an example of the working of these principles. When he arrived in the camp in October, 1942, the "queen" offered to intervene for him (for a price, of course) with the German commander so that the latter would provide a truck and several *Werkschutz* escorts to enable him to bring various possessions and money from his home.[27] Indeed, the entire "royal family" was obsessed with greed. With each new transport that arrived, agents were sent to "check things out" and drop hints in the right places that all sorts of favors could be arranged for a price: transfer to a different camp, a good work assignment, appointment to a junior post in the camp or plant, or a job as a policeman. Indeed, it was possible to effect a transfer to another camp for purposes of uniting families, if Ipfling's permission was obtained, or if one prisoner was exchanged for another.[28] Although very rare, there were also cases in which entire groups were transferred. Jeszajahu Rechter was sent to Werk A with 24 other prisoners in exchange for 500 zloty a head. A German escort took the "happy" group to their new camp, where they were welcomed by Kuehnemann himself!

In order to get a good work assignment, a prisoner had to pay not only a commission to the Jewish administration, but also a fee to the Polish foreman and a "tip" to the Jewish policeman on duty. Two work assignments required friends in the very highest places and were closed completely to newcomers. These were the plant's vegetable garden and the kitchen, where only Markowiczowa's personal friends from Skarzysko worked.[29] She had exclusive control over the appointment of functionaries, including policemen, and it was well-known that only those with "*dos Hitl*" – a black cap with a red band, a belt and a truncheon – had paid dearly for the honor. The chief officer, H. Eisenberg, commanded the

---

[26] Israel Rom-Rotbalsam, Testimony, YV, 0-3/2357; S. Goldhar, op. cit.

[27] I. Friedman, Bletlech, op. cit., p. 121.

[28] A. Lewkowicz, H. Albert, op. cit.

[29] Masza Szopil, Testimony, YV, 0-33/1853.

plant police, while his second-in-command, Feldman from Warsaw, was in charge of the camp police. In 1944, there were, all in all, some 40 policemen in Werk C.[30]

This police force presents a special problem. On the whole, they were alone in the camp with no family or friends for support, so that they were totally dependent on the "White House". Being a policeman in Werk C was much more a matter of life and death than in the other two camps. Their behavior, characteristically condescending and contemptuous of the ordinary prisoners, was largely influenced by their "queen's" concept of power and the example she herself set. Many testimonies depict the police as treating the prisoners like animals, and from here it was only a short way to cruelty and the drive to get rich at the prisoners' expense. From both the instructions they received and their own experience, the policemen knew who had no protection and who were the ones with the "strong backs" who should not be touched. The latter included the skilled laborers who enjoyed German protection, the "friends of the authorities" who knew too much, or people such as the two "orderlies" who worked hand in hand with the *"commandanta"* to loot the ill. Not surprisingly, it was generally believed that all abuses and punishments in Werk C could be traced back to one source: the "White House".

At the same time, it must not be forgotten that this situation was created first and foremost by the policy of the Hasag management, which determined not only living conditions in the camp, but also the composition of the internal administration. Without a doubt, the German authorities would have unhesitatingly removed the "queen" from her position of power had her policies not served Hasag's purposes.

In addition, the prisoners' state of mind was also influenced by their awareness that they were in an extermination camp, a fact which blunted their will to fight for their survival. As we have seen, the population of Werk C consisted largely of the human dregs of each new transport, along with the debilitated prisoners from the other two camps. This affected the social structure of the "Radom Tier," composed of the following "classes":

1) The "queen" and her family who lorded over everyone else. Entry to the "royal family" was only through marriage (as in the case of Dr Haendel).

---

[30] Jerzy Adryanowicz, Testimony, AGKBZH, SWK, sygn. 218, p. 189.

2) The *prominente*, a total of some 200 people including the police, functionaries, wealthy merchants and Markowiczowa's personal friends. Entry to this class required a large investment or procurement of a major post.

3) The middle class, while quite large in Werk A, was very small here since few prisoners brought any "capital" into the camp and anything they did have was very soon exhausted. The members of this class faded quickly and only few of them survived. (Thus, for example, only very few members of the Piotrków transport of Spring, 1943 remained alive in Werk C, while the majority of the same transport in Werk A survived.)

4) A very large class of "pariahs" continually added to and continually losing members to every 'selection'. Quite accurately, Strigler remarked that "there were generations in Werk C, one came and one went, but here *it happened much more rapidly*" [31] [emphasis mine – F.K.].

The constant turnover in a large part of the camp population on the one hand, and the stability of the "White House" rule on the other, created an unparalleled social and economic gap. Róża Bauminger testifies that "in no camp were there contrasts like in Werk C in Skarżysko. On the one hand the most abject poverty and on the other unheard-of luxuries." [32]

The "*picryners*," whose barracks stood at the edge of the camp, were among the pariahs of Werk C. The stench of the picric acid kept even lice and fleas away. Even when blankets or mattresses were distributed to the other prisoners, the "*picryners*" received none since they would immediately turn them yellow. There were no heaters here, either, for fear of fire. The men, who, because of the quantities they drank, often had to go to the latrine several times during the night, were afraid to be shot by a guard and so dug a trench beneath the door to the barracks. The police tried to combat the filth by beating the prisoners mercilessly, but even this did not help. Here no one had a shirt, and four prisoners would chip in to buy one cigarette for 40 *grosz*. Some crawled back and forth to the plant

---

[31] M. Strigler, Werk "Ce", op. cit., vol. 2, p. 181.

[32] R. Bauminger, see n. 4, ib., p. 6.

for months, while others ran aimlessly about the camp until one evening they simply lay down and died. The other prisoners treated these yellow skeletons like the walking dead and kept their distance. Nobody even knew their names, so that it could often be heard that "at the 'selection' they took away Moshe and Ya'akov and a few *picryners*."

The sad state of these "damned" prisoners is preserved in the "Picryner Anthem" penned by an anonymous poet:[33]

> We work with picric acid – the yellow poison!
> Which paints us from the top of our heads to our toes...
> It poisons our lungs and weakens our hearts
> Striking down even the strongest of us!
> On top of that, they all shoo us away,
> Shouting at us, Go away, picryner!
> They beat us and chase us, breaking our bones,
> As if their hearts were all made of stone.
>
> (from the Yiddish)

The New Pariahs – "Kaelniks" in Werk C

Such was the kingdom and such were its laws when, in the Summer of 1943, some 1,000 prisoners from Majdanek arrived in the camp. They still remembered the unguarded remark of one of the capos: "You're in luck, you're going to Skarżysko." [34] However, not even the ones with the most experience of German camps ever dreamed of what they would find in Werk C.

The first shock came in the very first roll-call. "Out of the office came *Werkschutz* men and behind them a young woman in a white raincoat who strode with a regal bearing. Impatiently, she tossed a leather whip in her hand.... The policemen all stood at attention before her." The "*commandanta*" spoke gently to the men, but used a different tone toward the women (many of whom were young and still attractive): "You, whores, where did you come from?" When the roll-call was over, the police began urging the "riff-raff" into their barracks, making considerable use of their clubs. There the second shock awaited them:

---

[33] M. Strigler, Goirolois, op. cit., vol. 2, p. 88.

[34] Simcha Engerest, op. cit.

What a stench! And who were those people wrapped in paper crowding together on filthy pallets? The newcomers discovered, to their amazement, that both men and women were quartered here. And the strangest part of all – where were the Germans!? [35] After Majdanek with its ubiquitous SS officers, Werk C looked like a *reine yidishe medine* (a purely Jewish country).

When work assignments were handed out, many of the women were fortunate enough to be sent to "Schmitz". Most of the men were assigned to the transport brigade or the Shell Department. They were glad at least not to have been sent to work with the picric acid. After several days in Hall Number 6, they were not so sure. The kaelnik Mosze Lestny writes: "Once when I was coming into the hall the foreman asked me what my name was. I answered according to form in Majdanek 'Number 1172'. When he asked to know my last name, I couldn't for the life of me remember it and I was beaten again." [36] The lot of the newcomers was no better in the camp. The Radomites suddenly realized that there were prisoners inferior even to them, and they took out all of their anger and bitterness on them. They kept them from reaching the water tap, would not let them into the barbershop, and accused them of being thieves and informants. For the *kaelniks*, there was never an extra piece of bread. As Ryszard Mittelberg states: "We were the worst of them all. We were ready to steal because we were starving to death." [37]

Thus, a unique social phenomenon evolved in Werk C – two classes of pariahs. As a result, competition for every spoonful of soup was even greater. But while the locals at least knew where to look for it, the prisoners from Majdanek died like flies. It may have been one of their number who left behind these melancholy lines of "Transport Workers Song": [38]

Werk C – the worst of all!
Thousands have already found their death here

How many heroes have fallen, have gone
Like a candle's wick, so quickly burnt up...

---

[35] M. Strigler, In di fabrikn, op. cit., pp. 104–107, 298.

[36] Mosze Lestny, Testimony, YV, M-1/E/2493/2608.

[37] R. Mittelberg, op. cit.

[38] See n. 33, ib., p. 84.

At night we return, exhausted and broken
From dragging the shells and pouring tetryl
But nobody here can help us at all!
So we live and we die all alone, unknown...

We work till we drop – in sunshine, in rain
No rest whatsoever for a Jew in this place!
And there's no one to ask, no one to petition
Oh when, oh when, will it come to an end?

(from the Yiddish)

No one knew the answer to this question, and once again there was a rash of escape attempts. In the Summer, 1943, Abraham Szmajser, a member of Zionist Youth from Staszów, escaped with two others, one of whom was Jehuda Wittenberg. They were caught by Polish partisans. Two managed to flee, but Jehuda was held and interrogated at length. When he asked to join forces with his captors, their officer replied: "Only 110 cm underground." Eventually, he was left with no choice but to return to the camp. Miraculously, he was not put to death, but sent to Werk B to work for Leidig.[39] The kaelniks made their escape in the Autumn - first seven, and then 15 men from the night shift of the transport brigade and several from Hall Number 54.[40] As a result, security was tightened, and the prisoners were faced with the problem of surviving under the cruelest of conditions.

"Words can not describe what it was like in Werk C," recalls Mejer Ryzenberg. "Today I can't understand how people in this death camp managed to stay alive."[41] How, indeed? Every now and then a miracle occurred. Kuzimiński was saved by the murderer Schneider; Ryzenberg escaped on the way to the firing range; Meir Guza eluded the guards chasing him by jumping through a barracks window; Friedmann was listed in the Picric Acid Department as deceased so that he could stay at "Schmitz". The kaelnik Hersz Bitter, marked for death at a night "selection," asked one of the Germans if he could bring a flashlight. The latter laughingly agreed, and Bitter, naturally, never returned.[42] Strigler

---

[39] J.Wittenberg, op. cit.

[40] M. Strigler, In di fabrikn, op. cit., p. 314 ff.

[41] M. Ryzenberg, op. cit.

[42] Hersz Bitter, Testimony, YV, 0-16/2584.

was saved from starvation by daring to write a letter to Markowiczowa asking for help.

Although a "camp economy" also grew up in Werk C, it operated along two parallel lines which virtually never met: the elite traded in valuables, foreign currency, etc. for profit, while the ordinary prisoners, despite the disparities among them, made "deals" for an extra piece of bread. This was nothing more than a "beggars' economy." The women from the Picric Acid Department brought bits of bread, an onion, a handful of barley, a few pieces of sugar or one or two cigarettes into the camp. Despite the bitter taste of everything they touched, they could always find a buyer. Here a slice of bread went to three men for 5 zloty, there a clever barterer offered potato peels, a "picryner" exchanged buttons for a cigarette, another sold a piece of his trousers to be used for a patch. At "Schmitz," Edzia brought a daily jug of coffee for sale. A woman lucky enough to buy the soup bones out of the Poles' dinner cooked up new "soup" and sold it. Apple peels thrown away by the privileged ones were dried and used to make "tea."[43] Middlemen also flourished: someone would get a few tins from a tinsmith and sell them for a 50 *grosz* commission; clothes were sold to the Poles on consignment; the cleverer businessmen opened "exclusive bazaars," as did Rubinek Zisskind, who used his "income" to help his friends as well.[44]

There were also artisans, such as several tailors, in the camp. One of these, Herszel Goldwasser, together with two other prisoners, sewed a whole suit for the manager Szarata's son in one night.[45] The tinsmiths used the aluminum they found in the "Schmitz" storerooms to make pots, buckets and bowls. The only craftsmen who truly prospered were the shoemakers. They took the backs of the shoes from wooden clogs, the leather from the handles of ammunition crates, the uppers from old bags purchased from the Poles, and the sewing cords from rope. A Polish customer who wished to order shoes would bring an old pair from which to measure the size to a middleman who would wear them into the camp. The new pair would be delivered to him in the same way.[46] Those who

---

[43] Pauline Schneider-Buchenholz, "Memoirs from the war and concentration camps", YV, 0-33/E/142-2-1.

[44] Awraham Ahuvia, "B' Buchenwald k'bnei adam", a diary, (Hebrew), AHJF, p. 9.

[45] Herszel Goldwasser, Testimony, YV, 0-33/1825.

[46] I. Rotbalsam, op. cit.

were afraid to take such risks ferreted through the garbage where they found all sorts of saleable goods that only needed cleaning, like buttons, rags, or tins.

For less enterprising prisoners, the only chance of survival was help from fellow prisoners. Opinions are divided as to the question of self-help in Werk C. Some speak disparagingly of the thorough bestiality of the prisoners and the abuse of the weak by the strong,[47] while others cite examples of "extraordinary" relationships among the prisoners.[48] There were also displays of genuine friendship among the men. The "picryner" David Schvarzmer never forgot his friend Finkelsztajn who once a week gave him bread for free. Szmuel Białywłos painfully recalls two friends who helped him in his time of need and found their death in the camp.[49] Every once in a while a policeman would exhibit a humane side. Mosze Lestny aptly defines this phenomenon by stating: "Among those to whom I owe my life were Jews from the underworld and Jews from the 'overworld'."

The lot of a few prisoners was made easier through connections with the outside. The Skarzyskoans regularly received packages from their Polish friends; Rogler, the mayor of Staszów, sent his townspeople money, sugar cubes and tobacco; and prisoners from the Piotrków ghetto continued to receive parcels from their relatives until Summer, 1943.

Religiously observant Jews had their own way of fighting for their survival. Several rabbis and religious teachers gathered groups of the devout around them, periodically organizing public prayers. A number of the bolder ones smuggled prayer shawls, phylacteries and prayer books into the camp. Although they risked their lives to do so, prayer brought them together and shored up their hope. Schvarzmer distressingly recalls his own personal crisis: "When someone stole my shoes I walked to work barefoot and felt that the end was near. I had lost all hope. I stopped washing, and, what was worse, I even stopped praying." In Hall Number 51, a group led by the yeshiva scholar Lemit recited the Minhah prayer even during work, organized anonymous charity for religious scholars, and at the request of mourners, arranged public prayers, the reciting of

---

[47] F. Bannet, see n. 4, ib., p. 7; S. Kurz, R. Mittelberg, op. cit.

[48] Frania Siegmann, Testimony, YV, 0-3/2979.

[49] Letter of Szmuel Białywłos, see testimony of J. Rechter, op. cit.

Kaddish, and even a Shiv'ah vigil for several hours. A small community of Bobow hassids also prayed together and helped each other.[50]

The women sought to preserve their traditions in their own ways. On the eve of the Sabbath, a special atmosphere pervaded the barracks. There was no more shouting and squabbling over a place near the heater, the heart of the barracks which also served as kitchen, laundry and baking oven. Each of the women found a corner in which to be alone with her own thoughts, and anyone who had managed to get hold of a bit of candle lit it on the edge of her pallet. Friends and relatives would visit. Here and there a singer would begin a solo performance for which she was rewarded with a potato or other delicacy.[51] Later, when the "visitors" had left, one of the women would start a song and the others would join in.

There were also attempts to celebrate the holidays. On April 19, 1943, Eliezer Lewin organized a Passover Seder for some of the religious figures, including the rabbis from Jasznica, Otwock and Falenica. Lookouts were stationed outside while eight rabbis gathered in the barracks. The table was covered in white paper on which were placed matzos baked during the night. Beet borscht was poured into tins in place of wine, and a bowl of eggs, sent by the "*commandanta*" as a gift, stood in the center of the table. They recited the Haggadah from memory. "There was an awesome silence when the four questions were asked and we had no answers, just as there were none for the questions each of us carried in his heart and which remain unanswerable to this day. The candle flames burned like the souls of the thousands of Jews tortured in the camp of horrors, Hasag, and quiet weeping accompanied each passage from the Haggadah." [52]

The Wolbrom rabbi, who was under the protection of the elderly Mrs. Gutman (the "*commandanta's*" mother), organized a public prayer in his barracks in honor of Rosh Hashanah, 1943, and even members of the "royal family" honored the occasion with their presence. Yom Kippur was also felt strongly in the camp, although the special atmosphere of this holy day was always fraught with the fear that the Germans would again surprise them with an unannounced "selection".

---

[50] M. Strigler, In di fabrikn, pp. 167, 357; Werk" Ce", vol. 2, pp. 12, 23.

[51] Ilona Karmel, An estate, op. cit., pp. 141, 292.

[52] E. Lewin, see n. 5.

Late September, 1943 saw the first signs of a new "liberal era". The large-scale "selections" ceased. Construction on the new barracks, begun in the summer, was resumed. A breach was opened in the fence through which building materials could be passed into the camp, and this immediately became the site of systematic smuggling. In view of the shortage of workers in the plant, several doctors who had arrived from Majdanek were assigned to the "hospital". They included Dr Rotbalsam, Dr Wassserstein, and Dr Świsłocki. An infirmary for the injured was set up and equipped with a few jars of salve and rags for bandages. The doctors were empowered to grant the ill several days "sick leave," and as a result a good many mussulmen wandered about the camp.[53] To everyone's amazement, attempts were made to improve the neglected physical conditions of the camp. Even the police underwent a certain change, and sensing that a "liberal" wind was blowing from above, they tempered their behavior somewhat. The prisoners were infused with new hope, and all waited impatiently to see what was coming.

The answer came in November. One morning, Kurt Schumann suddenly appeared in the camp and *Werkschutz* men were posted all around the fence. One hundred and eighty of those on "sick leave" were caught and loaded onto trucks. Schumann stopped them near the kitchen and ordered the cook to dole out soup to everyone since they were still "on the list." The condemned prisoners believed a miracle had happened. They lined up and seemed to forget everything that had gone before. When they had finished, they were herded back on the trucks. Bitter shouting and weeping ensued, as if their fate had been sealed all over again. Some tried to leap from the trucks and resist. "For the first, and perhaps only time, even some of the German managers looked away and many Poles shed a tear." [54]

On the night of November 16, 1943, a new transport from Płaszów arrived at the camp gate.

---

[53] Adam Wasserstein, Testimony, YV, 0-16/1043.
[54] M. Strigler, Werk "Ce", vol. 2, p. 179.

Chapter 11

"Life Can Be Good – Even in Werk C"

Meetings at the Cannons

All the camp "nobility" gathered by the gate through which hundreds of men and women from Płaszów were being herded into Werk C. Markowiczowa and the *prominente* had waited impatiently for this moment, and now they were convinced of the truth of the rumors that had spoken of new prisoners who were elite, intellectuals, rich! The newcomers marched in perfect order, carrying parcels and bags. The experienced eye of the police immediately noted how perfunctory the *Werkschutz* search was. These people could buy up Werk C lock, stock and barrel!

It was only the next morning, when the fog lifted, that the new prisoners saw where they had been brought. Why was everything yellow? The barracks, the mud ... it was a world gone mad! Those greenish specters – were they creatures from outer space? This place meant certain death. Curiosity got the better of some of the veteran women prisoners, and they dropped in on the newcomers' barracks. "Do you want to stay alive here? Without help you won't hold out for even three months!" [1]

Late at night, when the camp yard was empty, the sound of singing

---

[1] F. Immerglueck, op. cit.

could suddenly be heard from the next barracks over. Here? In this hellhole, they could sing? The voices grew increasingly stronger:

Oyf di kanonen veln mir zich bagegnen!
Unter di kanonen veln mir zich gezegnen!
(O'er the cannons we shall meet!
Under the cannons shall be parted!)

" 'Do you know what that is?' one of the girls asked. 'They're singing in Yiddish "We shall meet on the cannons' " !!! We were utterly astounded. In Płaszów a young boy caught humming a Russian song had been given a public hanging, and here they sing songs of rebellion!? This was totally crazy.... In the dark we thirstily lapped up every drop of music and weren't even aware that we too had started to whisper 'O'er the cannons we shall meet'." [2] Thus a spark of hope was lit. If the Germans let them sing, maybe they'd let them live, too. How had the others kept alive until now? How did a song like that find its way into the valley of tears that was Werk C?

"The Song of the Cannons" had been introduced into the camp in an earlier period, when each of the prisoners sought some form of support to help in the fight for survival. As a result, *new frameworks* were formed. With no real families, "camp families" came into being – groups of girls who lived together and shared whatever they had. "Cooking groups" of men and women were organized, where each member provided some item for the common pot from which they all ate together. Remnants of some of the old *Landsmannschafts – organizations* of people from the same town – still existed. Zeev Szenwald felt it was a miracle when five friends from his hometown of Sochaczew arrived on the Majdanek transport. "We would get together, reminiscing about our old home, and it encouraged us. I was the most veteran prisoner in the group, so I could help them a little, but in the end only two of us survived." [3] The prisoner's home was the crowded *Stube* (room) in the barracks. If they were lucky enough to get a good "overseer," as Friedland was in Barracks No. 2, he would make sure that the place was clean, that the food was distributed fairly, and that the haves shared their rations with the have-nots. Here youth groups met,

---

[2] H. Zorska, op. cit.
[3] Zeev Szenwald, Pinkas Sochaczew, p. 742.

some of which were organized by young policemen fed up with the lonely "ivory tower" existence advocated by their commander, Eisenberg.

The *prominente*, hungry for a social life, were responsible for the creation of the "good barracks" *(Guter Barak)* which housed the metal-worker Henoch Edelman together with the engineer Mosze Hartman, the attorney Neumann, and privileged prisoners such as Stanisław Kanczer, the former industrialist Sznitbaum, and the camp writer Strigler. Topics for debate were supplied by the chief politician in the camp, Jakow Kurz, who in some miraculous way managed to get hold of the German newspaper *Krakauer Zeitung* regularly. Here Markowiczowa found her "upper class" friends with whom she could chat or play a game of cards.[4]

For very different purposes, prisoners gravitated to the laundry which was run by Ungerowa, an illiterate with a grotesque body. She held sway over an oven, two vats of hot water, and even a bathtub. The prominente ordered cakes and meals from her, or came to bathe. This was the business center of the camp. Since Ungerowa knew many secrets, this woman, with her very spicy language, was highly feared.[5] There was also a social life in the police barracks which was the site of wild parties, accompanied by drinking and singing, in the company of the "cousins." "Troubadours" were sometimes invited to sing for the revellers in exchange for an extra bread ration or chit for the clothes store.

The "common" prisoners socialized in other places. The men chatted as they waited in line for the barber. They spoke of small-scale business dealings, cursed out the commanders of all sorts, and tried to make sense of the latest rumors from the front. The women turned the *waschraum* into a social club, gossiping avidly about the "pallet lovers" as they did their laundry. In the evenings, couples walked hand in hand along the camp paths. On warm summer days, they would spread a paper sack under a tree and have a starving man's "picnic".

As early as the "Radom Period", ideological and political groups began to form in an effort to add another dimension to the substandard life of the prisoners. The first were members of Hashomer Hadati from Staszów, among them Mączyk, Jakow Milgram, Goldberg, Szaul Goldhar, David Najman, Herszel Tochterman, and the brothers Zeev, Israel and Meir

---

[4] M. Strigler, Goirolois, op. cit., vol. 1, pp. 70–74.

[5] Anna Hauser, Testimony, YV, 0-16/4696; F. Bannet, see Chapter 10, n. 4.

Blusztajn. They had a common kitty from which they bought bread and shared it out among them all every day. On free evenings they met for talk and community singing, the special province of Najman and the Blusztajn brothers. Goldhar was their leader by default, since he had managed to make contact with other members from Staszów in the Poniatowa camp from whom he received money and a list of people for whom it was intended. The list was signed by "a man named Mordchai Tenennbaum." We cannot be sure whether or not this was the hero of the Białystok Ghetto uprising, although it has been suggested that he was indeed sent to Poniatowa after the rebellion was crushed.[6]

A second group, allied with the Poalei Zion movement, included two engineers, Mosze Hartman of Radomsko and Jakow Kurz of Warsaw. Both had a rather unusual status since they were not only popular with the prisoners, but also favored by Markowiczowa who sought to ally herself with intellectuals. Other members of this group were Starowiński, the former director of Keren Hayesod in Warsaw, Mosze Lestny, Baruch Szapira, and two doctors, Israel Rotbalsam and Adam Wasserstein.

The Bund group had a somewhat different nature. Its veteran members came from the cities and towns of the Radom district, such as the metalworker Edelman who despised the bourgeoisie, his colleague Mendel Rubin, Aharon Ciok, the second-in-command of the police Feldman, the policeman Treper, and Aharon Szichter, a Bund official from Szydłowiec.[7] They were joined by functionaries of the Bund who arrived from Majdanek: Bluma Klug, Solnik, Herman Goldberg, and others. Their leader was Henoch Ross, who had been a senior official of the movement before the war and was known for his educational and cultural work in which his wife Hedzia was also very active.[8]

The initial meeting between the veteran Bund members and their new colleagues was a spontaneous one. A group of girls had gathered in the forest for some community singing, and their voices attracted a large audience who joined in enthusiastically for the popular Yiddish songs.

---

[6] Szaul Goldhar, op. cit; cf. Nina Tennenbaum-Backer, The hero of the ghettoes, (Hebrew), (Tel-Aviv: Misrad habitachon, 1980) pp. 195, 351–358.

[7] M. Strigler, Werk "Ce", op. cit., vol. 2, pp. 107–111; B.Z. Rozenberg, op. cit.

[8] M. Kligsberg, "Henoch Ross", (Yiddish), in "Dorot Bundisten", 2, ed. J.S. Herz, (New York: 1956), pp. 412–415.

Suddenly, one of the *kaelniks* began to sing "Di Shwue", the well-known anthem of the Bund:

> Brider un shvester fun arbet un noyt,
> Ale vos zaynen tsezeyt un tseshpreyt...
>
> (Brothers and sisters, in toil and need
> All who are scattered all over the world...)

The familiar words sent shivers down everyone's spine. Even some of the exhausted "*picryners*" tried to join in. The prisoners were shocked when they saw the second-in-command of the police, Feldman, who had come running to shut them up, suddenly remove his hat and stand at attention as they sang his anthem.[9]

This incident was a turning point for the organization. At night, Feldman would meet clandestinely with his fellow members, periodically bringing them a bit of bread. Blumcia Klug, the daughter of Lazar Klug, a Bund official from Warsaw, became his "cousin". Henoch Ross, who had been sent to the picric acid department and was near collapse, was transferred at the insistence of Feldman and Edelman to a better assignment. During that same Autumn of 1943, the camp anthem was born. One day, as the girls were being marched to work and the bored *Werkschutz* ordered them to sing, two *kaelniks* remembered a song that had been popular in the proletarian streets of Jewish Warsaw and, unaware of what they were doing, entered history with the very first word:

> Haynt, libe Marion,
> Trefen veln mir zich oyf dem kanon,
> Un eyder vos ven
> Nem a sher in di hand!
> Sher op dayne tsep,
> Tu on a mantl mit di soldaten knep
> Nem arum, gib a kush un kum!
>> Oyf di kanonen veln mir zich bagegnen,
>> Unter di kanonen veln mir zich gezegnen,
>> Biks tsu biks veln mir zich bagrisn,
>> Kol tsu kol veln dunern un blitsn,
>> Oyf di kanonen, unter di kanonen,
>> Biks tsu biks!

---

[9] M. Strigler, Werk "Ce", op. cit., vol. 1, p. 106 ff.

(Today, sweet Marion
We shall meet by the cannons
But before all else
Take scissors in hand
Cut off your braids
Dress in soldier's coat
Hug me and kiss me – and come!
    O'er the cannons we shall meet
    Under the cannons shall be parted
    Rifle to rifle, each other greet
    Cannon roar to cannon roar,
    Flashing lightning, rumbling thunder
    Cannons o'er and cannons under
    Rifle to rifle!)

This song had an unusual effect. Within days it was being sung by everyone, men and women alike, and everywhere, in the barracks, the washroom, on the way to work.[10] It had been eight months since the victory at Stalingrad, yet freedom still seemed far away. Nonetheless, each and every prisoner knew that the German defeat would come and dreamt at night of the Soviet cannons moving slowly but surely closer. The song, with its motifs of rebellion and battle, was the total antithesis of the prisoner's condition, of the endless degradation and utter helplessness. It thus touched everyone, arousing hope and creating a sense of unity. The transport from Płaszów was greeted with this song, and under its wing a new element began to emerge in camp life.

That Autumn of 1943 saw the first signs of organized political, social and cultural activity in the camp. A meeting was called at the laundry, and it was decided to establish a camp Rescue Committee in order to aid the neediest prisoners and to recruit the help of the *prominente* and prosperous prisoners in this endeavor. The two political groups were represented on the committee, the Zionists by Hartman, Dr Wasserstein, Starowiński, Baruch Szapira and Jakow Kurz, and the Bund by Mendel Rubin and Feldman.

Towards the end of that year, Dr Rotbalsam was invited to a secret meeting with the engineer David Efrat who gave him 3,000 zloty from an unknown source and asked that a Distribution Committee be set up in

---

[10] M. Strigler, ib., p. 206; H. Zorska, op. cit.

Werk C to determine who was most in need of help. Rotbalsam called on Dr Wasserstein and Kurz to join him on the committee, and the money was distributed to members of the intelligentsia.[11] Through other channels, the Bundists managed to inform the movement's central office in Warsaw of the presence of Henoch Ross in the camp and received a letter promising assistance.[12] In the meanwhile, however, they heard that the money for the Distribution Committee had come from the *Komisja Koordynacyjna*, and that Berman and Feiner had stipulated it be meted out in accordance with party affiliation. As a result, the Bund demanded a new Rescue Committee be formed with representation proportional to the number of members of each party. The parity committee now consisted of Hartman, Kurz and Wasserstein for the Zionists, and Ross, Feldman and Edelman for the Bund.[13]

Very little is known of the extent of aid, since both the distributors and the recipients prefer to remain silent. Strigler reveals that he was one of the recipients and knew of others. Szaul Goldhar was chosen to help distribute money from the group led by Henoch Ross who brought him into his group and held underground meetings. As to the manner in which the money was doled out, Icchak Friedman offers a typical comment in stating that he himself knew nothing of financial aid but is certain the distributors helped in the best possible way "since they were very decent people." [14]

In time, political and welfare activities became part of the constant and independent cultural activities that distinguished Werk C. More sources have survived regarding Werk C than the other camps, making it possible to learn of the types of original creations, their roots, and their development. The most characteristic feature was the three distinct channels in which creative energy flowed: barracks lyrics; "court songs"; and the works of camp writers from among the intelligentsia. The cultural foundations were laid by a fund of popular Yiddish songs brought into the camp by the thousands of prisoners from the Radom district.

---

[11] I. Rotbalsam, op. cit; David Efrat, see Chapter 7, n. 30–31.

[12] Antek Bagniewski (Cukierman), Protokół przesłuchania w sprawie dr. Weicherta, YV, 0-21/7, p. 28;   see Chapter 7, ib.

[13] I. Rotbalsam, op. cit; M. Strigler, Werk "Ce", vol. 1, pp. 226–229.

[14] I. Friedmann, Bletlech, op. cit., p. 126.

The "barracks lyrics" were composed during rest hours in the barracks in a spontaneous and collective manner by anonymous bards. Although never written down, they were quickly learned by heart. They combined the elements of folk ballads with motifs of protest, familiar from the poor neighborhoods of the Jewish proletariat. The *"Picryner Anthem"* or "Transport Workers Song" reveal the grievances over the bitter fate of the heroic Jewish workers brought down by hard labor. This tone of secret class pride is joined by open criticism of the camp *prominente*.[15]

> Werk C – the worst camp of all!
> How many victims it has claimed for no reason,
> Because of the commandants – cruel souls –
> A barrel of vodka is all they desire.
>
> And we shall say – the day will come!
> When our crying is recalled by the children...
> The heart will rebel – the fist will form
> Against those who here sold out their brothers!
>
> (Translated from the Yiddish)

The "court songs" were sung at police drinking parties, wild revels at the "White House," and public performances first organized by Markowiczowa. When the "queen," hungry for entertainment, – relates M. Strigler – heard that Halina, a cabaret singer from Warsaw, was among the kaelniks, she decreed that a special show be arranged for the camp elite. The first court concert was held in a barracks with a stage and special lighting installed. It featured Halina, who danced and sang the current hits, and the policeman Dawid Najman who had written songs in Yiddish, including one on "The Beautiful Girls of Majdanek" which captivated the camp nobles. Among the amusing songs were also those that expressed the undying hope for a better future, popular lyrics that had been passed from one prisoner to the next:[16]

> Although here there is only despair and sorrow
> Still the desire for life burns on!
> For our end is yet a far tomorrow!
>
> (Translated from the Yiddish)

---

[15] M. Strigler, Goirolois, op. cit., vol. 2, p. 86.

[16] M. Strigler, Werk "C", op. cit., vol. 1, pp. 209–210.

In late Autumn, 1943, the Rescue Committee decided to organize a public concert, collecting an entrance fee which was to be used to help the needy. This was also a ruse to conceal the true source of the money smuggled into the camp. Unlike the first show, this was a publicly arranged performance for welfare purposes, but despite fears to the contrary, Markowiczowa gave her consent. She was motivated not only by her desire for amusement, but also by her concept of her "royal" status. She saw herself entitled to lend her patronage to the arts and the artists, and wished to keep an eye on "her" intellectuals who she regarded with guarded respect. Thus, for example, she confiscated the diaries of Strigler, the "camp writer," but returned them once she was convinced that he sought only to immortalize the people of Werk C, including herself.

The concert was held in a barracks with the inner partitions removed and a stage erected. The program was quite eclectic, including humorous couplets on the camp police, popular songs, and a poem by Strigler entitled "On the People of Werk C" and recited by Hedzia Ross.[17] This time, a very different note was sounded:

> To you, starving people of Werk C, there is little to say,
> No smiles can be seen on your faces, no laugh can be heard...
> Work! Toil in hunger! Live in filth and in excrement!
> Quotas! From you, bags of bones and yellow skin, they demand only work!

Here Hedzia turned to the *prominente* seated in the first row:

> And you! You neither see nor wish to hear!...
> Those are the plant Jews! They don't matter!
> And you have meat and money! You are rich...

> (Translated from the Yiddish)

Such sharp criticism had never before been openly voiced in Werk C. Strigler won instant popularity. Eisenberg assigned him to the humiliating job of collecting garbage, and the policeman Kaufman promised him extra soup. It became abundantly clear that even here poets were needed and "Werk C could not live on starvation alone."

As for the concert's objective, money was collected and distributed to the needy. But the prisoners soon had new concerns. The Płaszów transport arrived, and with it – typhoid.

---

[17] Ibid., vol. 2, pp. 118–120.

The Deadly Typhoid Epidemic

From the very first, the encounter between the autochthonous population
and the prisoners from Płaszów did not seem to promise any chance of a
communal existence. The Radomites now joined forces with the *kaelniks*
against the rich "intellectuals" who, as they saw it, filled the pockets of the
"White House" with gold and dollars in order to purchase good work
assignments for themselves, while the impoverished veteran prisoners
were shoved aside into the least desirable departments. Indeed, the money
brought into the camp encouraged trading. Nevertheless, a month later the
Werkschutz conducted a surprise search in the barracks and confiscated a
great deal of the newcomers' money.[18] Contrary to rumor, many of the
men from Płaszów were assigned to the Shell Department, the Transport
Crew, and the Picric Acid Department. The "Kingdom of the Damned"
struck terror in the hearts of all the prisoners. No one knows when or by
whom the following poem was composed.[19]

> Beyond the mountain, in the forest, in the wilderness,
> A very important product is being turned out,
> And people from all over the land
> Are soon destroyed there – by the thousands, the thousands..
>> The sons of Krakow in time arrived here,
>> And the girls came, too, from the city,
>> And the *kaelnik* girls express their condolences
>> And promise us a swift end...
> A new life awaits us
> Full of unknown surprises
> But the "picric" is the most terrifying
> And we all shiver at the thought.
>
> (Excerpts translated from the Polish)

Their fear did not protect them, and some of the new women prisoners
were sent to Halls 13 and 15. They were assigne several pallets in the
barracks of the veteran picric acid workers. Their "reception" in the
barracks is vividly described by Maria Lewinger: [20]

---

[18] Werkschutz Hasag-Werke, 11.12.1943, see Chapter 3, n. 32.
[19] Felicja Szachar, Testimony, YV, 0-33/3334.
[20] Maria Szechter Lewinger, "W baraku pikryniarek", YV, 0-33/1802.

When we entered the women's barracks we were appalled. The scene before us was so horrifying that it didn't seem real. From the filthy yellow pallets, yellow-green ghouls looked out and in screeching voices invited us to draw near them. The goods they had for sale were arranged on the edges of their pallets.... Yellow eyes peered out at us from all sides.... With what profound envy, what amazement, these ugly wrinkled women with rusty-colored hair stared at us! We were still dressed in coats and shoes, while they were wrapped in rags or paper with wooden clogs on their feet. We still looked young and fresh, while they looked old, bitter, gnawed to the bone by the yellow picric acid.... We lay down on our pallet.... Beside it was a bucket, and one woman after another came up to it to relieve herself in it. The urine spilled everywhere and we couldn't breathe for the stench. No one paid any attention to our protests. At most, someone uttered a sarcastic comment: 'Look at those spoiled princesses from Krakow! Don't worry, you'll soon look just like me!'

This sense of helplessness accompanied the Plaszowites wherever they went. Luna Fuss-Kaufman recalls:

One night I decided to go to the latrine. The camp paths were utterly deserted and I was surrounded by a terrifying darkness and silence.... Fearfully I crept towards the latrine, when I suddenly bumped into a huge crate with weird objects sticking out of it... I thought it was a garbage crate and chills ran down my spine when I saw that they were skeletons, human bones covered with thin yellow skin. I went back to the barracks frightened to death. This was what awaited us here.[21]

The experienced *kaelnik* women advised their new friends to find a "*kuzyn*". This was such a common arrangement during the "Majdanek Period" that no one thought anything of it anymore. Here in Werk C the poor were most dependent on the rich, and this fact was even apparent in their sex life. More and more private corners were closed off in the women's barracks and love-life flowered. At first the women from Płaszów stuck to their own men. Indeed, considering the immense mortality rate of the men from Majdanek, potential "cousins" were scarce, and the men often took advantage of the situation. The camp's "daily press" noted the new situation:[22]

---

[21] Luna Fuss-Kaufman, op. cit.

[22] Fela Blum, Testimony, YV, 0-33/1839.

> Come and I'll whisper a secret in your ear:
> Pickings are pretty slim with the "cousins" here!
> They have their cake and they eat it too,
> "Kuzynka" makes one and their wife makes two!
>
> (Translated from the Polish)

The girls from the "Kraków intelligentsia," however, were reluctant to become friends with shoemakers. In late 1943 they still had things they could sell, had become better acquainted with the Poles in the plant, and those who knew German could even converse with the German managers. It seemed as if the Plaszowites had a good chance of surviving. When the first cases of typhoid appeared, they attracted little attention, and the doctors, hoping to avert a "selection," reported them as influenza.

Suddenly, an epidemic swept through the camp like a storm. It struck down the women from Płaszów who had not yet contracted typhoid and thus lacked the natural immunity of the men. At first, some four women a day would die, and later 8 to 12. The ill lay in the "hospital", two to a pallet, covered in rags. There were no medicines. The orderlies, Alek and Melech, the policeman Bugajski and the "nurse" Lusia competed savagely for the gold teeth or money of each dying woman. For this reason, they tried to fill the "hospital" with the richest patients. In some cases, women managed to overcome the disease, but remained in a half-conscious state and starved to death in a puddle of their own excrement, covered in lice.[23] When there were more sick women than healthy ones in one of the barracks, it was turned into an improvised infirmary. Picric acid workers served as male practical nurses, bringing the patients soup and emptying their buckets in exchange for soup or bread.[24] "Selections" and consequent executions of the ill continued until January 1944. When they ceased, the doctors were able to issue work exemptions.

The victims of the disease suffered hallucinations which became etched on their memories. At times the fear of death brought the prisoner to the brink of madness.

> Death is a burning cave, a furnace! The flames rage... and death dances within them. His body twists and turns, striking the walls, clutching at them with his nails in wild laughter. He dances and dances... fire and

---

[23] Anna Hauser, Testimonies, YV, 0-16/4696; 0-16/1391.

[24] I. Karmel, An estate, op. cit., p. 293.

dancing, dancing and fire, build like a storm!... Stop! Stop! My brain is exploding! My brain is burning like a furnace![25]

In the following poem by Henia Karmel, the author offers a naturalistic description of the epidemic's terrors.[26]

Covered in rags, drained by hunger
Drowning in filth up to the neck...
And there in a whitewashed crate
The stench of corpses, spoils of the epidemic...
    The deadly stink from the sewage pits,
    The hallucinations of typhoid... human refuse.
    Is thrown out of life, which is never sated
    With any horrifying vengeance...
And the lice – fattened, despised
Cover human rags...

(Excerpts translated from the Polish)

The epidemic raged for close to three months, claiming some 900 victims, most of them women.[27] Enjoying immunity from the disease, few men were infected. Day after day they marched off to work and were sent to dig pits in the forest for the dead. Awraham Eliasziw lamented bitterly at this duty.[28]

Thirty victims I buried with my own hands,
Yet my own grave I never shall know...
    On the stony earth, the wooden clogs drum mutely,
    Rows and rows of human shadows, stretching endlessly.
    Shifts change morning and evening,
    But you will never find your brothers, lost along the way...

(Excerpt translated from the Polish)

The Three-Part Revolution and its Consequences

Those who survived the epidemic, recovering in the Spring of 1944, did not always know who had saved their lives. It may have been family

---

[25] M. Lewinger, cited by Felicja Karay, Boded mul hamavet, (Hebrew), (Jerusalem: Misrad hachinuch w'hatarbut, 1980) p. 48.

[26] Henryka Karmel-Wolf, "Wszy", Poesies, YV,0-33/1852.

[27] R. Bauminger, Przy pikrynie, op. cit., p. 64.

[28] Awraham Eliasziw, Testimony and poesies, YV, 0-33/1760.

members, as in the case of Mrs Karmel and her two daughters, Henia and Ila. Hela Szechter helped her sisters who were deathly ill. In other cases, a friend gave support. Mrs Karmel took devoted care of her friends. If it weren't for Dorka Miller, Fela Blum, with no family in the camp, would not have survived. Mala Zuckerbrot fondly remembers her friend Fela Boguchwał. It was this self-help that determined a victim's fate more than the work of the doctors who were often faced with the moral dilemma of whom to treat first. As a result, one finds a highly ambivalent attitude towards them, and they are mentioned both favorably and critically.

In late 1943, several Krakowites managed to obtain more help from outside as a result of private initiative.[29] Paulina Buchholz and Maria Szechter received letters and parcels from their fiancés still in the Płaszów camp. Frania Siegman made contact with the Janusz family who sent her money and clothes. In all such cases, the intermediary's fee was 400 zloty out of every 1000 Zloty. Recipients of such aid, however, were few in number and debilitation kept the mortality rate high. Schneider of the Shell Department went completely wild for fear that shipments to the front would not be delivered in time! Only a decisive change could improve the prisoners' condition. This came in the wake of a three-part revolution: the appearance of a new German commandant; a "coup d'état" in the "White House", and a boost to the prisoners' social and cultural life.

The new commandant, Friedrich Schulze, around 30 years old, short, and with one arm amputated, was a former *Wehrmacht* officer. He was given the nickname "*Rączka*" (little arm) for the prosthesis he wore in place of his missing arm.[30] When he assumed command, security and inspections in the camp were tightened and at the same time steps were taken by the Hasag management in the Spring of 1944 to improve the prisoners' living conditions. As soon as he arrived in the camp, Schulze declared himself a socialist concerned for the good of the workers and instituted a series of reforms. In order to improve his "soldiers'" appearance, he ordered that clothes be distributed from the clothing store and forbade the prisoners to sell them. The prohibition was ignored; bread was more vital.

---

[29] Eliezer Jurysta, Testimony, YV, 0-33/1800; Maria Madejska, AGKBZH, SWK, sygn. 219, p. 130.

[30] Schulze Friedrich, Zwischenbericht Nr. 1, T-A, 20.8.1963, YV, TR-11/61159, Nr. 16.

The camp began to take on a new look. Several new barracks were erected and the old ones were disinfected and their outer walls even painted. For the first time in the history of Werk C, lime was spread in the latrine and a prisoner assigned to clean it regularly. The endless mud paths were "paved" with branches over which gravel was scattered and even flower beds were marked off! A sign reading "Better work – good food!" was hung, as well as other signs identifying the "Infirmary," "Office," and so on. Naturally, when any military delegation was to visit, the picric acid workers and the ill were kept hidden.[31] The most important reform was the improvement in the food ration: 350 grams of bread (instead of 200) and 25 grams of sausage *(kaszanka)* once a week. In the Picric Acid Department the workers were periodically given a glass of milk. This brought about a significant improvement in the condition of the debilitated prisoners who had already begun to eat their clothes and their teeth – literally.

Around April, 1944, Schulze devised the idea of obtaining clothes and shoes from Majdanek, which were then distributed to the prisoners who found there not only the work papers of Jews murdered in the "Erntefest", but also money and jewelry concealed in the soles of the shoes or in buttons and hems. This was a well-kept secret in the camp, since it might one day save a Jewish life.[32] As a result of the epidemic, the prisoners were penniless and had nothing left to sell... and suddenly – a miracle! Trade again began to flourish! The Poles, who had long become used to seeing the yellow skeletons licking up the dregs of the soup vats, couldn't believe their eyes. How come these Jews had money and diamonds again?! Did they get help from outside, or did God send it down from heaven? And under the new commandant, even the beatings at the plant had been stopped.

The prisoners received the changes with mixed emotions. Their confusion was intensified even more by the "coup d'état" at the "White House". With the arrival of a new transport, there was a need for more policemen, and the tension was great. Who would be awarded a "cap"? Those close to the court among the veteran prisoners eyed their potential rivals, the policemen from Płaszów, with suspicion. The "queen" had her

---

[31] Niusia Kandel, Testimony, YV, 0-16/1372; R. Bauminger, p. 50.

[32] M. Strigler, Goirolois, op. cit., vol. 1, p.173; D. Schvarzmer, op. cit.

own ax to grind. She was tired of Feldman with his Bundists, and, most important, was in the market for a new "cousin". The surprise was not long in coming. After interviewing the Płaszów police representatives, one of whom was Fragner, a handsome blond, she made her pronouncement: Fragner would be the second-in-command of the police and commander of the camp police.

The prisoners were struck dumb when a new commander appeared at the morning roll call wearing a cap displaying three stars and walking arm in arm with the *"commandanta"*. His wife, standing in the back row, fainted dead away. The new police commander wasted no time in letting everyone know why he had been given his post. The affair sent shock waves through the camp. The veteran prisoners, familiar with their "queen" and her eccentricities, were not particularly dismayed, but the Plaszowites roundly cursed this modern Jezebel who had stolen a man from his wife.[33]

In the wake of this "coup d'état," policemen from the Płaszów transport were appointed to the force. Although they were well aware of their total subjection to the "White House, they did not wish to let this hurt their relations with their fellow Plaszowites. Some therefore sought to demonstrate their "efficiency" at the expense of the veteran prisoners, and the *kaelniks* from the Transport Crew complained bitterly of the lashings they received at their hands. The policeman Henoch sometimes helped his friends, but treated the others with particular cruelty. When he was asked why he beat them so savagely, he replied candidly: "The day I was given a truncheon, I became a different person." [34] Opinions were divided in the camp as to who was worse: Henoch or Bugajski from Radomsko who beat everyone and openly hinted that respite from his truncheon could be bought at a price. It is no surprise that he was the subject of a sarcastic ditty on "short-legged Bugajski who collected 'alms' – twice as many." [35] The long-suffering prisoners gave voice to their view of the brutal behavior of all the policemen:[36]

---

[33] M. Strigler, ib., pp. 15–42; Szraga Knobler, op. cit.

[34] R. Cypres, op. cit.

[35] Erna Nessel, op. cit.

[36] M. Strigler, Goirolois, op. cit., vol. 2, p. 84.

They seek with money or however they can
To get from "her" a cap of red,
In the end they become cold-blooded killers
Beating the young and the old 'til they're dead.

(Translated from the Yiddish)

There were also positive aspects to the integration of the Płaszów transport into the camp. Gradually, legal and illegal contacts were formed with Dr Weichert and the JUS in Kraków. Food and medicines reached the camp, the ill were given special soup, and extra bread rations were distributed to the worst departments. In May 1944, it was decided to erect a new hospital and a new infirmary was put into operation. The prisoners did not know where the funds for these activities came from, but rumor had it that they were from Jewish sources to which Schulze agreed to turn a blind eye. In regard to the extent of the aid received in Werk C from the JUS, opinions are divided. According to Henoch Ross, parcels fell into the hands of the camp authorities and the prisoners received nothing but bread and a few medicines.[37] In contrast, Róża Bauminger maintains that the JUS helped many of them. The claim of Dr. Gottesmann, representative of the RPŻ in Warsaw, that a monthly allotment of 3,000 zloty was sent to Werk C, is vehemently denied.[38]

The Spring, 1944 also saw an upsurge in social life in the camp. The overall improvement in living conditions and plain youthful spirit made their mark. The reinvigorated prisoners looked about them and suddenly realized that "life can be good – even in Werk C."[39] "A period of prosperity began. Tailors and shoemakers went about their work and trade flourished. The prisoners 'sowed their wild oats' and men and women came together as '*kuzinen mit kuzinkes*'." Those who had not yet made their choice looked on the love life of their friends with a mixture of envy and fear. Indeed, there was a cause for fear. Several women became pregnant, and there was no way that abortions could be performed in Werk C. Although automatic executions of pregnant women ceased in early 1944, birth inevitably meant the death of the baby. Many testimonies

---

[37] Antek Bagniewski, see n. 12, ibid.

[38] Felicja Bannet, Testimony, 12.1.1947, YV, 0-21/8.

[39] M. Strigler, Werk "Ce", op. cit., vol. 1, p. 106.

relate finding the bodies of infants in the death crate, the latrine or under a pallet.[40]

Whatever form la *dolce vita* took in Werk C, it was always diluted by a heavy dose of fear. And then, out of the blue one summer day it began to be rumored that the Germans were planning a massive search of the camp. Everyone had cause for concern, since, as business had picked up, there were numerous hiding places holding merchandise and items stolen from the plant. Moreover, the prisoners knew that four Jews had already been seized at the plant, among them Grzebień who did business with the Poles. The day of judgement arrived. The entire camp was ordered out for a roll call while the *Werkschutz* conducted a thorough and lucrative search of the barracks. The four detainees were brought before the assembled prisoners. Schulze delivered a speech on the "equity of German justice", adding that the death sentence handed down on the four defendants was a warning for the others. The most horrifying aspect was the presence of the notorious hangman Sander, who struck terror in the hearts of the prisoners in all three camps. Before the eyes of hundreds of prisoners petrified with fear, he murdered the four unfortunate men. Grzebień's "cousin", brought to the site at the last moment, was shot in the back by Kurt Schumann.[41]

In the "liberal" Spring of 1944, no one had expected such butchery. And this was just the beginning. Some time later the camp was again called out for roll call. This time several men were seized for stealing scraps of rubber from the pipes. All the knives found in the prisoners' pockets were confiscated. For the first time in Werk C, after the sentence was read out Jews were ordered to hang the condemned. When the deed was done, the Germans tried to reward them with bread and cigarettes. They refused to take them.[42]

The reasons for the shift in the authorities' "liberal policy" can be found in the deterioration of security in the Radom district as a whole. It will be recalled that in the second half of April, 1944, 25 *Werkschutz* men escaped with their weapons to join the partisans in the surrounding forest.[43] In early May, 1944, it was rumored that Poles had been arrested in the plant.

---

[40] A. Wasserstein, I. Rotbalsam, S. Kurz, op. cit.

[41] Arie Walach, Testimony, YV, TR-11/01159; B. Grossmitz, op. cit.

[42] A. Wasserstein, op. cit.; M. Strigler, Goirolois, vol. 2, pp. 11–20.

[43] See Chapter 4, n. 35.

Rumors reached the camp of the approach of the Red Army, and the prisoners again wavered between fearfulness and hope.

Singing in the Shadow of the "Frying Pan"

One of the groups that stood out among the Plaszowites were the young members of the Akiva movement from Kraków. This movement advocated a combination of political Zionism and the ideas of pioneering and a communal life, while at the same time remaining faithful to Jewish traditions and religion in liberal form. In August 1942, the movement initiated the founding of the Pioneering Youth Fighting Organization in Kraków, whose members, such as Szymek Drenger and Dolek Liebeskind, launched military actions against the Germans.[44]

The Akiva members in Werk C gathered together in a united group led by Mosze Imber, a violinist and musicologist. Before the war, Imber had conducted a choir of the Kraków branch of Akiva that was famed for its performances of Hebrew and Yiddish songs. Imber managed to bring his violin into Werk C, and the policemen, who knew him from Płaszów, invited him to play for them in the police barracks. He consistently shared the food and clothes he received for his performances with the other members of the group, among them Rut Kornblum, the sisters Mania and Hela Szechter, and others. They were joined by Zwi Kaner, Szmuel, Awraham and Meir Gottlieb, Reuwen Ziskind, the three Blusztajn brothers, Sala Diamant, and Mala Zuckerbrot. Ila and Henia Karmel also allied themselves with this group. Thus, a band of Zionist youngsters was formed who helped each other in the fight for survival and constituted something of an oddity in the ruthless world of Werk C.[45]

The members of Akiva found a social order alien to them in Werk C. Particularly in the women's barracks, the rift between the veteran prisoners and the "Duchesses of Kraków" was great. There was constant fighting over a place at the stove to cook soup or bake *peniclech* (bread in garlic), and frequent shouting, now in Yiddish, now in Polish. But there

---

[44] Hechalutz Halochem, Organ of the Underground Movement in Occupied Cracow, August–October 1943, (Hebrew), (Ghetto Fighter's House: Hakibutz Hamyuchad, 1984), pp. 9–11.

[45] Rut Kornblum-Rosenberger, Neder, (Hebrew), (Tel-Aviv: "Moreshet" & Sifriat Poalim, 1986), pp. 54, 62–67.

were also moments of fellowship. Maria Lewinger writes: "One evening
I read out my memories of my mother, how she would light the Sabbath
candles in our home…. There was utter silence all around. The women
were listening attentively. Only the sound of a woman's strangled weeping
could be heard from one dark corner of the barracks." And then someone
would begin singing the sad song which dated back to the first days of the
camp.[46]

> In lager in Skarżysko iz zeyer biter,
> In lager in Skarżysko, oy, Goteniu guter!

> In Skarżysko camp, a bitter world,
> In Skarżysko camp, O hear my Lord!
> The very thought is enough to make
> My hands and feet begin to shake.
> Oh if only I had never
> Known Skarżysko, no not ever.

> > There in the forest,
> > Not far from the town
> > Behind bars and fences,
> > Barbed wire all round
> > Oh, that is my prison,
> > Alone, no family near,
> > And no one, when I die,
> > To shed a tear.

(Excerpt translated from the Yiddish)

Within a short time, the Akiva youth's Sunday meetings were devoted
to organizing Oneg Shabbat concerts of Hebrew music and songs of
longing for Eretz Israel. They were motivated, among other things, by the
conspicuous presence of the Bundists with their songs in Yiddish. And so
on the banks of the Kamienna river they sang of the Kineret and the
Galilee. From time to time, Henia Karmel added one of her moving poems
about the Skarżysko forest.[47]

> In Skarżysko woods,
> The echo bears
> My tormented song.

---

[46] M. Strigler, In di fabrikn, op. cit., p. 408.

[47] Henryka Karmel-Wolf, "Wspomnienie ze Skarżyska", see n. 26.

And they sway, the trees
To its musical beat
As they sing along.

    *   *   *

And when I'm gone,
Never to return
Forgotten and lonely,
In their shade I'll find
Eternal peace of mind
Forgiving and holy.

(Excerpts translated from the Polish)

But the Bundists fought back, and in answer to the Jordan River and the Polish forests, they offered their listeners the birthplace of the revolution, *Matushka* Rassia and its wide expanses. They had no fear that the *Werkschutz* would hear them from across the fence, for in Skarżysko no one was hanged for singing, only for stealing rubber pipes. Thus even in Werk C, the songs reflected dreams of the three homelands, so typical of the soul of the Wandering Jew.

Unknown talents were discovered on the "cultural evenings." Hela Brunnengrabber (also Blumengraber), Rut Kornblum and others wrote poetry; there were entertainers and comedians; some recited poetry, like the small baldheaded *picryner* Fela Szechter (who had lost her hair in the typhoid epidemic) who recited "Lokomotywa" and "Ptasie radio" by Julian Tuwim and was sometimes rewarded by a policeman in the audience with an extra soup ration.[48] Malka Zuckerbrot-Hottner recalls: "Those were the best moments of my life in the camp. They ... carried us on the wings of imagination into a better, earlier world now lost to us.... The will to find an escape from the humiliation and despondency was very strong." Lunka Kaufman adds: "We spent many evenings curled up on our pallets listening breathlessly to recitations and songs of the good life that would some day come and dreaming of delicacies to eat and elegant clothes.... Starving and freezing, we forgot out bitter fate for a brief moment."[49]

The men sought in their own way to endow an ancient tradition with new meaning. On Passover 1944, a group of prisoners gathered to celebrate the anniversary of the Warsaw Ghetto uprising. The cantor

---

[48] Felicja Karay, Testimony, YV, 0-33/1812.

[49] Malka Zuckerbrot-Hottner, Testimony, YV, 0-33/1655; L. Kaufman, op. cit.

Josele Mandelbaum recited a prayer in memory of the fallen and the others joined in.[50] It was a moving and uplifting moment which helped the prisoners to forget the cruel reality of their lives. This was not an easy task, however. Their unrelieved exhaustion led to the spread of a new disease whose symptoms were high fever and debilitation. It was given the name "*hasagówka*". For its many victims, the illness exhausted whatever they had left from the short "period of prosperity". Suddenly it was rumored that the SS was about to take over direct control of the camp. But it was also said that the Russian front was drawing closer. In this atmosphere of alternating fear and hope, the prisoner never knew where to look for reassurance. David Schvarzmer writes: "I will never forget the second day of Shavuoth. It was the 29th of May, 1944. A group of us men gathered to pray in secret. Josele Mandelbaum was there and he recited *Yizkor* [the memorial prayer]. It was an unforgettable experience which left a deep impression on me and all the others."

At this time, a large part of the forest in Werk C was fenced off and huge signs warned that anyone approaching would be put to death. Thick smoke could be seen rising beyond the tall fence, and the prisoners from Majdanek could tell from their experience that human bodies were being burnt there. Black trucks began to drive down side roads to the fence where they would unload their mysterious cargo. The installation, soon given the name "*patelnia*" (Polish for "frying pan"), struck terror in the hearts of everyone. The prisoner Mendel Rubin, who was seized and sent to join the *Sonderkommando* in charge of burying bodies, managed to get a secret letter to his friends in the camp warning that the Germans throughout the district had started to eliminate the members of the Polish underground and unnecessary Jewish prisoners. It would soon be the turn of Werk C.[51]

As the smoke rose above the "*patelnia*", Schulze ordered that a dance floor be erected in a corner of the forest. Somewhere a violin, harmonicas and a trumpet were found, and as if by the wave of a magic wand, a small band came into being. In the evening the *prominente* would come to dance, while across the fence the Poles crowded together, watching in astonishment. Were these Jews prancing about? Several *Werkschutz* men

---

[50] S. Kurz, op. cit.

[51] See Chapter 4, notes 40, 41.

and even Germans came into the camp to watch the dancers. At the same time, Schulze gave the order to have red stripes painted on the prisoners' clothes to prevent them from escaping. But who even thought of escape? Even those who had received Rubin's warning had no idea what to do, since they knew that without help from outside there was no chance of organizing an uprising or mass escape. And why try anyway? After all, *"Rączka"* had commanded the "White House" to arrange a large show for the whole camp!!

The feverish preparations began. Markowiczowa sought out actors and singers; the tailors sewed costumes for the dancers; the chemical engineer Bień readied a pantomime act; the attorney Hornung volunteered to write an oral newspaper about camp life; various groups rehearsed their programs and devised new acts. The high point of the evening was to be the appearance of a choir led by Mosze Imber which rehearsed incessantly.

The great day arrived. The stage, erected especially for the performance, was decorated with colored paper and lanterns, and benches for the guests were set up before it. Groups of prisoners from Werks A and B were invited as well. Hundreds of Poles looked on from across the fence and found the strange sight totally incomprehensible. Thousands of prisoners lolled on the grass around the stage. Suddenly a convoy of cars appeared, bringing Dr Rost, Hecht, Krebs, and other executives. Even Sander was there! Markowiczowa and Eisenberg greeted the honored guests and led them, smiling graciously, to the front rows of benches.

The show began with German marching songs sung by the Blusztajn brothers, but Schulze asked to hear national Jewish songs in Yiddish, Hebrew and Polish. And indeed the men and women singers presented the finest songs in Yiddish, led by the works of Gebirtig. The excellent mime was rewarded with unusually enthusiastic applause, and the "oral newspaper", whose satiric barbs were well-understood by all the prisoners, aroused waves of laughter. The audience was highly entertained, and particularly enthralled by a solo dance choreographed to the music of "Kol Nidrei" (from the Yom Kippur liturgy).[52]

The highlight of the evening was the appearance of Mosze Imber's choir. Some twenty young men and women stood on the stage. They

---

[52] R. Bauminger, *Przy pikrynie, op. cit.*, p. 52.

opened with the popular Yiddish song: *"Hemerl, hemerl, klap!/ Klap
starker a tshwok noch a tshwok..."*. They sang in two-part harmony, their
voices carrying far into the distance. Naturally, they did not forget the
camp's revolutionary anthem "On the Cannons".

The guests enjoyed the performance and applauded as loudly as the
rest of the audience. The prisoners, however, were troubled by the strange
sense that a grandiose pageant was being staged and that they were
playing a part in it as well. Why? The Germans were not there by chance.
It had to be some new ploy....

The choir returned to the stage, this time singing in Hebrew:

> Kineret, Kineret, elayich,
> Nimshekhet kol nefesh meaz
> (Kineret, Kineret, to you is drawn
> Each soul since time long gone).

Imber conducted the choir as if they were performing a psalm. The
delicate harmonies rose and filled the forest, filling the prisoners' hearts
with a rare warmth. This was followed by the remarkable "Song of the
Bells" in four-part harmony, with the choir producing the full rich sound
of ringing bells. Let those Germans hear how young Jews can sing!

Finally, the choir arranged itself in two rows, linked arms, and, stepping
in unison from side to side, sang "Horat Ha-Galil".

> Hey, harmonika, nagni-li, shirat kol clil,
> Od ezkora et hahora, horat hagalil.
> (Oh, harmonica, play a gay song for me,
> I'll not forget the hora, the dance of the Galilee.)

The prisoners' hearts and feet moved in time to the dizzying beat. They
would yet live to dance in Eretz Israel! Only someone actually standing on
that stage and singing "Horat Ha- Galil" in that time and place could
understand its effect on those young people.[53]

The applause was thunderous. After this finale, the guests took their
leave from Markowiczowa with a handshake. Schulze was ecstatic.
The prisoners scattered. Until late that night the camp was abuzz with
arguments, rumors and gossip. What did it all mean?

There is no doubt that these performances were part of the authorities'

---

[53] Zvi Kaner, Testimony, YV, 0-33/2833; F. Karay, M. Lewinger, D. Schvarzmer, op. cit.

"delusionary policy" aimed at maintaining quiet in the camp. Yet in terms of the camp history, they were the apex of internal cultural life. No order handed down from above could have produced something out of nothing. A number of the prisoners were aware of the strange phenomenon, that within the hellish conditions that prevailed in Werk C, "cultural life there flourished." [54] All of the various forms of creative expression typical of the camps in general could be found here: anthems, protest songs with the themes of worker solidarity and vengeance against the cruel masters, satiric lyrics in Yiddish and Polish, lyrical poetry, macabre pieces describing the horrors of the epidemic, social criticism, and even religious lamentations calling God to account. And together with the writing were the shows, whether spontaneous or organized.

Why in Werk C of all places? Because here several interests came together, each employing cultural activity as a means of achieving its goal. For the *prominente* it was a form of entertainment; for the functionaries, a convenient cover for the operations of the Rescue Committee. The major reasons, however, were the support of the internal administration on the one hand, and the initiative of the organized political groups on the other. To Markowiczowa's credit, it must be said that her concept of "*noblesse oblige*" impelled her to encourage these activities, and in a number of cases she even saved the lives of "her" artists.

As for the Bund and Akiva, both groups saw cultural activity as a form of resistance and a means of preserving their movements' traditions. This is vivid evidence of the link between ideology and cultural-social activity in the camp. The adoption of an active stance in the face of the dismal reality was undoubtedly the result of a deliberate decision, both individual and collective, stemming from a clearly defined ideology and not merely from personal character or coincidence. Those taking an active part in these activities had the profound sense that they might be the last remnants of the immortal cultural heritage of a nation in the throes of extermination. Finally, the gifted prisoners naturally sought a stage for their talents as well as the consequent popularity which might serve them in the daily struggle for survival.

---

[54] Bina Hersztajn, Testimony, YV, 0-33/1796.

The Final Whistle

At one of the roll calls in late June, 1944 it was suddenly announced that security and discipline in the camp were to be stepped up. Rumors spread wildly. It was said that SS units were deployed in the surrounding forest. There was a feeling in the air that the end was near. More and more talk of escape was heard. Groups of youngsters huddled together making plans. The Bundists again gravitated around Henoch Ross in the hope that his money and connections would aid them in escaping when the time was ripe. The young Plaszowites, split into several groups, hatched their own plots, and naturally, for reasons of security, one group knew nothing of the plans of the others. No overall plan for mass escape was possible. Everyone kept a watchful eye on the "White House". What would they do? It was said that at night mysterious discussions were held there and sacks were being filled with dry bread! Were they really planning to escape? To abandon all the rest?

Deep down inside, everyone was waiting for the final whistle which would call them out to freedom. Meanwhile, the only whistles still heard were from the police calling them out to work. The more veteran policemen began to think twice about using their truncheons. They suddenly realized there were people here who might some day testify to their conduct. The prisoners began to take a different attitude to those of the police who still swung their truncheons, and threatening noises could be heard from the men's barracks.[55]

> They don't understand that we shall remember
> Not forgive, not forget a single one
> And if anything at all remains of Hasag
> The police from their bellies will be hung.
>
> (Translated from the Yiddish)

When the Russians crossed the border into the Radom district, the pace of evacuations accelerated and there was increasing unrest in the camp. On July 25, 1944, two separate lists of all the men in the camp began to be compiled in Schulze's office, arousing instant panic. Since the men tried to evade inclusion on the lists, Schulze ordered that registration be

---

[55] M. Strigler, Goirolois, op. cit., vol. 2, p. 88.

ceased. A few days before Tisha B'Av, 20 prisoners were commanded to dig a pit 20 meters long and 5 meters wide near the firing range.[56]

Nevertheless, the large-scale "selection" begun on Saturday, on the eve of Tisha B'Av, came as a surprise. The night shift was not sent out to work and the camp was surrounded by a cordon of SS and *Werkschutz* men. First, the debilitated, the ill and the picric acid workers were sent out. The men accepted their fate quietly, knowing there was no point in resisting. But wailing and sobbing filled the yard when women began to be taken out of the rows. Dora Rosenblat, 17 years old, was shot to death together with her mother from whom she refused to be separated. The Fortgang sisters and the doctor Mina Krenzler all went to the firing range together with their mothers.[57]

On the following day, July 30, 1944, the "selection" continued. All the patients were removed from the infirmary. Melech Goldberg barely managed to save two sick girls. Several were able to hide themselves.[58] Dr Wasserstein and Dr Aptowicz saved a number of other prisoners. Towards the end of the "selection," German executives arrived from the plant, including Hecht, Walter, Hoffman, Krebs and others. They passed among the rows indicating all those they wished to be rid of, some of them healthy young men. For a moment these prisoners were sure they were being chosen for some work assignment, and only when they were shoved out of line by the *Werkschutz* did they realize what was happening to them. They began shouting and putting up a fight. Some, refusing to go to the firing range, were shot where they stood.[59]

But the tragic night of Tisha B'Av was not yet over. The rumors of an escape attempt being planned at the "White House" proved to be true. It may be assumed that Markowiczowa's plans were based on a bargain she had struck with Schulze whereby he had agreed to give her and her entire family the chance of escaping in exchange for a pretty penny. Yet, it is unlikely that Schulze, as directly responsible for security in the camp, would have taken such a risk on his own. It is more reasonable to

---

[56] Jakow Zilberberg, Testimony, YV, 0-16/2586; E. Jurysta, op. cit.

[57] F. Bannet, see Chapter 10, n. 4, ib., p. 114; M. Strigler, Goirolois, op. cit., vol. 2, pp. 211–214.

[58] L. Kaufman, A. Hauser, op. cit.

[59] R. Mittelberg, S. Goldhar, op. cit.; M. Strigler, ib. pp. 253–263.

believe that, with the consent of the Hasag management, he had worked out a grandiose scheme to get Markowiczowa and her family out of the camp. Within its perimeters, he would have had no excuse for acting against her, while outside the camp they would become escapees subject to punishment. This speculation is strengthened by the fact that Schulze warned several people (such as Strigler and Dr Aptowicz) not to try to escape since only certain death awaited them outside the camp.

As a first step, Schulze started a large-scale "selection", informing Markowiczowa in advance, and she then fell into his trap. Assuming that immediately following the "selection" evacuation of the camp would begin, she proposed to Schulze that in exchange for a special fee, the *Werkschutz* would be removed from the camp that night making it possible for her to escape. Several policemen got word of the plan, and they demanded to be included among the escapees. With her back to the wall, the "*commandanta*" agreed, although she had intended only for her own family to accompany her. She had no inkling that several other groups were also planning to flee. When a few of the policemen reported Markowiczowa's plan to their friends (as the Bundist Feldman did to Henoch Ross), preparations for escape escalated.

That night, after the "selection," the police briskly herded the prisoners, who did not understand what was going on, back to their barracks. From this point on, things started to go from bad to worse. As agreed upon with Schulze, the *Werkschutz* began to leave their posts at around two o'clock in the morning, at which time the escapees cut the fence in three places. The first to leave were all the people of the "White House," some 15 in number. The second group included the police and their intimates, followed by the Bundists with Henoch Ross and his wife. It did not stop here, however. The prisoners in their barracks had kept watch all night, and when they saw their officials escaping, they decided that they would follow! A mass escape began as prisoners in pairs or small groups fled through the breaches in the fence.[60] Strigler puts the number at 800 (unquestionably an overly high figure), while other estimates run from 250 to 600.[61]

---

[60] M. Kligsberg, see n. 8; Stella Obremska, Testimony, YV, 0-33/1854.

[61] M. Strigler, Goirolois, op. cit., vol. 2, p. 284.

About an hour after the fence had been cut, whistles were heard and the *Werkschutz* appeared from out of their hiding places in the forest. They were the first to begin a mass slaughter of the escapees. There can be no doubt that this was done with the full knowledge of Schulze. No one will ever know into whose hands fell the diamonds of "Katerina the Second" of Werk C, who was murdered together with her whole family. The only survivor was, by chance, her elderly mother.

The following day the prisoners heard various accounts of the slaughter from the Poles in the plant. It was said that many had reached the nearby villages where they were killed and looted by the local peasants, while others were shot in the forest by Polish partisans. This latter version is supported by the survivors, apparently some 20 people. Three Jews who preferred to remain anonymous testified that of the 11 escapees in their group, 8 were murdered by the A.K. partisans.[62]

In the German canteen at the plant it was told of 71 escaping prisoners who were killed by the "Polish bandits." Rumor had it that they were shot after being ordered to line up to swear allegiance to the Polish flag. The Werkschutz found many Jews in the forest who had been wounded by the Poles, and took them to the firing range. Others, such as the policeman Awner Lederman, were arrested. He told Hartmann, who was allowed to see him before he was executed, that Poles had shot at the escaping Jews. The policeman Ullmer, who survived, related to Herszel Goldwasser the fate of his group, which included Dr Haendel and his wife. They came across partisans who welcomed them warmly and Dr Haendel was immediately put to work giving medical aid. After a short time, several strangers arrived and took the Jews out one at a time under the pretext of an interrogation. They were each shot. Ullmer's son managed to warn his father who overcame his partisan escort and fled together with his daughter. All of the others were killed.[63]

On that "Night of the Great Escape," as shots heard from the forest told the tragic tale, there was total confusion in the camp. The despised internal officials had vanished and neither Germans nor *Werkschutz* had yet made an appearance. The two storehouses holding bread and clothes were broken into and frenzied prisoners grabbed whatever they could get their

---

[62] Testimony, YV, 0-16/4715 (anonymous).

[63] Herszel Goldwasser, Szraga Knobler, R. Aptowicz, op. cit.

hands on. Many raced about as if they had run amok. No one knew what fate the next day held for them. Before dawn, Schulze entered the camp and ordered a roll call. He showed no surprise whatsoever at the number of escapees and gave his solemn word that those remaining in the camp would come to no harm.[64]

On August 1, 1944, the train arrived. Sixty women were crowded into each car and told they were going to Germany. At the very last minute, they were given bread and water. Few believed these assurances, and the general feeling was that they were being taken to their death. The same atmosphere prevailed among the men herded into one car. Finally, 20 policemen, who had hoped to remain in the camp with the men who were to continue the loading of munitions, were shoved inside as well.

The train started moving west, to the next stage of the prisoners' wandering and torment.

---

[64] M. Strigler, Goirolois, op. cit., vol. 2, pp. 336–342.

Chapter 12

The Last Act

The Fate of the Survivors

Only a small part of the Skarżysko prisoners, those who were lucky enough to remain in camps in Częstochowa, were freed in January, 1945. Between August 1944 and January 1945, most of the men were sent, either directly from Skarżysko or through Częstochowa, to Buchenwald. Two incidents are associated with this camp.

The first concerned four-year-old Jurek Zweig. Literature has it that he was brought to Buchenwald by his father, the attorney Zacharia Zweig, in a suitcase. At that time, the camp was controlled by an internal administration run by political prisoners, among them the German Communist Wili Bleicher who took it upon himself to save the child. Zweig, who left a detailed testimony, was by force of circumstances made privy to the secrets of the underground. He took part in their meetings where denunciations of the Jews for not resisting the deportations were sometimes voiced. When the SS began evacuating the Jews in 1945, Zweig turned to the leaders of the underground to ask why they were not putting up any resistance despite the weapons they had managed to procure. They replied that the matter had been debated, but since opinion was divided, no decision had been taken.[1] The rescue of Jurek Zweig, "the boy in the

---

[1] Zacharia Zweig, Testimony, YV, 0-3/2192 ; cf. F. Pingel, Haeftlinge unter SS-Herrschaft, op. cit., p. 228.

valise," gained international attention as a result of Bruno Apitz's book, "Naked Among the Wolves".[2]

The second affair was the kangaroo court at which police and informers from the Skarżysko camp were brought to trial. Despite considerable disparities among the many testimonies, all claim the trial was justified. Menasze Hollender writes: "The day after we arrived, something extraordinary happened, something incomprehensible which filled us with joy and pride, something which gave us the sweet taste of vengeance and sense of freedom." [3] Two Jewish officials of the internal administration (one of whom seems to have been Gustaw Schiller), conducted an interrogation in which prisoners serving both as prosecutors and defenders appeared before them.[4]

Hollender goes on, reciting the names of the infamous ones of Skarżysko:

> "Here they were – *commandenten*, policemen, spies and informers. People ... who had the deaths of hundreds of their brothers on their conscience.... They peer out of corners, creep about. Not long ago they were so sure of themselves in their elegant uniforms, but now they are submissive, obedient. Grave questions are posed: "Was it you who informed on?... Was it you who turned... over to the authorities? Did you abuse helpless women, steal the soup and bread out of the mouths of your starving brothers?... The crowd was becoming more incited.... The accused tried to justify themselves and begged for mercy.... The vengeful crowd fell on them. Some managed to flee. Others were brought down by the blows of the prisoners. Two lay dead. They were killed with wooden clogs.... This was the first act of the drama of vengeance. Others followed. Quiet and premeditated. Each day a few disappeared, snuffed out for good.... The organization moved carefully and ruthlessly."

According to testimony, close to 20 people from this transport were killed at the instruction of the court at Buchenwald. They included: the *commandanten* Krzepicki, Teperman, Imerglik, and Mosze Finger; the informers, Zenek Milsztajn, Josef Wajcblum and Jonatan (family name unknown); and the orderly Alek from Werk C. (The policeman Najman

---

[2] Bruno Apitz, Nackt unter Woelfen(Halle: Mitteldeutscher Vlg, 1959).

[3] M. Hollender, Likwidacja obozu w Skar.-Kam., see Chapter 7, n. 48.

[4] A. Gastfrojnd, M. Horowicz, A. Jagoda, op. cit.; Chaim Camit, Testimony, YV, 0-3/3116.

saved the Melech orderly from a lynching.) Offenders from later transports were also tried, among them the policemen "Grobe Abram," David Bugajski, Pantel, Dr Sax and others.[5]

The prisoners brought from Hasag labor camps in the *Generalgouvernement* did not stay in Buchenwald, but by and large were divided up among the camps that had been established in the Summer of 1944 by Hasag beside its plants in Germany: at Schlieben, Altenburg, Colditz, Floessburg, Leipzig, Meuselwitz, Taucha, and Herzberg, which were all *Aussenkommandos* of Buchenwald. In Autumn, 1944 some 11,650 prisoners were put to work in these camps, most of them Jews.[6] In April, 1945, Menasze Hollender made up a list of the dead who had been buried in the Schlieben camp. Sixty-one of them had come from Hasag-Skarżysko.[7]

In April, 1945, the evacuation of all the Hasag camps in Germany was begun. The Jews from Schlieben were marched for two weeks to Theresiendstadt where the survivors were released. Many had died of starvation on the way. Some of the men from the camps at Floessburg and Meuselwitz were released, half dead, along the way, and others at Mauthausen.[8] The women from Skarżysko, most of whom had been sent to the women's camp at Leipzig, were sent, along with thousands of other women, on a two-week "death march" during which many died. The survivors were released at various places in the region of the Elbe River. Some women had been shifted interminably from Częstochowa to Ravensbrück to Burgau to Tuerkheim, their war ending either on the death march or at Bergen-Belsen.[9]

The lack of German sources, dispersion of the evacuees, and death of many witnesses, makes it impossible to estimate the total number of survivors from the Skarżysko camp. Purely as speculation, we might expect the number of survivors to be some two-thirds of the nearly 7,000 Jews evacuated from the camp in the Summer of 1944.

The final act of the tragedy entitled "Skarżysko Camp" took place in

[5] Chaim Milsztajn, Testimony, M-1/E/1183/53; S. Goldhar, M. Goldwasser, op. cit.

[6] M. Kaiser, Monopolprofit und Massenmord im Faschismus, Blaetter fuer deutsche und internationale Politik, Heft, 5, 1975, p. 570.

[7] M. Hollender, "Cmentarz obozowy w Schlieben", YV, 0-3/1012, p. 45.

[8] J. Barkai, W. Monderer, op. cit.; item: see n. 5.

[9] R. Potasz, E. Kohen, op. cit.; Chaja Szapira, Skarżysko Book, p. 104.

that very town in the Winter of 1945–46 when a small group of Jews returned to liberated Skarżysko. Among them was a couple who, in January 1946, received an anonymous threat letter promising that soon "the Jews here will be slaughtered" and therefore "advising" them to leave the town.[10] They did. But a few former citizens remained, including Icchak Warszauer and Eliezer Lewin who had come to investigate the possibility of regaining their property which was being held by the Poles. The town's residents, as well as the local authorities, received them with undisguised hostility. After prodigious efforts, Warszauer was able to obtain an apartment in his former home, to which several Jews moved. One night in early February they were all killed: Icchak Warszauer, Szmuel Milet, Zelig Warszauer's son, Blacharz's son, and Mrs Lewit. When Eliezer Lewin and others demanded that those responsible be put behind bars, they were informed by the local authorities that the Jews had been killed after attempting to retrieve a Jewish child from a Christian family by force. The secret police at Kielce eventually found the three murderers: the commanders of the civil guard at Skarżysko, a policeman, and a woman named Grzymkowa. They were sentenced to death.[11]

Today the town of Skarżysko is totally "Jew-free". Memorials and monuments to the Poles killed by the Nazis have been erected in every corner and grove of the town. The regional museum is filled with photographs and mementoes of the Polish partisans and their operations. Here and there are notices from the Hasag management to its Polish workers. Several pictures from the ghetto appear on one wall. A monument erected in 1965 rises opposite the gate to what is now a metalworks and was once the main entrance to Werk A. It bears a plaque commemorating the victims of the camp and reading:

> In memory of the 35,000 killed in the Nazi slave labor camp (of the Hasag Company) at Skarżysko-Kamienna between 1940 and 1944, members of the resistance movement, citizens of the city and prisoners of war who gave their lives so that others could live.
>
> Citizens of Skarżysko-Kamienna
May, 1965

---

[10] "O pogromie w Skarżysku w 1946 roku", Kontakt i dialog, ed. by Coordination Committee for Activities for Polish–Jewish Youth in Scandinavia, no. 19, May 1982, p. 20.

[11] Eliezer Lewin, Skarżysko Book, pp. 158–159; M. Szopil, op. cit.

Was there nary a Jew in Hasag-Skarżysko?

In 1986, Skarżysko-born Jews who had settled in the United States decided to raise a monument to the former Jewish community. On May 18, 1987 the monument was unveiled at a national ceremony in the presence of guests from America, the former camp prisoners Hersz Krys, Szalom Nugel and others. The monument bears a short inscription in Hebrew and Polish: "In eternal memory of the Jews of Skarżysko-Kamienna murdered by the Nazis in the years 1939–1945." The Polish authorities seem to have given their consent only to this phrasing which contains no mention of the camp.

When the time came for the speeches, there was no getting away from it. Finally, all those present knew precisely where the Jews had been murdered. Stanisław Kubiatowski, the manager of the metalworks, spoke of the Hasag camp. In his address, he stated that on average close to 2,000 (!) Jews had been in the camp, and noted the "long list of Polish workers who bore the tragic consequences of their attempt, despite their own poverty, to help the Jewish workers with whatever means were available to them". If the guests sought to correct the "inaccuracies" in his speech, there is, of course, no record of their comments. We can, therefore, only end with the remarks of the mayor of Skarżysko, Lubosław Langer: "Many of the events still await to be reported and commemorated lest they be forgotten." [12]

Until the day when some other monument is raised, may this volume serve to commemorate the memory of the 20,000 forgotten Jews who found their death in the Hasag slave labor camp at Skarżysko-Kamienna.

---

[12] Renata Saks, "Pomnik pamięci w Skarżysku Kamiennej", Folks-Sztyme, nr. 21 (4832), 30.5.1987, p. 11.

Conclusions

At the "Kamienna Trial" in Leipzig in 1948, the judges ruled that through out the years of its operation, the Hasag Concern had given "unusual support" to the National Socialist regime. After considering the company's five-year history in the *Generalgouvernement*, we may arrive at the opposite conclusion: it was Hasag which enjoyed the solid support of governmental institutions, both in the Reich and in the G.G., most particularly in regard to the supply of manpower.

As for the relations between the German firms and the institutions of the Third Reich, the various schools of historiography hold highly contradictory views regarding the supply of manpower from the occupied countries. Western scholars (Hans Pfahlman, Franz Kannapin, Louis Lochner), despite their different approaches, all maintain that in view of the shortage of workers, the companies were forced to employ foreign labor because of the pressure brought to bear on them by the Nazi dictatorship. In contrast, East German historiographers (Dietrich Eichholtz, Eva Seeber, Juergen Kuczynski) contend that the governmental institutions served the interests of the monopolies, and each and every one of them – the army, the WVHA, and the commissioner Fritz Sauckel – did their utmost to supply these concerns with workers in great numbers, and, most importantly, at low cost.

The history of Hasag reveals that in view of the functional collaboration between the government and the monopolies and their overlapping authority, it is extremely difficult to determine who was in control and who was being controlled. Paul Budin is an excellent example for the many hats he wore in his various functions: general manager of Hasag, member of the advisory council of the Armaments Office of the Third Reich, and senior official of the SS.

As we have seen, Hasag enjoyed privileges not afforded the other German firms operating in the territory of the *Generalgouvernement*. These are apparent in the unique features of the external history of the Skarżysko camp. In terms of time, the camp was established in Spring, 1942, when the dismantling of "open" labor camps had already begun and preparations were being made to transfer responsibility for Jewish labor from the G.G. authorities to the SS commanders. In terms of type, this was the first "company camp" *(Betriebslager)* anywhere in the *Generalgouvernement* that was set up by an industrial concern on its plant grounds and run by a "plant guard" *(Werkschutz)*. Following this precedent and model, additional company camps were erected in the Radom district in 1943, five of them at other Hasag plants.

As compared to other munitions plants, Hasag enjoyed special assistance in the procuring of Jewish labor, especially for its factories at Skarżysko. In general terms, there is a correlation between the frequency of Jewish transports to the camp and the needs of the front: the many transports of the "Radom Period" coincided with the Stalingrad campaign; Jews were brought from Majdanek in Summer, 1943, before the new offensive on the eastern front; 2,500 prisoners from Płaszów were transferred to Skarżysko in November, 1943 when it became imperative to hold back the advance of the Red Army.

The entire "external history" of the camp reveals the surprising fact that all the authorities of the *Generalgouvernement* administration joined in the effort to supply Hasag with Jewish workers. What was the principal authority interested in the existence of the Jewish "company camps," and what was Budin's ace in the hole that enabled him to maintain the independence of his camps? Joseph Billig's suggestion that it was the local district SS commanders who took up and even won the fight to control the Jewish labor camps in their jurisdiction does not accord with the facts. It was precisely in regard to the labor camps under their direct command that the SS failed. Against Boettcher's will, responsibility for the Jewish camp at Radom was transferred to the WVHA, and contrary to the interests of the SS commander of the Krakow district, Płaszów became a concentration camp.

As I see it, the major factor accounting for the inviolability of Hasag is associated with the production of munitions. It will be recalled that a problem in this regard arose from the disparity in the strategic approaches of Hitler and General Georg Thomas. In the wake of the *Munitionsstop* (a halt in ammunitions production) called from time to time by the munitions companies in the Reich, the *Wehrmacht* periodically suffered a shortage of ammunition. Affording minimal profits, ammunition was not a popular industrial undertaking among the large German concerns, and thus Hasag was able to obtain a monopoly in the field in the *Generalgouvernement*. In March, 1944, the G.G. – which is to say, the Hasag plants led by Skarżysko – supplied fully one-third of the total ammunition needs of the infantry on the eastern front. This was the advantage that enabled Budin to dictate terms to the authorities and demand, above all, that they supply him with cheap labor (that is, Jews). Budin's ultimatum – no Jews, no ammunition – was, in my opinion, the primary factor underlying the existence of Hasag's six company camps in the G.G. and the fact that they were not turned into concentration camps.

This may account for the extraordinary efforts made by Gen Maximilian Schindler in order to obtain Jews for Budin, since the Hasag plants were the lynch pin and *raison d'être* of the G.G.'s Armaments Inspectorate. Schindler viewed the local and independent munitions industry and its control over the Jewish labor camps as the backbone of his influence, and he was unanimously supported in this regard by the local authorities who were also seeking to advance their own interests: Hans Frank, who was fighting against the gradual erosion of his authority by the central government; and the local businessmen who rejected the notion that Eastern Europe was no more than a market for German industry. This coalition was joined by the local SS commanders who did not look with favor on the intention of the WVHA to centralize power in its own hands. They were all united by a common fear of Himmler's interference in their affairs. It would thus seem that the role played by the Skarżysko camp in the internal power struggles in the G.G. determined its status more than did developments on the front, and its fate was affected not by ideological concerns but by the particular interests of those in positions of authority.

The dependency on Hasag led Albert Speer and the military authorities to pressure Frank's government to sell Hasag the Skarżysko factories at the ludicrous price of 10,000,000 zloty. "Hasag Werke Skarżysko-Kamienna" was registered as a local firm in which Budin held total control as a stockholder together with Hasag. Without a doubt, this state of affairs was the major, although not the only, factor which determined the size of the Jewish work force, living conditions in the camp, and the extent of the extermination.

It must be stressed that the recruitment of thousands of Jewish laborers was not the result of a shortage of Polish workers. In contrast to popular opinion, there was never a lack of manpower in the *Generalgouvernement*. Although thousands of Poles had been sent to work in Germany, unemployment, which had been high in independent Poland, remained unabated and even increased in the wake of the refugees streaming into Poland from the territories annexed to the Reich. There was a seeming shortage of workers in 1942 because of the thousands of Poles who evaded work, making their living on the black market, which grew to monstrous proportions in the G.G., unmatched anywhere else in occupied Europe. Its feverish expansion began in 1942, facilitated, among other things, by the "final solution" when Jewish property fell liberally into the hands of former neighbors and from there found its way into the local markets. Polish historiographers (such as Piotr Matusak, Czesław Madajczyk, Czesław Łuczak and others) totally ignore the causal relation between these two developments, attributing the evasion of work to patriotic motives alone.

In the Radom district especially, there was never a lack of Polish workers for the local munitions industry which offered high wages and good food and obtained exemptions from compulsory work in Germany for its employees. Even here, however, more and more workers shirked their jobs, both because of the opportunity to earn profits on the black market and because of the propaganda spread by the Polish underground. Nevertheless, the number of Poles employed in the Skarżysko plants increased steadily. It was only in late 1942, when it was discovered that Jews could be put to work in production, that the Hasag management sought to procure more Jews, whose upkeep was negligible compared to the expenses incurred in maintaining a Polish staff.

Another question that might be asked is whether the prisoners' living conditions were in line with the definition of Hasag-Skarżysko as a labor camp? Evidence shows that both the food rations and the barracks at Skarżysko were sub-human, even below the level prevalent in concentration camps. The massive mortality rate of the prisoners led the court at Leipzig to state in its verdict that the Skarżysko camp was in fact intended to serve the goal of exterminating Jewish prisoners in the spirit of the National Socialist theory of racial purity. The court's decision coincided with the dominant school of Eastern European historiography which maintains that beginning in 1942, all the Nazi camps fulfilled the same function, no matter what their formal designation. At the same time, many scholars (such as Hermann Langbein, Eugen Kogon, Falk Pingel and Józef Kamiński) claim that as the economic activities of the SS increased, there was an essential conflict between its interests as employer and the political–ideological demand for the extermination of prisoners.

In the opinion of the prosecution in the Leipzig trial, this conflict appeared unfeasible in the case of Skarżysko. Indeed, indications of their resulting consternation can be found in the language of the bill of indictment: "These Jewish labor camps, attached, at the personal initiative of the general manager of Hasag, the Nazi murderer Budin, to the Skarżysko factories, can not be categorized in the terms of the Nazi dictatorship as divisions of political extermination camps, denounced by the court at Nuremberg. Rather, they must be seen, because of their structure designed specifically for production purposes, as particularly sinister means for exiling helpless people to labor camps established for imperialistic purposes" [Anklageschrift, p. 19]. In other words, if Hasag as an imperialistic institution established a labor camp in order to exploit the free labor of Jews in such an important industry as munitions production, why did it use the very same camp as an instrument for their annihilation?

The answer is that the Skarżysko camp was not designed for the extermination of Jews per se. Hasag's policy was "*Austausch der Juden*" – "Jew exchange" – the replacement of debilitated prisoners, who were sent to their death in Werk C, the local extermination camp *(Betriebliche Vernichtungslager)*, by healthy ones. This system generated no conflict between Hasag's economic interests and ideological dictates, since the Jews served as unskilled labor in the production process, while the professional jobs were reserved exclusively for Poles, who were not "exchanged".

Thus, economically, it was more expedient for Hasag to constantly replace the Jews, maintained as "apprentice laborers" incurring negligible outlay, than to turn them into skilled workers which would entail improving their living conditions. The system could be implemented as long as new transports continued to arrive in the camp. When in Spring, 1944, it became clear that there was no chance of procuring more Jews, Hasag decided to improve the prisoners' conditions in order to reduce the mortality rate.

*   *   *

In political terms, Hasag was faced with the same problem confronting the Third Reich in organizing the continental system of forced labor: by what means could the few control the many?

At the Skarżysko plants, this meant that thousands of Poles, scattered over a vast area, had to be overseen by a small German staff and 170 *Werkschutz* guards. The existence of the Jewish camp played a significant role in the solution to this problem, for several reasons.

1. By appointing Polish instructors and inspectors to oversee the Jews, Hasag was assured of the Poles' cooperation with the German plant management. This compensated them for the degradation they themselves were forced to suffer. The presence of the Jews made it possible for the Poles to use them as an outlet for their anger and frustration at the occupation and their subjugation to the Germans.

2. The Jewish camp represented a political enemy common to the Germans, Volksdeutsch, Ukrainians and Poles, and thus the deep-seated anti-Semitism of these groups healed the rifts opened by their hatred of each other, uniting them and thereby serving the needs of the plant management.

3. The plant management encouraged its staff to join in the looting of the Jewish property which arrived in Skarżysko with each new transport. Some of this property was confiscated by the Germans and *Werkschutz*, while the rest enriched the Poles in exchange for goods supplied to the Jewish prisoners.

The Jewish camp therefore became a prodigious political tool aiding Hasag to control the entire staff of its Skarżysko plants, and most particularly the thousands of Poles employed there.

When it came to establishing the internal organization of the Jewish camp, the Hasag management applied the same principle of controlling the many by means of the few, and at minimal cost. Their solution was to set up an independent administration *(Selbstverwaltung)* run by prisoners who collaborated with the Germans in exchange for better physical conditions, assurances of their own survival, and the illusion of power.

We may conclude, therefore, that in organizing forced labor at all levels, the Germans employed the tried and true three-part method: "divide and conquer"; give one group of slaves control over another; and afford them a share of the loot. The Germans added to this system a political weapon in the form of extermination of the Jews. It enabled the Nazi occupiers to control the economic activities of subjugated Europe and to bring them into line with its broader policies. This weapon turned the wheels of the entire continental system of forced labor by means of "graduated terror". In other words, each class or group lived in fear of descending to the next lower rung, with the bottom of the ladder being physical extermination. For each sector, the threat took a different form: the terrorized European nations saw before them the vision of Auschwitz; for the Poles at the Skarżysko plants, the condemned Jewish prisoners were a constant reminder of what their own fate might be; in the Jewish camp itself, every prisoner in Werk A or B lived in fear of being transferred to the extermination camp, Werk C.

This view of the extermination of the Jews as an integral part, and even precondition, of the system of forced labor does not detract from its ideological and propagandistic aspect. However, just as it would have been impossible to slaughter six million Jews without the foundation of the principles of Nazi ideology, so it is unreasonable to assume that this genocide was perpetrated for ideological reasons alone. One might wonder what would have happened had the Third Reich been victorious and the last of the Jews within its borders annihilated. It is fortunate for the other European nations that this question never arose.

Thus it appears that the complex interrelations among the various national groups at the Skarżysko plants recreated in miniature the situation in the entire system of continental forced labor. Since the same laws operated in the micro-system as in the macro-system, the results were also the same.

First, like the Poles and Jews at Skarżysko who produced munitions intended for use against themselves and their brothers, so every nation in Europe collaborated with Nazi Germany in its own destruction. In each of the occupied countries, millions of workers were employed to fill the Wehrmacht's orders. In 1944, within the area of Germany itself there were 7,000,000 foreign laborers, and every fourth item of munitions sent to the front was produced by Russians, Poles, Frenchmen and others, some of whom were prisoners of war. A similar situation prevailed in the concentration camps where prisoners of all nationalities became production workers. Whatever acts of sabotage there were, they cannot alter the fact that all of these foreigners strengthened the military potential of their enemy, the Third Reich.

Secondly, nowhere in Europe was there any attempt to destroy the system of forced labor from within, in the same way as there was none at Skarżysko. Rebellions were not mounted by the prisoners of concentration camps or by foreign workers in Germany and elsewhere. In no country was there a popular uprising which succeeded on its own in routing the occupiers. The bonds of slavery were broken only by the blows of outside forces.

*   *   *

The attempt to arrive at conclusions from the internal history of the Skarżysko camp presents problems which are considerably more complex. Here common denominators must be drawn from the recollections of prisoners, each of whom has his or her own subjective truth.

All the prisoners brought to the camp underwent the same processes as those in any camp: the initial shock, followed by adaptation to camp life and learning of the stratagems that could help in the struggle for survival. The information a prisoner managed to obtain from the "veterans" gave him or her a realistic picture of the chances of survival. Those aged from 20 to 30 had a better chance of standing up under the hard labor in the plant, and women proved to be more adaptive than men. Skilled craftsmen and doctors had a singular advantage. Social status did not appear to be a significant factor, although members of the *petit bourgeoisie* seemed to adapt to camp life better than the intelligentsia and upper-class individuals. Only in rare cases did a prisoner's level of education, devotion to religion or Jewish tradition, or political–ideological orientation affect his or her ability to adapt.

Two criteria determined the degree of success of each prisoner's struggle for survival in the factory: the type of job and relations among the workers. In regard to the first factor, there was extreme diversity, ranging from the privileged Automatic Weapons Department in Werk A to the deadly picric acid section of Werk C. As for relations among the workers, despite the differences between departments, an atmosphere of violence and terror pervaded the entire plant. In this sense, Hasag's Skarżysko factories were decidedly worse than its plants at Kielce and Częstochowa. Direct responsibility for this situation must be laid at the feet of the Skarżysko management, headed b Egon Dalski, and Budin, who gave Dalski a free hand. Together with his cohorts, Dalski created the atmosphere of a madhouse in which there were no restraints on abuse, murder, rape, thievery and extortion. Worthy of note is the fact that the Germans' treatment of the prisoners was not affected by their political affiliation: there were former Communists among the sadists, and Nazi party members among the more decent managers. The Leipzig trial found no basis in the defendants' argument that their treatment of the prisoners was dictated by orders from above. Indeed, witnesses singled out several German executives for their humane behavior.

The atmosphere riddled with violence also affected relations between the Jews and the Poles. Typically, insofar as human relations are concerned, the prisoners condemned the Poles more than the Germans for violence. The Jews saw the Germans as agents of the devil, alien and hostile, but had known the Poles as former friends or neighbors. They attributed the enmity of the Poles not to Nazi propaganda, but to "homegrown" anti-Semitism and greed, which masked unconscious feelings of guilt: "They live in our homes and for that reason they hate us."

As for "economic relations" between the prisoners and the Poles, attitudes are diametrically opposed. Polish historiographers (such as Piotr Matusak and Longin Kaczanowski) unanimously laud the aid given by the Poles to their Jewish friends. In contrast, the Jews note the outrageous exploitation, exemplified by the price of bread, sold by the Poles to the prisoners for four times its value on the black market. Objectively speaking, the possibility of purchasing food saved many Jews from death by starvation. On the other hand, however, the Jewish camp became a major source of income: the Poles filled their pockets with money, dollars, jewelry, gold teeth and clothes in exchange for food. This state of affairs served Hasag's interests admirably, since the brisk trade earned the Poles profits and fed the Jews at no cost to the company.

Sources concerning military cooperation between the Jews and the Poles reveal that the Polish underground offered the camp no organized assistance. All instances of cooperation, both in the theft of ammunition and in acts of sabotage, were carried out at the personal initiative of an individual Pole. Only very few prisoners escaped with the help of local Poles, and a small minority of these survived. Nearly all of them were caught and murdered or handed over to the *Werkschutz* by local residents. The Polish partisans in the region were controlled by the rightist and anti-Semitic Armia Krajowa (AK) which balked at admitting Jews to its ranks and certainly had no interest in arming them. As a result, the Jews reached the mournful conclusion that their lives were safer inside the camp than out. That they were right was proven by the mass murder of hundreds of escapees during the evacuation of Werk C in late July, 1944.

The darkest pages in the annals of the Skarżysko camp were written by the *Werkschutz*. In addition to their guard duties, escort jobs and search and inspection functions, all of the guards took part in the executions of camp prisoners. Nevertheless, the German tribunal in Nuremberg ruled in 1967 that the rank and file members of the *Werkschutz*, were only carrying out orders and so could not be held responsible for their actions as their German commanders could. The post-war Polish management of the Skarżysko factories took a difference stance when they demanded that the *Werkschutz* as a whole be declared a criminal organization. They based their demand on trials of *Werkschutz* members where it was revealed that they had committed acts of murder and brutality against the Jews at their own initiative and had severely abused Poles charged with various offenses at the plant.

Within the confines of the camp, the prisoners were subject to the authority of the internal administration which was granted total control. Admittedly, from Hasag's point of view, appropriate people could always be found to fill the post of head of administration. The distinction made by certain scholars between cooperation and collaboration with the German authorities does not appear relevant to the camps in general or to Skarżysko in particular. If collaboration means full identification with the occupier and his objectives, this is something no Jew could be suspected of, and thus the officials of the administration must be judged by their actions alone. On the whole, appointment to a position of authority brought about a drastic change in a prisoner's conduct. One policeman confessed: "When I was handed a truncheon, I became a different person." In the testimony of prisoners, the members of the internal administration are depicted as a collection of underworld characters, extortionists and brutal individuals. Yet in many cases, these same people helped the camp inmates. They warned of "selections," managed to get prisoners out of the hands of the *Werkschutz*, offered a piece of bread or a shirt. Judgement, therefore, cannot be unequivocal.

1. The administration and police generally checked to see the way the wind was blowing from above and then conducted themselves accordingly, both when terror tactics were intensified and during more "moderate" periods.
2. As a "governing body", the *prominenten* at Skarżysko took no steps to improve the lot of the prisoner population as a whole, although they did offer aid to individuals.

It is worthy of note that although the prisoners never forgave the Germans and Poles their crimes, they understood that these were the actions of tyrants. In regard to the Jews, the situation was reversed: they could not understand, but often forgave. "I never understood how a Jew could beat another Jew," wrote one of the prisoners. I have, however, encountered numerous instances in which former prisoners refused to testify in trials of Jews who had brutalized them in the camp.

In each of the three camps, a prisoner society developed over the more than two years of the camp's existence. It was characterized by a three-tier structure of the groups who arrived in the camp one after the other: from Radom, Majdanek and Płaszów. Sources provide evidence of a total of more than 50 transports brought to the camp containing at least some 23,000 Jews, men and women, all told. Each tier maintained its identity and mixed little with the others. This was the result both of differences in the mentality, education and cultural background of the three groups, and of the policies of the Hasag management interested in destroying the solidarity of the prisoners. Such solidarity was also sabotaged by the vertical division of the prisoner society into classes of "*prominenten*", "proletarians" (the ordinary prisoners), and "musselmen". Hence, a society fragmented into numerous small sub-sections evolved in the camp.

Each of the transports walked the same treacherous path. Entrance to the camp included confiscation of most of one's property and a "selection" at which the frail prisoners were weeded out. The filthy lice-ridden barracks were intolerably overcrowded. Sanitary facilities consisted of a public latrine and cold-water faucets. Within two months, each transport fell victim to typhus, which claimed hundreds of lives as there were no medicines whatsoever and doctors were in short supply. Up until 1944, an average of two "selections" a month were conducted in all three camps and the condemned executed at the "firing range" in Werk C. Shortly before the evacuation in Summer, 1944, the mass graves were opened and the bodies cremated.

The prisoner, who was given 200 grams of bread and a liter and a half of watery soup per day, was compelled to fight for his or her survival in any number of ways: by joining in the "economic activities" of the camp, by self-help, or with the aid of a "cousin".

The camp's economic activities were based on the pilfering of a variety of raw materials from the plant. These were used by the camp craftsmen to manufacture different goods: shoes, cooking utensils, combs, clothes, bags, etc. The goods were sold within the camp or offered to Poles at the plant, with a long line of middlemen taking their cut along the way. The prisoners' ingenuity, resourcefulness, and skill seems to have known no bounds, not to mention their courage, since smugglers who were caught were sent directly to the gallows.

Self-help existed in a number of different frameworks: families, *Landsmannschafts*, couples, or "camp families" formed by a few friends. Several groups established their own "rescue committees", and a certain amount of help was proffered by the doctors. Groups of observant prisoners did their best to support each other and at times were aided by the camp *prominenten*. The institution of "cousins", that is extramarital intimate relations, was common in all three camps. The lack of fences separating the men's and women's barracks, the young age of the prisoners, loneliness, and most of all, hunger, impelled many girls to seek the patronage of one of the *prominenten* by becoming his *kuzynka*.

Some of the Jewish prisoners in the camp had been allied with various political movements even before the war, but only in Werk C do any associations seem to have organized around these affiliations. Here there were small groups of Hashomer Hadati and Poalei Zion members and a large group of Bund members, including several party officials from Warsaw. In addition, a number of members of the Zionist Youth Movement Akiva arrived from Płaszów. The illegal monetary assistance which filtered into the camp in mysterious ways in late 1943 was associated with these political groups. The members of the Bund and Poalei Zion received aid from fellow-members who were active in the *Żydowski Komitet Narodowy* (National Jewish Committee) in Warsaw. The underground Polish organization *Rada Pomocy Żydom* (Council for Aid to Jew), represented by the historians Marek Arczyński and Teresa Prekerowa, claims also to have gotten extensive aid into the camp, but this is not confirmed by any other sources. Legal and unofficial assistance provided through the services of Dr Weichert, the head of the Jewish Welfare Office (JUS) in Kraków, reached former Krakowites.

In all three *werks* the prisoners sought to maintain some semblance of cultural activity in one form or another. Yet the greatest miracle is that there is evidence of a much more extensive religious and cultural life in the terrifying yellow kingdom of Werk C than in the other two camps. This activity took three major forms.

1. Spontaneous community singing and poetry readings during the rest hours in the barracks.
2. Shows put on by the members of the Bund and Akiva,

alongside performances arranged to entertain the officials of the Jewish administration.

3. Public "concerts" organized with the consent of the German camp commandant and including solo performances of singers and dancers, recitations and pantomime, and the choir led by Mosze Imber.

There were writings (in Yiddish and Polish) of all the types known from other camps as well: the camp anthem, religious laments, satires of the *prominente* and their way of life, humorous verses on camp personalities and aspects of the prisoners' daily life, literary prose, songs of yearning, protest and vengeance, and more. The great majority were written by anonymous authors and passed by word of mouth, but the works of Maria Lewinger, Henryka Karmel, Ilona Karmel, Mordchai Strigler and others have also survived.

Among the reasons behind the "cultural opulence" of Werk C, we might include:

1. The presence of organized groups of Zionist youth group, Akiva, and Bund members who initiated such activities for ideological–political reasons.
2. The support of the Jewish administration and "Rescue Committee".
3. The presence of a relatively large number of people with literary and artistic gifts.

In each of the three camps there were religious prisoners who succeeded in gathering groups for prayer and observed the holidays. The non-religious sought comfort in friends, community singing, or debates over the latest war news garnered from the Poles in the plant or from a newspaper miraculously smuggled into the camp. For these few moments, the prisoners were reinvigorated and able to maintain their personal identity, steadily being eroded by the merciless struggle for survival.

Employing a carefully calculated and deliberately planned system devised by the National–Socialist ideologues, the German tyrant attempted to carry out the most extreme and nefarious experiment in human history: to create a new society and a new man operating by the moral precepts of the *"Neue Ordnung"*. Each of the hundreds of camps scattered throughout occupied Europe served as a laboratory. By means of starvation, a political weapon of whose efficacy Hitler became aware early in his career, they succeeded in destroying prisoner solidarity in every camp, and directing the prisoners' enmity toward their fellow inmates. In each camp there was a life and death struggle for any crumb of power which might ensure survival. Everywhere, there was blind obedience to the most demonic of orders. In all camps, prisoners helped to exterminate their brothers. Under this system, the prisoners were taught to despise the weak and revere the strong. A thousand times a day the individual was faced with the choice, not between good and evil, but between a greater and a lesser evil, and he or she had to make the decision alone.

The system was applied in Skarżysko, just as it was in every other Jewish camp, leading of necessity to the conclusion that the Jews, subject to this system, responded in the same manner as all other prisoners, even though only they were destined for annihilation. They were neither better nor worse than prisoners of other nationalities, nor were they less vulnerable.

To the eternal question of whether the German experiment succeeded in general and in Skarżysko in particular to create a new society and a new man according to Nazi precepts, there must be two answers, one in reference to the whole picture and the other in reference to the individual. In general terms, I believe the system was thoroughly successful. The lesson to be learned from this is that certain experiments must never be allowed to recur anywhere in the world, since the results will inevitably be the same. It was this realization that led more than a few former prisoners to take their own lives after their release.

In terms of the individual, I must conclude that the system failed. In a state of total helplessness, facing the highly sophisticated and powerful German enemy, the prisoners fought not only to preserve their lives, but also to preserve their identity. They therefore used the only manner of resistance available to them: self-help and social and cultural activities. Only at such times could they feel a sense of solidarity, of shared destiny. A chat, a song or a simple word of encouragement strengthened the prisoners' hope, maintained their sanity, and added a spark of humanity to their hellish existence. In this way they also expressed the political fight aimed at thwarting the attempt of the Third Reich to establish in the camps a model of their future "new order".

I do not mean in any way to absolve the individual prisoners from moral responsibility for their actions by reason of their subjection to the Nazi system. On the contrary, they must bear that responsibility, for they brought their knowledge of good and evil into the camp with them, even if all their other links to the past had been severed.

At a convention of scholars of the Holocaust in London in July 1988, all of those present agreed that the Holocaust in Europe testified to the failure of Western civilization. One of the participants suggested that research into the Holocaust deals not only with a study of human evil, but also with a study of human courage, holding out the possibility of hope. The *pikryner* girls already knew this as they marched through the yellow woods of Werk C singing "The Song of the Cannons".

Bibliography

Archives

Yad Vashem Central Archives – Jerusalem

"Wiener Library", Collection of Testimonies, London	0–2
Testimonies Department of the YV Archives, Tel-Aviv	0–3
Trials of Nazi Criminals	0–4
Adam Rutkowski Collection	0–6/37–3
Jewish Historical Commission in Poland, Collection of Testimonies	0–16
Yad Vashem Manuscripts Collection	0–19
M. Weichert Collection on Jewish Welfare in the General-gouvernement	0–21
M. Silberberg Collection Archives of the Polish underground Research Institute (Studium Polski Podziemnej), London	0–25
Collection on Various Testimonies	0–33
D. Boder, Collection of Testimonies	0–36
Central Committee of Liberated Jews in Munich, Testimonies Collection	M–1/E
Collections of Historical questionnaires	M–1/Q
Office of Dr I. Schwarzbart, Member of the Polish National Council, London	M–2
International Tracing Service, Arolsen, Basic Documents of Concentration Camps	M–8/BD
S. Wiesenthal Collection, Linz	M–9
War Criminals Section, Legal Department of the Central Committee of Liberated Jews	M–21

International Military Tribunal (IMT) – Pohl Case	TR–2/N–IV
"Zentrale Stelle", Ludwigsburg – Investigations of Nazi Criminals	TR–8
Indictments and Sentences in Trials of Nazi Criminals	TR–10
Israeli Police Investigation of Nazi Crimes	TR–11
Microfilm Collection	JM
Personalakte und die Offizierskartei der allgemeinen SS-NSDAP beim 6889 Berlin Documents Center	APO 742

Bundesarchiv Koblenz (BA)

Reichsministerium fuer Ruestungs- und Kriegsproduktion – Ministerbuero Speer	R 3
Wirtschaftsgruppe Eisenschaffende Industrie	R 13 I
Wirtschaftsgruppe Chemische Industrie	R 13 XII
Wirtschaftsgruppe Metallindustrie	R 13 XXIV
Reichsamt fuer Wirtschaftsausbau	R 25
Beauftragter fuer den Vierjahresplan	R 26 I
Regierung des Generalgouvernements	R 52
Kanzlei des Generalgouvernements	R 52 II
Hauptabteilung Wirtschaft	R 52 VI
Hautabteilung Ernaehrung und Landwirtschaft Polizeidienststellen in eingegliederten und besetzten Gebieten Polen	R 52 VII R 70

Militaerarchiv Freiburg (MA)

OKW/Wehrwirtschafts- und Ruestungsamt	RW 19
Wirtschaft und Ruestung – Polen	WiIF5
OKH/Heereswaffenamt	RH 8 I
Kriegstagebuecher des Wehrwirtschaftsoffiziers des Wehrkreiskommando im GG, 1943–1944)	RW 46
Militaergeschichtliche Forschungsamt, Dokumentzentrale (Wehrkreiskommandos Generalgouvernement)	RH 53-23
"Reports on Poland 1935–1939"	WiID/3
Ruestungsdienststellen im Generalgouvernement: Kriegstagebuch der Ruestungsinspektion im Generalgouvernement:	RW 23 (WiID.1)
1. Oktober – Dezember 1942	RW 23/2
2. Januar – Dezember 1943	RW 23/3
3. Januar – September 1944	RW 23/4

"Geschichte der Ruestungsinspektion im GG vom
   1. Juli 1940 bis 31. Dezember 1941   RW 23/5
"Anlageband zur Geschichte der Rue In im GG"   RW 23/6a
"Lageberichte der Ruestungsinspektion XXIII (Oberost
   GG) vom 20. November 1939 bis 15 Mai 1941"   RW 23/7
"Lageberichte der Rue In im GG vom 13 January 1941 bis
   Mai 1941"   RW 23/8
"Lageberichte vom 15.6.1941 bis 15.2.1942"   RW 23/9
Kriegstagebuch des Ruestungskommando Krakau:
   1942   RW 23/10
   1943   RW 23/11
   1944   RW 23/12
Kriegstagebuch-Aussenstelle Radom des Rue Kdo
   Warschau, Juli 1942   RW 23/16
Kriegstagebuch des Ruestungskommando Radom, vom
   1. Juli 1943 bis 30. September 1943   RW 23/17
Ktb des Rue Kdo Radom fuer 1944   RW 23/18
Ruestungswirtschftliche Lageberichte der Rue In im GG
   fuer die Zeit 1940–1941   RH 53-23/27,28
Staatsarchiv Leipzig (STAL)
Handbuch der deutschen Aktiengesellschaften, 1943

Archives Beit Lohamey Hagettaot (HJF)

Testimonies Collection

Archiwum Głównej Komisji Badania Zbrodni Hitlerowskich w Polsce, Warszawa (AGKBZHwP)

Akta prokuratora wojewódzkiego w Kielcach w sprawie Jerzego Adryanowicza,
   Sąd Wojewódzki Kielce, SWK, sygn. 212–242
Akta Okręgowej Komisji Badańia Zbrodni Niemieckich w Radomiu, Dane staty-
   styczne odnośnie strat ludności polskiej i żydowskiej.
Akta Sądu Okręgowego w Radomiu w sprawie:
   Franciszka Gajowczyka, SORd 196
   Romana Koperka, SWK 211
   Wincentego Wójcika, SORd 200
   Michała Czepila, SWK 211.

Muzeum Miejskie w Skarżysku-Kamiennej

Dział dokumentów

Document collections

Anatomie des Krieges, Neue Dokumente ueber die Rolle des deutschen Mono-
polkapitals bei der Vorbereitung u. Durchfuehrung des zweiten Welt krieges,
hrsg. von D. Eichholtz und W. Schumann (Berlin: VEB Deutscher Verlag
der Wissenschaften, 1969).

Deutschlands Ruestung im zweiten Weltkrieg, Hitlers Konferenzen mit Albert
Speer 1942–1945, hrsg. von A. W. Boelcke (Frankfurt a/M: Athenaion, 1969).

Das Diensttagebuch des deutschen Generalgouverneurs in Polen, 1939–1945,
Quellen und Darstellungen zur Zeitgeschichte (Stuttgart: DVA, 1975).

Documents on the Holocaust, (Hebrew), Selected Sources on the Destruction
of the Jews of Germany and Austria, Poland and the Soviet Union, edited
by Y. Arad, Y. Gutman, A. Margaliot (Jerusalem: Yad Vashem, 1978).

Documenta occupationis teutonicae, vol. VI, Hitlerowskie prawo okupacyjne
w Polsce, Generalna Gubernia (Poznań: Instytut Zachodni, 1958).

Documenta occupationis teutonicae, vol. X, Praca przymusowa Polaków pod
panowaniem hitlerowskim 1939–1945 (Poznań: Instytut Zachodni, 1976).

Dokumenty i materiały, vol. I, Obozy, edited by N. Blumental, (Żydowska
Centralna Komisja Historyczna, Łódź 1946).

Dokumenty zbrodni i męczeństwa, edited by M. Borwicz, N. Rost, J. Wulf
(Kraków: Żydowska Komisja Historyczna, 1945).

Eksterminacja Żydów na ziemiach polskich w okresie okupacji hitlerowskiej,
Zbiór dokumentów, edited by T. Berenstein, A. Eisenbach, A. Rutkowski
(Warszawa: Żydowski Instytut Historyczny, 1957).

Faschismus – Getto – Massenmord, Dokumentation ueber Ausrottung und
Widerstand der Juden in Polen, hrsg. von Juedischen Historischen Institut
Warschau (Berlin: Ruetten u. Loening, 1960).

Hans A. Jacobsen: 1939–1945, Der zweite Weltkrieg in Chronik und Dokumenten
(Wehr u. Wissen Vlg, Darmstadt 1961).

Korherr Fritz: Die Endloesung der europaeischen Judenfrage, Statistische Bericht,
April 1943, YVA, 05/DN/33-3.

Okupacja i ruch oporu w dzienniku Hansa Franka 1939–1945, edited by Zofia
Połubiec (Warszawa: Książka i Wiedza, 1972).

Prel Max Freiherr du: Das Deutsche Generalgouvernement Polen (Wuerzburg:
K. Trueltsch, 1942).

Ungerer A.: Verzeichnis von Ghettos, Zwangsarbeitslagern und Konzentrations-
lagern, Muenchen 1953.

Ursachen und Folgen, Eine Urkunden und Dokumentensammlung zur
Zeitgeschichte, hrsg. von H. Michaelis u. E. Schraepler Berlin.

Verordnungsblatt des Generalgouverneurs fuer die besetzten polnischen Gebiete.

Books

Adamczyk Mieczysław: Prasa konspiracyjna na Kielecczyźnie w latach 1939–1945 (Kraków: Wydawnictwo Literackie, 1982).

Arczyński Marek, Balcerak Wiesław: Kryptonim "Żegota" (Warszawa: Czytelnik1979).

Backer-Tennenbaum Nina: The hero of the ghettoes, (Hebrew) (Tel Aviv: Misrad habitahon, 1980).

Bagel-Bohlan Anja: Hitlers industrielle Kriegsvorbereitung 1936 bis 1939 Beitraege zur Wehrforschung, Band 24, (Koblenz: Wehr und Wissen Vlg, 1975).

Bauminger Róza: Przy pikrynie i trotylu, Obóz pracy przymusowej w Skarżysku-Kamiennej (Kraków: Centralna Żydowska Komisja Historyczna w Polsce, 1946).

Billig Joseph: Les camps de concentration dans l'économie du Reich hitlerien (Paris: Presses Universitaires, 1973).

Broszat Martin: Der Staat Hitlers (Muenchen: DTV, 1969).

Catalogue of camps and prisons in Germany and German occupied territories, International Tracing Service (I.T.S.), vol. I–IV.

Czech Danuta, Kalendarium der Ereignisse im Konzentrationslager Auschwitz-Birkenau, Hefte von Auschwitz, nr. 4 (Państwowe Muzeum w Oświęcimiu, 1961).

Daitz Werner: Der Weg zur Volkswirtschaft, Grossraumwirtschaft und Grossraumpolitik, hrsg. vom Zentralforschungsinstitut fuer Nationale Wirtschaftsordnung u. Grossraumwirtschaft (Dresden: Meinhold Verlagsgesellschaft, 1943).

Donat Alexander: The Holocaust Kingdom (London: Becker a. Warburg, 1965).

Dunin-Wąsowicz Krzysztof: Ruch oporu w hitlerowskich obozach koncentracyjnych 1933–1945, Warszawa: (Państwowe Wydawnictwo Naukowe, 1979).

Eichholtz Dietrich: Geschichte der deutschen Kriegswirtschaft 1939–1945 (Berlin: Akademie Vlg, 1971).

Eisenbach Artur: Hitlerowska polityka zagłady Żydów (Warszawa: Książka i Wiedza, 1961).

Encyclopedia of the Holocaust, ed. Israel Gutman, (New York: Macmillan Publishing Company, 1990).

Frey Hans: Die Hoelle von Kamienna, unter Benutzung des amtlichen Prozessmaterials (Berlin-Potsdam: VVN-Verlag, 1949).

Friedman Icchak: Bletlech fun a lebn, (Yiddish) (Tel-Aviv: "Naj Leben", 1981).

Gadolin Axel von: Der Norden, der Ostraum und das neue Europa (Muenchen: G. Roehrig, 1943).

Gilbert Martin: Atlas of the Holocaust (London: Michael Joseph, 1982).

Granatstein Jechiel: Hod vegvura, (Hebrew) (Jerusalem: "Zekher Naftali" 1986).

Hechalutz Halochem, Organ of the Chalutz Underground Movement in Occupied Cracow, August–October 1943, (Ghetto Fighter's House, 1984).

Heilbrunn Stefania: Children of dust and heaven (Cape Town: Irgun Yotzey Radomsko, 1978).

Hilberg Raul: The Destruction of the European Jews (Chicago: Quadrangle Books, 1961).

Homze E.L.: Foreign Labor in Nazi Germany (Princeton: Princeton University Press, 1967).

Janssen Gregor: Das Ministerium Speer, Deutschlands Ruestung im Krieg (Berlin: Verlag Ullstein, 1968).

Kaczanowski Longin: Hitlerowskie fabryki śmierci na Kielecczyźnie, (Warszawa: Książka i Wiedza, 1984).

Kannapin H.E.: Wirtschaft unter Zwang (Koeln: Deutsche Industrie Verlag 1966).

Felicja Karay: Hamavet b.tzahov, mahane avoda Skarżysko-Kamienna slave (Hebrew), (Jerusalem: Yad Vashem & Tel-Aviv University, 1944)

Karay Felicja: Boded mul hamavet, (Hebrew) (Jerusalem: Misrad hahinukh v'hatarbut, 1980).

Karmel Ilona: An estate of memory (Boston: Houghton Miffling Company, 1969).

Keilig Wolf: Das Deutsche Heer 1939–1945 (Bad Neuheim: H.H. Podzun, 1956).

Kogon Eugen: Der SS-Staat, (Muenchen: Kindler Verlag, 1974).

Krakowski Shmuel: Jewish Armed Resistance in Poland 1942–1944, (Hebrew) (Tel-Aviv: Sifriat Poalim, 1977).

Kuczynski Jurgen: Die Geschichte der Lage der Arbeiter unter dem Kapitalismus (Berlin: Tribune Verlag, 1964).

Kwintner-Merder Flora: Haiti sham b'gil nekhaday, (Hebrew) (Tel-Aviv: Moreshet, 1985).

Landau Ludwik: Kronika lat wojny i okupacji (Warszawa: Państwowe Wydawnictwo Naukowe, 1962).

Leszczyńska Zofia: Kronika obozu na Majdanku (Lublin: Wydawnictwo Lubelskie, 1980).

Ludwig H. Karl: Technik und Ingeunieure im Dritten Riech (Duesseldorf: Droste Verlag, 1979).

Lochner P.L.: Die Maechtigen und der Tyrann (Darmstadt: F. Schneekluth, 1955).

Madajczyk Czesław: Polityka III Rzeszy w okupowanej Polsce (Warszawa: Państwowe Wydawnictwo Naukowe, 1970).

Matusak Piotr: Ruch oporu w przemyśle wojennym okupanta hitlerowskiego na ziemiach polskich w latach 1939–1945,(Warszawa: Ministerstwo Obrony Narodowej, 1983).

Meducki Stanisław: Przemysł i klasa robotnicza w dystrykcie radomskim w okresie okupacji hitlerowskiej (Warszawa: Państwowe Wydawnictwo Naukowe, 1981).

Nonnenbruch Fritz: Die dynamische Wirtschaft (Muenchen: Zentral Verlag der NSDAP, 1937).

Nonnenbruch Fritz: Neue Ordnung in Europa (Berlin: E.R. Alisch, 1939).

Obozy hitlerowskie na ziemiach polskich, Informator encyklopedyczny (Warszawa: Państwowe Wydawnictwo Naukowe, 1979).

Orenstein Benjamin, Churban Czenstochow, (Yiddish), (Central Farwaltung fun der Czenstochower landsmanszaft in der amerikaner Zone in Dajczland, 1948).

Pamiętnik Dawida Rubinowicza, ed. Anna Piliszek, (Warszawa: Książka i Wiedza, 1987).

Petzina Dietmar: Vierjahresplan und Ruestungspolitik, Wirtschaft u. Ruestung am Vorabend des 2. Weltkrieges, hrsg. von Friedrich Forstmeier u. H.E. Volkmann (Duesseldorf: Droste Verlag, 1975).

Pfahlman Hans: Fremdarbeiter und Kriegsgefangene in der deutschen Kriegswirtschaft 1939–1945 (Darmstadt: Wehr und Wissen, 1968).

Pingel Falk: Haeftlinge unter SS-Herrschaft, Widerstand, Selbstbehauptung und Vernichtung im Konzentrationslager (Hamburg: Hoffman u. Campe, 1978).

Piotrowski Stanisław: Dziennik Hansa Franka (Warszawa: Wydawnictwo Prawnicze, 1956).

Prekerowa Teresa: Konspiracyjna Rada Pomocy Żydom w Warszawie 1942–1945, (Warszawa: Państwowy Instytut Wydawniczy, 1982).

Reitlinger Gerald: Die Endloesung (Berlin: Colloquium Verlag, 1956).

Rosenberger-Kornblum Rut, Neder, (Hebrew) (Tel-Aviv: Moreshet & Sifriat Poalim, 1986).

Ryszka Franciszek: Państwo stanu wyjątkowego (Wrocław: Ossolineum, 1964).

Seeber Eva: Robotnicy przymusowi w faszystowskiej gospodarce wojennej (Warszawa: Książka i Wiedza, 1972).

Sesja popularno-naukowa poświęcona martyrologii mieszkańców miasta Skarżysko-Kamiennej oraz okolic w latach 1939–1945, (Skarżysko-Kam.: Towarzystwo Miłośników Miasta Skar.-Kamienna, 1974).

Speer Albert: Der Sklavenstaat, Meine Auseinandersetzungen mit der SS (Stuttgart: DVA, 1981).

Stabholz Tadeusz: Siedem piekieł (Stuttgart: "Ojf der Fraj", 1947).

Strigler Mordchai: Majdanek, (Yiddish) (Buenos Aires: Union Central Israelita Polaca en la Argentina, 1947).

Strigler Mordchai: In di fabrikn fun toyt, (Yiddish) (Buenos Aires: Union Central Israelita Polaca en la Argentina, 1948).

Strigler Mordchai: Werk "Ce", (Yiddish) (Buenos Aires: Union Central Israelita Polaca en la Argentina, 1950).

Strigler Mordchai: Goirolois, (Yiddish) (Buenos Aires: Union Central Israelita Polaca en la Argentina, 1952).

Thomas Georg: Geschichte der deutschen Wehr- und Ruestungswirtschaft (1918–1943/45), hrsg. von Wolfgang Birkenfeld (Boppard a/Rhein: H. Boldt, 1966).

Wroński Stanisław, Zwolakowa Maria: Polacy i Żydzi, 1939–1945, (Warszawa: Książka i Wiedza, 1971).

Wspomnienia Rudolfa Hoessa, ed. Jan Sehn (Warszawa: Wydawnictwo Prawnicze, 1960).

Zuckerman Itzhak (Antek): Sheva shanim hahen, (Hebrew) (Ghetto Fighter's House, 1990).

YIZKOR-BOOKS

Pinkas Chmielnik – Yizkor Book, published by Irgun Yotze Chmielnik b'Israel, and Chmielniker Landsmannschaften in USA, Canada, Argentina *et al.*, Tel-Aviv, 1960.

Jendrzewer Buch – Jendrzewer Yizkor Book, edited by S. Dow-Jeruszalmi, published by Irgun Olei Jendrzejow b' Israel, Tel- Aviv, 1965.

Sefer Mogelnica – Sefer Iskor Mogelnica-Blendow, edited by Israel Sander, published by Mogelnicer Blendower Societes in Israel, Argentina, USA *et al.*, Tel-Aviv, 1972.

Sefer Apt (Opatów) – edited by Zvi Yasheev, published by Apt organizations in Israel, USA, Canada, Brazil *et al.*, Tel-Aviv, 1966.

Sefer Piotrków – Piotrków Trybunalski Yizkor Buch, edited by Jakow Maltz & Naftali Law, published by the Landsmannschaften in Israel, USA, England, Canada *et al.*, Tel-Aviv, 1964.

Sefer Radomsk – Yizkor l'Khilat Radomsk, published by Irgun Yotzei Radomsk b'Israel, USA, Argentina.

Skarżysko Book – The "Yizchor" Book in memory of the Jewish community of Skarżysko, edited by Eliezer Lewin, Jerachmiel Shier, published by the organization of Skarżysko former inhabitants in Israel & USA, Tel-Aviv, 1973.

Pinkas Sochaczew – edited by A. Stein, G. Weissman, published by Irgun Yotzey Sochaczew b'Israel & America, Jerusalem 1962.

Sefer Staszów – edited by Elhanan Ehrlich, published by the Organization of Staszowites in Israel with the Assistance of Staszowite Organizations in the Diaspora, 1962.

Szydlowcer Book – Shidlovtser Yizkor Bukh, edited by Berl Kagan, published by Shidlovtser Benevolent Association, New York, 1974.

Sefer Wodzisław – Sefer Vojdislav-Sedziszow, edited by M. Szucman, published by Vaad shel Yotze Vojdislav-Sedziszow b'Eretz ub'Tfucot, Tel-Aviv, 1978.
Zwoliner Book – Zwoliner Yizkor Bukh, edited by Berl Kogan, published by New York Independent Zwoliner Benevolent Society, New York, 1982.

Journals & Periodicals

Biuletyn Głównej Komisji Badania Zbrodni Hitlerowskich w Polsce, Warszawa.
Biuletyn Informacyjny, Londyn.
Biuletyn Żydowskiego Instytutu Historycznego w Polsce, Warszawa.
Biuletyn Informacyjny A.K.
Biuletyn Informacyjny 1943–1944, Warszawa.
Blaetter fuer deutsche und internationale Politik, Koeln.
Echo dnia, Kielce.
Gazeta Żydowska, 1941–1942.
Głos Warszawy
Gwardzista
Folks-Sztyme, Warszawa.
Frankfurter Zeitung
Kurier Szczeciński, 1966.
Nasze Słowo, Skarżysko-Kamienna.
New Bulletin, Piotrków Trybunalski Relief Association, New York.
Przegląd Lekarski, Kraków.
Vierteljahreshefte fuer Zeitgeschichte, Stuttgart.
Zeszyty Oświęcimskie, (Hefte von Auschwitz), Oświęcim.
Zion, Jeruszalaim (Hebrew).

Index

The letter 'f' after a page number
indicates a figure, the letter 't' indicates
a table.

"2 cm Department" 143, 154–5
"500 section" 143

abduction of Jews 20
"Abram, Grobe" 231
absenteeism: Polish 25–7, 48, 54, 237
Abt. Kraft u. Waerme 175
ADCA (Allgemeine Deutsche Credit
  Anstalt) 4
administration of camp 43, 44–6,
  79–88, 113, 124–5, 238–41, 242–3
Adryanowicz, Georg (*Jerzy*) 44, 186–8
aid:
  external 120–1, 128–31, 157, 196,
    202, 204–5, 212, 215, 245;
  internal 160, 196, 200, 204, 207,
    211–2, 245, 247
Ajzenberg (shoemaker) 80, 127
Ajzenman, Etla 131
AK *see Armia Krajowa*
Akiva 217–8, 223, 245–6
Ala (prisoner) 112
Albert, Chaim 137
Albirt, Eljasz (Pinie) 84–6, 113, 138,
  139
Albirt, Hana 84

Alek (orderly) 185, 210, 230
Allgemeine Deutsche Credit Anstalt
  (ADCA) 4
Altenburg 231
Alter Flughafen 61
Altman, Rabbi Abraham 136
ammunition: theft of 48, 116–9, 132,
  163–6, 173–4, 179, 242
ammunition production 9, 67, 70–1,
  235–6
Andress, Richard 92
Anker, Israel 170, 175
Apelzweig, Neomi 145
Apitz, Bruno: "Naked Among the
  Wolves" 230
Apparatebau 71t
Aptowicz, Dr 225–6
Arbeitsdienst xvii
Arbeitserziehungslager 25, 42
Arbeitslager (open work camps) 20, 30,
  42
Arbeitspflicht xvii
Arbeitszwang xvii
Arczyński, Marek 129, 245
Armaments Command 3, 10, 26, 58, 67,
  70
Armaments Commission 16
armaments industry 6–7, 9, 13, 15–6,
  52–4, 235–6
Armaments Inspectorate Units: anti-

258

Himmler coalition 31, 62, 236; armaments plants 14–5, 41; control of 16; creation 3; Eastern Command 7, 9; Jewish workers 32, 61; Skarżysko plant 12; SS camps 47; transfer of workers to Germany 18; *Werkschutz* 24
armaments policy: Third Reich 3–4, 16
armaments production 39, 46–7, 70; *see also* ammunition production
Armia Krajowa (AK) 48, 118, 120, 227, 242
army *see* Wehrmacht
Aryanization of businesses 26
Aussenkommando 69
"*Austausch der Juden*" *see* "Jew exchanges"
authorities: camp *see* administration of camp
Automatic Weapons Department 89, 93

Bach Zelewski, Erich von dem 60
Badura, August 147
Bahntransport 168
Bałanowski, Chil 145
Barckhausen, General 7
"barracks lyrics" 206
barracks overseers 84–5
Bartenschlager, Fritz 43, 80, 100
Basserman, Felix 4
Baukommando 164–6, 180
Baumgarten, Renia 148–9
Bauminger, Róża 179, 191, 215
beatings: "official" 82–3
Beker, Awigdor 187–8
benefits, workers' *see* workers' benefits
Bergen-Belsen 231
Berliński, Abraham 149
Berman, Adolf 129–30, 205
Bertgram, Amalia 127–8
Betriebskarten see "factory cards"
Betriebslager 30, 32, 42, 71t, 235
Biała-Rawska 32
Białobrzegi: transports 51
Białywłos, Szmuel 196
Bielski, Bolesław 106

Bielski, Jan 164
Bień (prisoner) 221
Bierkamp (SiPo commander) 72
Biłas, Mirosław 43
Bilewicz, Tadeusz 129
Billig, Joseph 235
Bitter, Hersz 194
Blacharz's son 232
black market 26–7, 109, 237
Bleicher, Wili 229
Blemengraber, Hela 219
Blizyń 70, 71t
Blockaelteste 84–5
Blum, Fela 212
Blusztajn, Israel 201–2
Blusztajn, Meir 201–2
Blusztajn brothers 217, 221
Board of Directors: Hasag Concern 4
Bodalska, Wanda 129
Bodzentyń 22; transports 32
Boettcher, Herbert 11, 32–4, 66, 69, 81, 165, 235
Boguchwał, Fela 212
Bolsheviks: Polish hatred 47–8
Bormann, Martin 30
Bornes, Lejb 58, 121
Bosch (shop steward) 39
Bosch, Martin 92
"Boxer" *see* Faerber, Hans
Braeutigam (German) 168
Brandt (German) 97
Brauchitsch, General von 9
Braunschweig Stahlwerke Company 10, 14, 53t, 71t, 72
Breest, Will 92
Brellendin (German) 97
Brenner (prisoner) 130
Brest (German) 101
Briks, Genia 144
Bronner, Irena 148, 155–6, 159–60
Brunnengrabber, Hela 219
Brzeźnica: transports 36t, 40f
Buchenwald 72, 140, 229–31
Buchholz, Paulina 212
Budin, Paul 234, 241; authority 4, 6; conscription of Polish workers 29;

"Economic Strategist of the SS" 4; general manager of Hasag 2; invites Himmler to visit plants 18, 19f; Jewish workers 21–2, 29–33, 55, 70–1, 73, 236, 238; "Leader of the War Economy" 6; munition production started 2; personnel changed at Skarżysko 58; personnel policy 6, 23–9; purchase of plants 46–7, 236; Special Committee 2, 13, 16; suicide 2; takes over Skarżysko plants 15

Budzyń 61

Bugajski, David 210, 214, 231

Bund: aid for prisoners 120–1, 129–30, 245; camp group 202–5, 218–9, 223–4, 246

Burgau 231

Burzlaff, Kurt 93

"Bzinek atrocity" 63–5

"camp elders" 83–4

"camp families" 200, 245

camps 20, 41–2

cartelization of companies 2

Casing Department 92–3

Central Labor Department 17

Cesia (prisoner) 160

Chęciński (prisoner) 148

Chęciny 32

children 127–8, 142

Chmielnik: transports 36t

Cholewa (Volkdeutsch) 153

Chudin, Tola 105

Ciekierski, Pawel 106

Ciok, Aharon 177, 180, 202

"class" structure 74–5, 99, 158, 190–1, 244

clerical work 146

closed work camps 20

closure of camp 72–3

clothing 78, 212–3

Colditz 231

Comber, Felicja 130

commissary management 9–11, 13–5

"company camps" *see Betriebslager*

"compulsory labor" xvii

concentration camps 65–7, 71t, 72

conditions, living *see* living conditions

confiscated property: in *Generalgouvernement* 13–4; *see also* property of Jews

conscription: Polish workers 29

"construction commandos" (*Baukommando*) 164–6, 180

control of workers 23–4, 83, 238–9

"cooking groups" 200

costs: Jewish workers 42, 44, 71; Polish workers 54–5

Council for Aid to Jews *see Rada Pomocy Żydom*

"coup d'état": Werk C 213–5

"couplets" 137–9

"court songs" 206

"courtiers" 99

"cousins" (*kuzyns, kuzynkas*) 115–6, 125, 158–9, 201, 209–10, 215, 245

craftsmen 103, 150, 195

cultural activities 132–9, 204–6, 218–9, 223, 245–7

Cypres, Rina 174

Czaplicki, Dr 119

Częstochowa: evacuation to 140, 161, 229, 231; purchase of factory 46; transports 36t, 51, 62, 69, 72; work force 53t, 71t

Częstochowianka 54, 71t

Czop (overseer) 171

Czopyk, Stefan 43

Czopyk, Teodor 43

Dąbrowa Górnicza: transports 36t

"daily press" 137–9, 209–10

Dalski, Egon (Hugo) 11–2, 16, 21–2, 30, 39, 58, 96, 241

dance floor 220–1

Dance Hall *see Musiksaal*

D.A.W. (*Deutsch Ausruestungswerke*) 61–2

"death lists" 94

"death march" 231

"death train" 64
Dechant, Erich 97, 126
Deutsch Ausruestungswerke (D.A.W.) 61–2
Deutsche Bank 4
Deutscher, Rut 146–7
"Di Shwue" 203
Diamant, Sala 217
"dismissed" Jews 94, 141
Distribution Committee 204–5
Division of War Economy and Ordnance 14
Długoszcz (Pole) 180
doctors 114, 198, 245
Donat, Alexander 58
Drenger, Szymek 217
Dresdner Bank 4
"Dziadek" see Hecht
Dziewięcki (Pole) 152

Eastern Industries Co. (OSTI) 47, 55, 60–2
economy, underground *see* underground economy
Edek (prisoner) 119
Edelman, Henoch 201–3, 205
"Education for Work" camps 25, 42
Edzia (prisoner) 195
Efrat, David 130–1, 204
Ehrlich, Elhanan 130
Eichholtz, Dietrich 234
Eisenberg, Henek 183–4, 187, 189–90, 201, 207, 221
Eisenberg, Ruchana 81
Eisenschmidt, Otto 80
"Ekonomia" 75, 77, 113
Elaboracja 63, 166
Eliasziw, Awraham 211
Elza (prisoner) 160
"emergency committee" 102
entertainment 136–7, 160, 206–7, 221–3, 245–6
Entlassene Juden see "dismissed" Jews
entry into camp 78–9, 244
Erlich, Elhanan 86, 102
Erlich, Lolek 173

Erlich, Natanel 163
Ernest, Ewa 80
Ernst, Michael 168
"Erntefest" 60–2
escape attempts 100–1, 110, 118–9, 132, 139–40, 155, 242; drop in number 66, 132; "Great Escape" 72, 225–8; Werk A 101, 164; Werk B 142; Werk C 163–4, 166, 186, 194; *Werkschutz* 82
Espenhaym, Erich ("*Krimineller*") 93
"essential production workers" 23
evacuation of camp 72–3, 140, 161, 229, 231
evacuation of Jews 49–50
Ewa (prisoner) 112
"exchanges, Jew" 38–9, 101, 238
exchanges, prisoner 185–6, 189
executions 63–5, 103, 110, 118, 185–6, 216; *see also* "selections"
extermination of Jews 237–40

Fabrikslager 42
"factory camps" *see Betriebslager*
"factory cards" 5f, 54
Faerber, Hans ("Boxer") 94, 104, 126
"families, camp" 200, 245
family barracks 115–6
family groups 79, 87–8, 112, 200, 245
"family rooms" 149, 150
farm 151–2
Fass, Sala 171
Feiner, Leon 129–30, 205
Feldman (Fela Markowiczowa's brother-in-law) 183
Feldman (police commander) 190, 202–5, 214, 226
Feldman, Renia 183–4
Fersztendig, Rabbi Israel 162
Feucht, Paul 11, 81
"Final Solution" 26–7, 30, 32, 60, 237
Finger, Lola 84, 100
Finger, Mosze ("the gravedigger") 84, 100, 230
Finger, Regina 113
Finkelsztajn (prisoner) 196

Finkler, Malka 131
Finkler, Rabbi Yitzhak 135–6
"firing range" 63, 65, 244
Fischlewiczowa (prisoner) 153
"500 section" 143
Flajszakier, Noach 105
Flajszhakier (barracks overseer) 85
Flick 42
Floessburg 231
Flora (prisoner) 112, 114
Florstedt, Herman 55
food: from aid agencies 157; "Pikryna
    Soup Affair" 178; "Polish Soup
    Affair" 170–1; rations 59, 77–8, 90,
    126–7, 213, 244; sale of 133, 195;
    smuggling 104–5, 107–9, 151, 153;
    suppliers 12, 18, 54, 69, 77, 237;
    withdrawal of food allowance 27
food plant 150–4
"forced labor" xvii
forest ("green corridor") 163–6
"forest commandos" 163–4
Fortgang sisters 225
"Four Year Plans" 2–3, 6
Fragner (police commander) 214
Frajdenrajch, Staszek 105
Frank, Hans: conscription of workers
    29; labor camps 20, 236; ownership
    of munitions plants 13–4; purchase of
    Skarżysko plants 46; security
    problems 49, 59, 62
Frauendorfer, Max 17
Frenkel, Rabbi Yitzhak 159
Frey, Hans: *Die Hoelle von Kamienna*
    1–2
Friedland ("overseer") 200
Friedman, Wolf 145–6
Friedman, Zelig 145–6
Friedmann, Icchak 179, 189, 194, 205
Friedmann, Róża 160
Friedmann, Sala 153
Friedmann family 141–2
Frietsche, Kurt 93
"frying pan" 64–5, 220
Fuehrer, Hans 4
Fuks, Levi 87

functionaries 43, 83, 86–7, 116, 156,
    189; responsibilities 84–5
Fuss-Kaufman, Luna 178, 209

Gajda (Pole) 165
Gajowczyk, Franciszek 169–70
Gałczyński (garden manager) 152
garden, vegetable 152, 189
Gelberowa (prisoner) 129
Geldmacher, Paul 47, 58
Geller, Ahron 177–8
Generalgouvernement: black market
    26–7, 109, 237; confiscated property
    13–4; economic policy 10–11;
    industry 68f; labor relations xvii;
    political borders 8f; security 59–60,
    62
Genia (nurse) 114–5
Genthe, Karl 95
Germans 23–4, 46, 239
Germany: transferred workers 18, 23
Gerstel, Roman 179
ghetto workshops 20
ghettos: Radom district 22, 37f
Giesel, Martin 96–7
Giesser 168–9
Ginsburg (prisoner) 94, 107
Ginsburg, Hinda 127
Gizela (prisoner) 152
Glasner, Dr Roman 140
Glaue, Walter 143, 153, 155–6
Gleisberg, Walter 93
Globocnik, Odilo 20, 47, 55, 58
Głogowski, Tadeusz 110
Gnat (barracks overseer) 85
Goering, Herman 3, 6–7, 14
Goeth, Amon 62, 122–3
Gola, Genia 147
Goldberg, Herman 201–2
Goldberg, Lilka 160
Goldberg, Melech 225
Goldfarb, Gilek 86
Goldhar, Szaul 179, 201–2, 205
Goldszajder (prisoner) 107
Goldwasser, Herszel 195, 227
Goldwasser, Mordchai 144

"good barracks" 201
Gorlicki, Baruch 145
Gottesmann, Dr 215
Gottlieb, Awraham 217
Gottlieb, Meir 217
Gottlieb, Mosze 166
Gottlieb, Szmuel 217
"Granat" factory *see* Kielce
Granatenabteilung – Pociskownia 89–90
"grand search" 39
"Great Escape" 225–8
"green corridor" (forest) 163–6
Greichen, Erich 93
Greipner, Henryk 106
Greiser (German) 67
Grenade Department 89–90
Grinberg, Dr 140
"Grine Lente" 85
Griner, Szlomo 187
"Grobe Abram" 231
Gross, Edward 166
gross Filzaktion 39
Grundman, Ozer 103
Grzebień (prisoner) 216
Grzelka, Lucjan 164
Grzymkowa (murderer) 232
guard commanders 43–4
Guter Barak 201
Guterman, Bezalel 165
Gutman, Mrs 184, 197, 237
Gutman, Feigele 181; *see also* Markowiczowa, Fela
Guza, Meir 144, 175, 194

Haas, Leonard 147, 156, 160
Haeckel und Schneider 2
Haendel, Dr 180, 184, 190, 227
Haenicke, Gen 49–50
Haeussler, Dr 18
Halina (singer) 206
Hall 12 ("Schmitz") 172–4
Hall 13 176, 178
Hall 15 176
Hall 24 178
Hall 51 168, 196
Hall 53 168–9
Hall 58 170–2
Hana (singer) 137
Hannale (prisoner) 159–60
Hans ("*Pleitzes*") 179
Hartman, Adolf 4
Hartman, Mosze 201–2, 204–5
Hartman, Ziata 173
Hartmann (prisoner) 227
Hasag Concern: ammunitions "monopoly" 70–1, 236; anti-Himmler coalition 31, 62; beginnings 2, 4–6; control of Radom district industries 11–6; Fela Markowiczowa 190, 225–6; "Jew exchanges" 38; military plant status 2; munitions plant status 6; production costs and Jewish workers 21; purchase of plants 46–7, 236; records destroyed 2; size 1, 20, 53t, 54, 70, 71t; stockholders 4, 46–7, 236; support for 234–6; transferred workers 18, 23; *see also* Budin, Paul
"Hasag Five" 124
"Hasag trenches" 63, 65
"hasagówka" 220
Hashomer Hadati 201–2, 245
Hecht ("*Dziadek*") 176, 178–9, 221, 225
Hencke, Heinrich 90
Henoch (policeman) 214
Hercberg-Goldman, Bela 80–1
Hercke (overseer) 180
Hering, Georg 143–4, 149
Herling, Szmuel 104
Herman Goering Werke 1
Herold, Karl 23, 96–7
Herszkowitz (informer) 86
Herzberg 231
Hessen, Gustav 4
Himmler, Heinrich: capos 85; centralization plan 31; control of munitions plants 41; "Education for Work" camps 42; "Final Solution" 60; "gangs" 49, 59; invited to Skarżysko 18, 19f; Jewish workers agreement 32; power struggle 62, 236

Hitler, Adolf 2, 13, 29, 49, 73, 235, 246–7
Hławacz, Jarosław 43
Hławacz, Roman 43
Hochoefen-Ostrowiec 71t, 72
Hoehn, Carl 4
Hoelle von Kamienna, Die (Frey) 1–2
Hoffman (German) 168, 225
holidays, Jewish 136, 197
Hollender, Menasze 115, 230–1
Homze, E.L. 27
Horn, Rosa 129
Hornung, Dr 173, 221
Horowicz, Menachem 118
hospital 185, 198, 215
Hugo Schneider Stock Company xvi, 2
hunger: Werk C 170–1, 178

Ickowicz (transport worker) 173
ideological groups 201–4
I.G. Farbenindustrie 1, 4
Imber, Mosze 217, 221–2, 246
Imerglik (prisoner) 230
industrial companies: armaments production 3–4, 13, 15, 236; security 59–60, 62; SS work camps 47
industry 68f
Infanterie 89–93
infirmary 185, 198, 215
informers 86–7, 188, 230
Instrument Division 89, 93
intelligentsia *see* "Płaszów Tier"
internal transport section 168
Ipfling, Anton 43–4, 58, 81, 101, 122, 164, 189
Irchal (murderer) 81
Itzik (prisoner) 159–60
Iwanejko (*Werkschutz*) 164

Jakower, Izak 178, 180
Janina (prisoner) 112
"Jankale" (*Werkschutz*) 148
Jastrzębski (Pole) 155–6
Jędrzejów: transports 36t, 51
Jedwab, Raca 146
Jermelow ("Jeremia") 148–9

"Jew exchanges" 38–9, 101, 238
"Jew File" 43–4
Jewin, Eda 173
Jewish administration 83–5
Jewish Fighting Organisation (ŻOB) 130–2
Jewish holidays 136, 197
Jewish-Polish relationship 105–12, 131, 179–80, 232, 239, 242
Jewish slave labor camps xvi–xvii, 29–30, 41–2, 69–70, 71t
Jewish slave labor program 20–1, 32
Jewish Social Relief *see* JUS
Jewish uprisings 59–60
Jews: number died in camp 65, 73, 101–2; number entered camp 32, 51, 73, 101, 244; number evacuated from camp 73; restrictions on 22, 29
Jonatan (prisoner) 230
Józik (foreman) 165
Judenhertz, Mordchai 87
Judenkartei 43–4
Judenrats 20–1, 31, 75
JUS (Jewish Social Relief) 120, 123, 128, 157, 215, 245

Kaczanowski, Longin 242
kaelniks/kaelankas 113; *see also* "Majdanek Tier"
Kalinowski, Emil 94, 124
Kamiński, Józef 237
Kanarek (prisoner) 155
Kanarek, Leon 164, 166
Kanczer, Stanisław 201
Kaner, Zwi 217
kangaroo court: Buchenwald 230–1
Kannapin, Franz 234
Kapłański, Cesia 80
Karmel, Mrs 212
Karmel, Henia 211–2, 217–8
Karmel, Henryka 246
Karmel, Ila 212, 217
Karmel, Ilona 246
"Katyń in Generalgouvernement 65
Kaufman (policeman) 207
Kaufman, Lunka 219

Kielce: "Granat" factory 15–6, 20, 33, 46, 51, 53t, 71t; transports 32, 36t; workforce 53t, 71t
Kiessling, Else 80
Kiessling, Paul 80, 186, 188
Kinel, Jechiel 118
kitchen 153, 189
KK (*Komisja Koordynacyjna*) 120, 205
Klemm, Herman 156
Kłosek (Pole) 165
Klug, Bluma 202
Klug, Blumcia 203
Knobler, Jehuda 165–6
Knoeffler, Walter 92–3
Koch (German) 126
Koch, Dr Richard 4
Koczelnice: transports 36t, 40f
Kogon, Eugen 237
Kojfman-Sznitlich, Fela 128
Kokoć (*Werkschutz*) 148
Komendanten 85, 87–90
Komisja Koordynacyjna (KK) 120, 205
Końskie 22; transports 32, 36t, 142
Konsum 75, 105
Kopecki, Henryk 179–80
Kopernik (Pole) 165
Koppe, Wilhelm 61, 66–7
Kornblum, Rut 217, 219
Kotkowski (Bund official) 120–1
Kotlęga, Stanisław 164–5
Kotula, Mikolaj 164
Kowalik, Edward 170, 173–4
Kozakowa, Towa 179
Kozłowski, Petro 43
Kozo, Fela 153
Krakowites *see* "Płaszów Tier"
Krause, Kurt 43, 58, 80
Krause, Ludwig 92
Krebs, Felix 167, 174, 221, 225
Kremer, Bernhard 90, 92
Krenzler, Mina 225
Krosta, Friedrich 175
Krueger, HSSuPF xvii, 17, 20, 26, 32, 41, 49–50, 55, 61
Krueger, Ester 145
Krupp 42

"Kruss"-Pionki 72
Kruszyna: transports 51
Krys, Hersz 233
Krzepicka, Ewa 84, 105
Krzepicki, Josef 84–6, 113, 124, 157, 230
Kubiatowski, Stanisław 233
Kuczynski, Juergen 234
Kuehnemann, Paul 58, 122, 124, 128, 136–7, 140, 189
Kuhne, Gustav 12, 58, 77
Kundt, Ernst 11
Kurz, Jakow 201–2, 204–5
Kuzimiński, Emanuel 164, 166, 186, 194
kuzyns/kuzynkas see "cousins"

Labor Department 31
labor exchanges 17–8, 31–2, 48
labor market: changes in 29–33
labor relations xvii
"ladlers" 168–9
Lageraelteste 83–4
Landsmannschafts 79, 102, 112, 200, 245
Langbein, Hermann 237
Langer (prisoner) 129
Langer, Lubosław 233
Laskowski (German) 126
Laskowski, Henryk 101
Laskowski, Jan 151–3, 156
layout of camp 76f, 117f
Łęczycki, Lea 151
Lederman, Awner 227
Leeb, Emil 2, 4
Leidig, Wilhelm 143–4, 146, 151, 154
Leinkram, Giza 160
Leinkram, Janek 160
Leipzig: Hasag factory 2, 6, 73, 231
Lelów: transports 32
Lemit (yeshiva scholar) 196–7
Lepiasz (Pole) 131
Leśniewski (overseer) 171
Lestny, Mosze 193, 196, 202
Lewin, Eliezer 184, 197, 232
Lewin, Rywka 142

Lewinger, Maria 176–8, 208, 212, 218, 246
Lewit, Mrs 232
Lewkowicz, Hana 119
Lewkowicz, Perla 127
"liberal era" 198, 216
"liberal policies" 39
Lieberman, Maryla 160
Liebermann, Josef 159
Liebeskind, Dolek 217
Lipszyc, Lunia *see* Rozenzweig-Lipszyc, Lunia
Lis, Stanisław 187
living conditions 237, 244; improvements 69, 126–7, 131, 212–3, 238; Werk A 75, 77–9, 115–6; Werk B 149–50; Werk C 184–5, 191–2, 200, 209, 212–3
Lochner, Louis 234
Łódź: transports 69, 127
Lordenhaus 150
Łoza (Pole) 155
"Lucia" 129
Łuczak, Czesław 237
Ludwików: transports 62
Lusia ("nurse") 210
"luxury" items 105
Lwów-Janowska 61

'Maccabees' 50
Machtinger (prisoner) 130
Mączyk (prisoner) 163, 201
Madajczyk, Czesław 237
Majdanek: *Erntefest* 60–2
"Majdanek Girls" 160
"Majdanek Period" 34, 62; transports 55–8, 235
"Majdanek Tier" 74, 87, 112–6, 121, 127, 153–4, 192–3; and "Radom Tier" 113–5, 158, 193, 208
Malik (cart driver) 175
Malik (technician) 165
Mandelbaum, Josele 219–20
Maniszewicz (prisoner) 130
manpower shortage *see* workers: shortage of

Marek (Renia Feldman's assistant) 183
Marian (overseer) 173
Markowicz (Fela Markowiczowa's husband) 181–2
Markowicz, Lolek 183
Markowiczowa, Fela 181–2, 185, 192, 194–5, 197; business dealings 188; "*commendanta*" 182–4; concerts 206–7, 221–3; control of work assignments 189–90; "coup d'état" 213–4; entry into camp 182; escape attempt 225–7; friends 201–2; "selections" 187; "White House" agents 188–9
Matusak, Piotr 12, 237, 242
Maurer, Gerhard 55–6
Mauthausen 231
Melech (orderly) 185, 210, 231
memorials 232–3
Mendel (prisoner) 163
Mendelewicz, Lola 119
Meuselwitz: Hasag plant 73, 231
middlemen 26, 107, 165, 195, 212, 245
Milchman, Gucia 81
Milet, Szmuel 232
Milgram, Jacob 148–9
Milgram, Jakow 201
Military Economic Command *see* WWiStab
Miller, Dorka 212
Milsztajn, Zenek 87, 230
Ministry of Munitions and Armaments 13
Miriam (prisoner) 112
Mittelberg, Ryszard 193
Moehring, Artur 58
Moerschner, Kurt 144–6
Monderer, Marylka 152, 158–9
"money barons" 99
monuments 232–3
"Morcin" 92
mortality rate: need to control 69, 121; and production 54, 58, 67
Mumme, Dr Georg 4
Munitions and Armaments, Ministry of 13

Munitionsstop 39, 235
murders 80–1, 95, 163; *see also*
    executions; "selections"
Musiksaal (Music Hall) 144–5
"mussulmen" 99–100, 198, 244

Nagel, Awraham 87
Najman, David 201–2
Najman, Dawid 206, 230–1
Najman, Mosze 82, 84, 188
"Naked Among the Wolves" (Apitz) 230
names, prisoners: recording of 44, 45f
national differences: and control of
    workers 23–4, 83, 238–9
National Jewish Committee (ŻKN)
    129–30, 245
"Neue Ordnung" 246–7
Neumann (prisoner) 201
Neumerkel, Reinhard 126
Niechcicki, Mosze 117, 119
Niewiadów 53t
"Night of the Great Escape" 225–8
Nikielberg, Dr 114
Nirenberg, Zygmunt 148–9, 154, 156–7,
    159
"nobility" 25
Nowak, Tadeusz 110, 111f
Nowicki, Adam 89, 118
Nugel, Szalom 233

Ofir, Madzia 123
Ogniewicz, Leib 145
Opatów 22; transports 32, 36t
open work camps (*Arbeitslager*) 20, 30,
    42
Opoczno 32
"ordinary" work camps 42
organizacja (pilfering) 103, 244
organization of camp *see* administration
    of camp
Ost Industrie (OSTI) 47, 55, 60–2
Ostojowski, Frida 94
Ostrowiec transports 36t, 62; work force
    53t, 71t
Ostrowiecki (wagon driver) 152
Ozan, Stanisław 164

Ożarów: transports 32, 36t

Pacanów: transports 36t
Palestine: prisoner exchange 185–6
Pankiewicz, Tadeusz 128
Pantel (policeman) 231
"pariahs" 191–3
Patac, Josek 94
patelnia 64–5, 220
Pawlowski, Dora 94, 144
Pawlowski, Richard 94, 107, 126,
    143–4
penal camps 42
Perel brothers 104
Perlow (prisoner) 130
Perlstein, Bela 145
personnel policy 6, 23–9
Peterseil (prisoner) 124
Pfahlman, Hans 234
Pfefferman (policeman) 100
Picric Acid/TNT Departments 175–80
"Picryner Anthem" 192, 206
picryners 191–2
"Pikryna Soup Affair" 178
pilfering 103, 244
Pingel, Falk 94–5, 237
Pinno, Aleksander 170
Pionki 33, 54, 62, 71t, 72
Piotrków 71t, 191, 196
Piotrków Trybunalski: transports 51
Plant Guard *see Werkschutz*
Płaszów 61, 66
"Płaszów Period" 34, 69, 155–60;
    transports 61–2, 69, 127, 198, 235
"Płaszów Tier" 74, 87, 122–5, 127–8,
    199–200, 207–10, 214–5
"Pleitzes" 179
Poalei Zion 129–30, 202, 245
poetry 134, 208, 210–1, 218–9, 224,
    245–6
Pohl, Oswald 1, 61
police 83–5, 87, 125, 214–5, 224, 243;
    Jewish "plants" 126; Werk B 149;
    Werk C 189–90, 198, 201
Policjanten 84–5
Policzner Hof: transports 36t

Polish armaments industry: debate over
    6–7; promotion of 7, 9
Polish-Jewish relationship 105–12, 131,
    179–80, 232, 239, 242
"Polish Soup Affair" 170–1
Polish-Ukrainian relationship 24, 165
political groups 201–4, 245
Polizei 83–5, 87, 125
Pollmer, Walter 58, 125–6, 156
Polska Podziemna 120
Półtorak, Janina 144
Połynka, Michał 168
Pomeranzblum, Frania 152
Poniatowa 60–1; transports 51
Ponikowski (Pole) 114
Porzig, Hellmut 96, 173
potato mill 151
Power and Heat Department 175
Pozner (prisoner) 173–4
pregnancy 116, 152, 215–6
Prekerowa, Teresa 129, 245
Pressing Department (*Presserei*) 176–7
prisoner exchanges 185–6, 189
prisoner reports 44, 45f
Procher, Karl 89–90
production problems 54, 58, 67, 146
"professor" (Jewish capo) 178
"proletarians" 99, 116, 244
prominenten: administration of camp 83,
    87–8; attitudes towards 158, 206–7,
    243–4; children of 127; *kaelankas*
    115–6, 245; underground economy
    102–4; Werk C 191, 201
property of Jews: confiscation of 25, 27,
    29, 45, 78, 82, 124, 164–5, 208, 239;
    extortion of 82, 94–5, 179, 242; from
    Majdanek 213; "purchase" of 188,
    239
Przybyszewski (Pole) 106
Ptasznik (barracks overseer) 85

"*Rączka*" see Schulze, Friechrich
Rada Pomocy Żydom (RPŻ) 120–1,
    129–31, 215, 245

Radom 61; munitions plants 53t; Steyr-
    Daimler-Puch 10, 53t, 71t, 72
Radom district: administration system
    11; economic policy
    10–11; evacuation of camps 72–3;
    factories turned over to German
    companies 10; ghettos 22, 29, 37f;
    Jewish labor camps (1944) 69–70,
    71t; munitions plants work forces
    (1943) 53–4; population (1940) 10;
    security 47–51, 63, 216
"Radom Period" 34–51, 86; transports
    34–5, 36t, 38–9, 40f, 51, 235
"Radom Tier" 74, 78, 98, 102, 112, 139;
    children 127; hegemony 87–8;
    Komendanten 87; and "Majdanek
    Tier" 113–5, 158, 193, 208; and
    "Płaszów Tier" 208; Werk B 148;
    Werk C 190–1
Radomsko: munitions plant 53t;
    transports 36t, 51, 142
Radoszyce 32
rail transport section 168
Raków: factory 15, 20; transports 32
rapes 80–1, 95
Rattke, Leo 90
Ravensbrück 231
Rechter, Jeszajahu 124, 136, 189
recruitment 16–25, 29, 31, 39, 67,
    236–7
registration of prisoners 79, 91f
Reichssicherheitshauptamt (RSHA) 60
Reisler, Heidi 137
Reismann (policeman) 149
Reitlinger, Gerald 58
Rejów jail 64
religious differences: and control of
    workers 24, 83, 239
religious observance 135–6, 196–7,
    219–20, 246
repair shop (*Reparaturwerkstatt*) 175
Rescue Committee 204–5, 207, 223,
    245–6
"residual ghettos" (*Restghetto*) 30
Rina (prisoner) 173

Roechling 10–11, 13, 15
Rogler (mayor of Staszów) 196
Romanko, Iwan 43, 80, 82
Ronnenberger, Wilhelm 151–2
Rosenberg, Ben Zion 146, 151
Rosenblat, Dora 225
Rosenblatt, Dr 150
Rosenblatt, Pawełek 160
Rosenblum (work brigade escort) 173
Rosenzweig, Szlomo 117–8
Rosenzweig, Dora 146
Rosenzweig-Lipszyc, Lunia 146–7, 152
Ross, Hedzia 202, 207
Ross, Henoch 202–3, 205, 215, 224, 226
Rost, Dr Artur 38, 44, 167, 172, 174, 182, 221
Rotbalsam, Israel 198, 202, 204–5
Roter (Pole) 144
Rotmund (shift manager) 92
"royal family" 184, 189–90, 197
Rozenblaum, Hersz 118
Rozenzweig, Lunia 146
RPŻ *see Rada Pomocy Zydom*
RSHA (*Reichssicherheitshauptamt*) 60
Rubin, Mendel 65, 202, 204, 220
Rudolf, Walter 175
Ruebesamen, Hugo 96
Ruestungsinspektion see Armaments Inspectorate Units
Ruestungskommando see Armaments Command
Russian advance: effect in camp 139, 224
Rygier, Aharon 164
Rysińska, Józefa 129
Ryzenberg, Mejer 78, 194

sabotage 45–6, 48, 94–5, 156, 179–80, 242
Sachs, Dr 100
Sadza, Henryk 170–1
salary/wages 23–5
Sander, Georg 43, 216, 221
Sandomierz: volunteer workers 51
Sarnecka, Ewa 129
Sauckel, Fritz 29, 41, 234

Sawczak, Teodor 82–3, 188
Sax, Dr 231
Scharfherz, Golda 152
Schellin, Erich 55–6
Schiessplatz see "firing range"
Schiller, Gustaw 230
Schindler, Maximilian: Armaments Inspectorate 14–6, 41; food supplies 69; and Hasag plants 70, 236; Jewish workers 32, 50, 61–2; and Koppe 67; production problems 58; security problems 49, 59; uncompetitiveness of munitions plants 54–5
Schippers, Franz 35, 38, 80–1
Schlieben: Hasag plant 73, 231
Schmecher, Hans 77
Schmidtke, Gustav 148
Schmitz, Hermann 172–4, 182
"Schmitz" department 172–4
Schneider, Johannes 81, 186–7, 194, 212
Schoen von Wildenegg, Dr Ernst 4
Schoengarth, Karl 32, 49
Schulze, Friechrich ("Rączka"): concert 221–2; dance floor 220–1; external aid 215; "great search" 216; improvements to Werk C 212–3; prisoner list 224–5
Schumann, Kurt 147, 186, 198, 216
Schvarzmer, David 178, 196, 220
Schwinger, Fritz 92, 96
secondary camps 69
security: *Generalgouvernement* 59–60, 62; Radom district 47–51, 63, 216
Seeber, Eva 234
Seidel, Willi 39, 80, 93–6
Seidenbeutel, Dr 114, 118
"selections" 128, 180, 244; on arrival at camp 78, 112–3, 244; "death lists" 94; final 72, 128, 140, 160–1; large scale 41, 224–5; at Madjanek 57; Skarżysko 38; typhoid epidemics 100–2, 210; Werk B 145–6; Werk C 187–8, 191, 198, 210
self-help *see* aid: internal
Sendłak, Stefan 119–20
Serek (overseer) 106

service workers 84
Sewin (informer) 86
sexual relationships 46, 95–6, 152–3;
    see also "cousins"
shareholders 4, 46–7, 236
Shaul (prisoner) 178
Shell and Grenade Department 89–90
Shell Department 166–72
shop stewards 23, 39
"sick leave" 198
Siegman, Frania 212
Sikorski, Tadeusz 106
Silberman, Mania 81
Singer, Chaim 99–100, 102, 135
Singer, Salomon 168
SiPo commanders 60, 66
Skarżysko (ghetto) 22, 38, 141
Skarżysko (town) 9, 232–3
Skarżysko-Kamienna factory xvi, 9, 18,
    20, 53t, 67, 71t; "commissary
    management" 9–11, 13–5;
    establishment of labor camp 29–33;
    see also Werk A; Werk B; Werk C
skilled workers 50, 238
slave labor camps, Jewish 29–30, 41–2,
    69–70, 71t
Śledzik, Natan 127
Small Ammunition Department 89, 90–3
Smolarz (barracks overseer) 85
smuggling 104–5, 107–9, 151, 153, 198
Sobański (Pole) 173
Sobkowski (nurse) 114–5
Sobol, Melech 104, 137
social activities 135, 201, 204, 215, 247;
    see also cultural activities;
    entertainment
society, camp: structure 74–5, 244; *see
    also* "Majdanek Tier"; "Płaszów
    Tier"; "Radom Tier"
Solnik (prisoner) 202
Sonderkommando 64–5
songs 100, 133–5, 193–4, 202–6, 215,
    218, 222, 246
"Soup Affair, Pikryna" 178
"Soup Affair, Polish" 170–1
"soup song" 133–4

Special Committee 2 13, 16
Speer, Albert 16, 41, 46, 49, 55, 60–61,
    70, 236
Sperling, Bela 155
spy network, Jewish 126
SS 43–5, 59–60, 69
SS-WVHA *see* WVHA
Stabholz, Tadeusz 57
Stanko, Leon 146, 153
Starachowice 10, 53t, 62, 71t, 72
Starowiński (prisoner) 202, 204
Staszów: transports 32, 36t, 51, 142
"Staszower Barracks" 102
Stein, Willi 146, 154–5
Steinhaus 150, 159
Stelzner, Heinrich 97
Stępinski (Pole) 114
Stern (prisoner) 118
Steyr-Daimler-Puch 10, 53t, 71t, 72
stockholders: Hasag Concern 4, 46–7,
    236
Stolarska, Ludwicka ("Lucia") 129
Stopnica: transports 32, 36t, 142
Stosstrupp 43, 125, 187
Straflager 42
Strasser, Dr Stanisław 157, 160
Strenk, Leo 43
Strigler, Mordchai 5 6–7, 64–5, 169,
    191, 194–5, 201, 205–7, 226, 246
Stubenaelteste 84–5
Suchedniów 22, 36t; transports 36t
Sulejów 72, 140, 161
Suligowski (Pole) 144
Sundays 135
supervision of camps 42
survival: criteria determining 241
survival measures 98–121
Świsłocki, Dr 198
Szajbe, Moniek 131–2
Szajber (Elias Szajbe?) 84
Szajger, Bezalel 132
Szaniawski, Henryk 101, 106
Szapira, Baruch 202, 204
Szapira, Szymon 185
Szapsia (prisoner) 177
Szapszewski (*commandenten*) 149

Szarata, Andrzej 172–3, 195
Szaweslajn (nurse) 115
"*Szawues*" 163–4
Szczawnica: transports 36t
Szczotka (overseer) 171
Szechter, Fela 219
Szechter, Hela 212, 217
Szechter, Helena 178–9
Szechter, Mania 217
Szechter, Maria *see* Lewinger, Maria
Szechter-Lewinger, Maria *see* Lewinger, Maria
Szenwald, Zeev 200
Szewczyk, Józef 168
Szichter, Aharon 202
Szmajser, Abraham 194
Sznitbaum (prisoner) 201
Szotland, Chaim 187
Szparkowski, Zdzisław 121
Szwed, Stanisław 117, 119
Szydłowiec 22; transports 35, 36t, 38, 51, 141

Tanzsaal (Dance Hall) *see Musiksaal*
Tatarski (overseer) 107
Taubert (shop steward) 39
Taucha 231
temporary camps 20
Tenennbaum, Mordchai 202
Teperman, Lejzer 84–7, 113, 139, 230
Theresiendstadt 231
Thomas, Georg 3, 7, 16, 235
Tietge, Marianne 92
TNT/Picric Acid Departments 175–80
Tochterman, Herszel 201
Todt, Dr Fritz 13
Tomaszewski (Pole) 155
townsfolk groups *see Landsmannschaft*
"train, death" 64
transport sections 168
"Transport Workers Song" 193–4, 206
transports 31–2, 67, 69; *see also* evacuation of camp; "Majdanek Period"; Płaszów Period"; "Radom Period"
Trawniki 61

"Treblinka Song" 134
Treper (policeman) 202
Tuerkheim 231
Tuwim, Julian 137, 219
"2 cm Department" 143, 154–5
typhoid epidemics 67, 99–100, 102, 125, 185, 210–2, 244
Tyras-Ofir, Madzia 137
Tyrmand, Maryla 137

Ukrainians 12, 23–4, 165, 239
Ullmann, Otto 169
Ullmer (policeman) 227
underground activities 12, 47–9, 59, 63, 65, 116–21, 237; *see also* ammunition, theft of; escape attempts; sabotage
underground economy: black market 26–7, 109, 237; in camp 102–5, 107, 109, 133, 150, 195–6, 213, 242, 244–5
Underground Poland 120
Ungerowa (laundry manageress) 201
Urban (German) 127

vegetable garden 152, 189
Voigt (German) 97
Voigtlaender, Ernst 93
Volksdeutsche 12, 23–4, 239
volunteer workers 31, 39, 51
von dem Bach Zelewski, Erich 60
Vorarbeiter 85

Wachfuehrer 43–4
wages 21, 31, 42, 48, 54, 237
Wagner, Alfred 92–3
"*Waise Hoiz*" *see* "White House"
Wajcblum, Josef 87, 230
Waksman, Busiek 160
Waldkommando 163–4
Walter (German) 178, 225
War Economy and Ordnance, Division of 14
Warehouse 3, 172
Warschauer, Mrs 153
Warschauer family 141–2

Warszauer, Icchak 232
Warszauer, Zelig: son of 232
Warszawska (prisoner) 160
Warta 54, 62, 71t
Wasserlauf, Henryk 179
Wasserman (barracks overseer) 85
Wasserstein, Dr Adam 198, 202, 204–5, 225
Wehrmacht: armaments industry 3–4, 7, 13, 41, 62; Hasag plants 32–3, 46–7; security of plants 59–60; supply of workers 234
Wehrwirtschaftsstab (WWiStab) 3, 7
Weichart, Dr 120, 123, 128–9, 131, 215, 245
Weinstock, Yehiel 130
Weintraub, Chaim 86–7
Weintraub, Hayim 126
Weintraub, Mendel 86–7
Weissblum, Meir 130–2
Weizhendler (prisoner) 151
Werk A 32, 43, 63, 74–97, 101, 115–6, 117f, 121, 132–9, 164
Werk B 32, 43, 76f, 78, 123–4, 141–61, 189
Werk C 22, 32, 63–5, 76f, 78, 162–228
Werkschutz (Plant Guard) 81, 186–7, 242–3; composition of 24, 43; desertions 49, 63; escape attempts 82, 164; functions 12, 42–3, 45, 82–3; "Great Escape" 227; Pollmer appointed 125; property of Jews 45, 78, 82, 124, 164–5, 208; "selections" 100, 140, 146, 187; supervision of 24, 43, 60, 66; wages/benefits 24–5; Werk A 43; Werk B 43, 148; Werk C 43, 165, 186–8
Werkzeugbau – Narządziownia 89, 93
Wermus, Lili 127
Wertman, Simon 85
"White House" 149–50, 184, 190, 206, 213–4, 224–6
"White House" agents 188–9
Wildenegg, Dr Ernst Schoen von 4
Winterfeld, General von 10

Wittenberg, Jehuda 194
Włoszczowa: transports 32, 141
Wodzisław 36t
Wojciechowski (Pole) 144
Wójcik, Wincenty 101, 106
Wolbrom rabbi 197
work brigades 20
work camps 20, 41–2
work group escorts 85
"work service" xvii
workers: abundance of 12, 22–3, 236–7; control of 23–4, 83, 238–9; shortage of 18, 22, 27, 50–1
workers' benefits 12, 18, 23–5, 31, 48–9, 54, 237; suspension 28f
Woźny, Stefan 43
Wroclawski (prisoner) 184
WVHA 31, 47, 55, 60–2, 66–7, 69, 234, 235–6
WWiStab (*Wehrwirtschaftsstab*) 3, 7

Zahn, Walter 176
Zając, Jakow 186
Zajączkowska, Halina 110
Zajdenwerg, Hana 121
Zajfert (barracks overseer) 85
Żak, Rachel 129, 132
Zalcman ("camp elder") 84
Zeev brothers 201
Zellner, Rafael 170
Zieliński, Walerian 170–1
Zilberberg, Chaim 149
Zimmermann ("*Szawues*") 163–4
Zinna (prisoner) 104
Zinsser, Hugo 4
Zionists 130, 204–5, 217, 245–6
Zipfel, Oskar 94, 97
Ziskind, Reuwen 217
Zisskind, Rubinek 195
ŻKN *see Żydowski Komitet Narodowy*
ŻOB *see Żydowska Organizacja Bojowa*
Zonszajn, Fride 145
Zosia (nurse) 114–5
Zucker (goldsmith) 104
Zuckerbrot, Mala 212, 217

Zuckerbrot-Hottner, Malka 219
Zuess (informer) 86
Zukerman, Henryk 142
Zweig, Benjamin 101
Zweig, Jurek 229–30
Zweig, Zacharia 229
Zwoleń: transports 32, 36t
Żydowska Organizacja Bojowa (ŻOB)
   130–2
Żydowski Komitet Narodowy
  (ŻKN) 129–30, 245
Zylbersztajn (policeman) 178

DATE DUE			
DEC 0 7 2008			